FAT FREE SUCCESS STORIES

Dear Mrs. Steinback,

I want to thank you for talking to me on Tuesday afternoon; you have motivated me as no one has in a long time.

Some morning when you jump on your HealthRider, and you're dreaming your dreams, look at the stars that are out. You will see one star that shines brighter, know that it is me and I am thanking you for being the person that you are. Also know that the encouragement that you have shown me will not be in vain.

The very best to you and your family. I will keep you updated on my weight loss.

Thank you,
Bonnie Young, Appleton, WI

P.S. To date Bonnie has lost 25 pounds and is still living Fat Free! Yea Bonnie!

✦ ✦ ✦

Hi Jyl,

I have lost 40 pounds, thanks to FAT FREE LIVING and Jyl Steinback. I tried diets for ten years, and I was never successful. Fat Free Living has helped me make healthy lifestyle changes, that I can afford, and that I actually enjoy. I feel 100% better about myself. I tell everyone I see that FAT FREE IS THE WAY TO BE!

Brenda Hardy, Mesa, AZ

✦ ✦ ✦

Dear Jyl,

Just a quick note to let you know how much I enjoyed meeting you. I made your Orange Jello Mold and "Au Gratin" potatoes for Easter, both were a big hit. Even with Easter I still lost 2 pounds. I truly enjoy your cookbooks. I just ordered a breadmaker today so I am excited about your next cookbook. My husband has been impressed by everything I've made so far.

I am one of your biggest fans. Thank you again for your great cookbooks.

Betty J. Mahnke, Glendale, AZ

✦ ✦ ✦

Dear Jyl,

I think your enthusiasm is unmatched. You motivated me to try a little harder, persist a little longer and venture into new territory. Best wishes to you and your family.

Virginia M. Granger

✦ ✦ ✦

Dear Jyl,

I just wanted to let you know that I absolutely love all of your cookbooks. Every recipe that I tried was terrific! Thanks a lot! Keep up the good work!!!

Gloria Blankschein, Marinette, WI

✦ ✦ ✦

more . . .

Dear Jyl,

Thank you for returning my phone call. As I explained to you, my husband had a double heart bypass 2 years ago at age 47. He exercises regularly and is not overweight. His heart disease is hereditary.

Needless to say, our lives have changed. We both exercise even more than ever and are totally committed to a fat-free way of living. We have not found this hard to do. We have even converted his mother. She has copies of your *Fat Free Living* Cookbooks. I will be happy to recommend your cookbooks to all my friends.

Lynette Homes, Raleigh, NC

✦ ✦ ✦

Dear Ms. Steinback,

Since I have cut fat from my diet, I have lost 5 lbs. in a month. I need good recipes to fill me up, but without the fat in order to get my cholesterol down. The doctor doesn't think I can do it with diet alone. (I am 76 years old.) However, I haven't cheated once on my fat-free diet!

Mrs. Murray Force, Cairo, NY

✦ ✦ ✦

Dear Jyl,

I am 36 years old, and want to insure my physical health more than ever. I take the best supplements and have gotten very serious about exercise, and fitness. Again, you are an incredible example of being fit.

I have been going through the FAT FREE LIVING recipe books and what excites me most is how easy the preparation will be. Being extremely busy, I need quick, and easy recipes! Also, the way you promote these recipes is great! It's not what we say, but what we feel about what we say! You do a great job! My family is ready for variation and it's all FAT FREE!!

Jyl, thanks for your time!

Cheryl Swain, Billings, MT

✦ ✦ ✦

Dear Jyl,

It was a pleasure having you visit my First Grade classroom. Armed with your sparkling smile and eye-catching posters, you quickly captured the children's attention and kept it as you shared important nutritional information and eatable low-fat snacks. Your message was clear. YOU CAN HELP YOUR FAMILY AND YOU TO MAKE HEALTHY CHOICES when shopping for meals and planning menus.

I know my class is now more conscious of eating healthy. Thanks, Jyl, for sharing important nutritional information in such a fun and inspiring way.

Myra Cates, Scottsdale Public Schools, Scottsdale, AZ

✦ ✦ ✦

Dear Jyl,

Yesterday I went to Costco looking for a vegetarian cookbook, then I ran across all 3 of your books. I started reading them and just couldn't put them down. I love them. I bought all 3.

My Doc wants me to lose weight because I am diabetic and also have a cholesterol problem and heart problems. I've been starving myself trying to lose weight. But no such luck.

Well God has answered my prayers. He brought me to your books to help me. Thanks so very much to you and all your dear friends who helped. I'll let you know how I make out. Please keep up the good work and best of luck always.

God bless and keep you and your family safe always.

Betty Northcoat, Cypress, CA

✦ ✦ ✦

The Fat Free Living Super Cookbook

✦ ✦ ✦

Jyl Steinback

WARNER BOOKS

A Time Warner Company

The advice in this book can be a valuable addition to your doctor's advice, and is designed for your use under his or her care and direction. You should regularly consult a physician in all matters relating to your health, and particularly in respect of any symptoms that may require diagnosis or medical attention.

Warner Books, Inc., 1271 Avenue of the Americas, New York, NY 10020
Visit our Web Site at
http://pathfinder.com/twep

 A Time Warner Company

Printed in the United States of America

Library of Congress Cataloging-in-Publication Data
Steinback, Jyl.
    The fat free living super cookbook / Jyl Steinback.
      p.   cm.
    Includes index.
    ISBN 0-446-67313-7
    1. Low-fat diet—Recipes. I. Title.
    RM237.7.S8135 1997   97-3678
    641.5'638—dc21   CIP

First Printing: May 1997

10 9 8 7 6 5 4

Cover photos by Elliot Lincis, Camel Studios
Cover design by Mark Nickel, Graphics 4
Interior design by Charles Sutherland

ATTENTION: SCHOOLS AND CORPORATIONS
WARNER books are available at quantity discounts with bulk purchase for educational, business, or sales promotional use. For information, please write to: SPECIAL SALES DEPARTMENT, WARNER BOOKS, 1271 AVENUE OF THE AMERICAS, NEW YORK, N.Y. 10020

ACKNOWLEDGMENTS

✦ ✦ ✦

The "WORKS" IS HERE...THE FAT FREE LIVING SUPER COOKBOOK! The Steinbacks want to give you all a warm welcome of applause. YOU ARE THE GREATEST! Thank you all for helping make this healthy lifestyle a reality! It is because of you this book is possible and successful! Please continue to live a FAT FREE and HEALTHY LIFE ALWAYS!

"The future belongs to those who believe in the beauty of their dreams" (Eleanor Roosevelt). Thank you, Gary, for loving me "unconditionally" and helping make all of our dreams reality. You influence me with your unique gift of love, wisdom and a fabulous heart. I count my blessings every day for how lucky we are to work together and how lucky I am to have you as my husband and "bestest" friend. As they would say at the Olympics, "Let's go for the gold." Let's change the world to a healthier place to live. Together we can do it! You're the BEST and I love you so very much!!

Jamie and Scott, your playful spirit is addicting. You both have enriched my life beyond words. You make me smile in the morning when I wake up and I dream about you at night. The more time I spend with you, the more I love it! Of course, I am blessed with two of the greatest kids in the world! Lucky, lucky me! And Jamie, what a great food tester you are, as long as it's potatoes, spaghetti and white sauce, pizza, bread and chips, we've got it made. I do love you, Jamie, so very much! And, Scott, your hugs and kisses are to melt for...I love you both more than life. Thank you! Thank you for your support, your love and understanding. Thank you for both of YOU!

My mom and dad, Betty and Bill Levy, my very favorite babysitters in the whole world. Jacie, you're right up there! There's a great quote by Richard L. Evans, "Children will not remember you for the material things you provided, but for the feeling that you cherished them." I appreciate you for both! You taught me success is "The harder you work...the luckier you get." But, you also taught me, "The more you love...the bigger your heart." Thank you for both of you and for a very special life. I love you!

Jacie, my next favorite babysitter and sister. Thanks! I love you very much! Jeff, Diane, Alex, and Casey, Here's to YOU! I always think I'm busy until I talk to you. Keep up the fabulous job. I love you all so very much!

Snooky and Harlan Steinback (my mother and father-in-law). You are a blessing and I love you very much! Thanks for believing in our dreams!

I want to thank Larry Kirshbaum, Mel Parker, Sharon Krassney, Ann McCarthy, Anna Maria Piluso, and Diana Baroni at Warner Books for believing in me and "FAT FREE" Living and getting this book into the hands of millions of people who are trying to live healthier lifestyles. We are very excited about THE FAT FREE LIVING SUPER COOKBOOK and the wonderful opportunity! I appreciate you all and am extremely thankful for your unlimited energy and rewarding support! You are all truly a blessing, thank you!

I am also extremely grateful for the opportunity to work with the following people. My life has been enriched and without a doubt this book would not be possible without each and every one of them. I am gifted and blessed to know you all, and extremely lucky to be touched by each and every one of you in my life. Thank you!

Mikki Eveloff, you are a saint! I am so grateful for your support, dedication, warmth and fabulous friendship. Your commitment to helping make this book possible is magical. You are an amazing woman. You always do whatever is necessary to make THE FAT FREE LIVING SUPER COOKBOOK perfect. Thank you so very much, Mikki. I love you lots!

Debra Kohl, you are a doll. You paced yourself beautifully, and you did good! Debra is a Registered Dietician with a master's degree in Nutrition and Dietetics and you can reach her services at (602) 266-0324. I've been working with Debra for five FAT FREE books now, and your colors shine through each and every time. You are a gift to your field and thank you for joining forces with me to make a healthier world. I love you, Deb!

Elliot Lincis, you're a lot of fun and you always make me smile! The front and back cover are your best "shot"! Thanks for sharing your wonderful friendship and beautiful talents with me, my family and THE FAT FREE LIVING SUPER COOKBOOK! You're the greatest and I love you lots!

Mark Nickel, you are ONE IN A MILLION! And, a good cook besides. Thanks for everything! May life's successes be everything you always dream of...because you deserve it all! Love you lots, Mark.

Terri Weisz, you are a sweetheart! Thanks to you and Two Plates Full in Scottsdale, Arizona. Our front and back covers are SENSATIONAL! An awesome job you did! Thanks a million for all of your wonderful generosity!

Jim Peterson, general manager at Scottsdale County Club, made our background scenery an awesome sight! Thanks a million for your support!

Leslie Gross, you are the greatest! Thanks so much for all your wonderful support! We couldn't have done the front and back covers without you!

Mile Munson, thank you so much for all your positive energy! Our covers look extra special because of you and Barbeques Galore!

HINTS FOR SIMPLE
FAT FREE COOKING

The key to flavorful fat-free meals is to learn the right additions and simple substitutions for highly caloric and fat-filled ingredients. Experiment with different seasonings and spices to add a flavorful addition to basic foods. Learn the basic substitutions to make fat-free cooking tasty, tempting and tantalizing. Replace deep-fried or cream-sauce cooking with grilling, roasting, or poaching for meats and vegetables.

- Fat-free broths (chicken, beef, oriental, or vegetable) can be used in the following ways:

  - instead of oil for fried, sautéed, or stir-fried foods
  - instead of water to add flavor to rice, vegetables, fish or chicken
  - instead of fats or oil as a base in sauces and gravies.

- Marinate fish or chicken in fat-free marinades, fat-free broths, or fat-free salad dressings.

- Marinate or baste fish or chicken with concentrated fruit juice, fresh fruit juice, or vegetable juices.

- Marinate chicken and fish at least several hours in refrigerator to enhance tenderness and flavor.

- Poach (cooking in a simmering liquid) chicken or fish in wine, fruit or vegetable juices.

- Steam fresh or frozen vegetables and enhance their flavor with minced garlic, crushed spices, or low-sodium teriyaki sauce.

- Fruit juices, wine, and fat-free broths are great additions to steamed vegetables.

- Toss cooked pasta with fat-free broths instead of oil to prevent sticking.

- Toss fat-free seasoned bread cubes or crumbs with cooked celery, onion, and fat-free broth to make a delicious and simple holiday stuffing.

- Substitute fat-free ground turkey, fat-free ground chicken, or vegetable beef crumbles (Morningstar Farms Ground Meatless or Green Giant Harvest Burgers for Recipes) for ground beef in recipes.

- Spice up fat-free foods with fresh herbs at the end of cooking time.

- Fresh herbs will lose their flavor if cooked too long. Dried herbs can be added at the beginning of cooking to enhance the flavor. (See Spice Substitutions for suggested varieties.)

- Season cold foods more intensely than hot foods.

- Season pasta salads just before serving for best flavor.

- When increasing a recipe, gradually increase the spice portions; do not double or triple in the same equivalent as the increase in other ingredients.

- Fat-free substitutions to thicken soups include:

  - Add fresh or dried bread crumbs.
  - Remove ⅓ vegetables from the soup and purée in food processor or blender and mix into soup.
  - Add grated raw potato to soup and cook 5-10 minutes until thickened.
  - Use evaporated skim milk in place of high-fat creams.

- Fat-free substitutions to thicken sauces or dressings include:

  - Purée fat-free cottage cheese or fat-free ricotta cheese and substitute for part of the liquid in a recipe.
  - Blend one or more tablespoons of mashed potatoes into sauces.

- Add fat-free cream cheese to boiling liquid when making sauces, and stir constantly until melted.

- Baked casseroles can be sprinkled with fat-free cheese after baking; cheese will melt from heated food.

- Broil fat-free cheeses during the last 3 minutes of cooking.

- Fat-free cheeses should be added the last 5 minutes of cooking to soups and stews.

- A great cream sauce substitute: 1 cup low-fat buttermilk + 1 tablespoon cornstarch + tomato sauce or mustard.

- Make a corn purée as a substitute for oil in corn cakes, corn muffins, corn pudding or tamales. In a blender or food processor, process corn and a small amount of water until puréed and blended.

- Blend cottage cheese in a food processor or blender and use in place of butter or oil in baked foods.

- Make or purchase fat-free pie crusts and top fruit pies with fat-free crunch toppings for a great summer dessert.

- Frost fat-free cakes with marshmallow cream instead of frosting.

- Use fat-free sour cream or yogurt for marinating and baking.

- Coat chicken with fat-free sour cream or fat-free yogurt; roll in fat-free seasoned bread crumbs or seasoned cornflake crumbs for a simple fat-free meal.

- Use fat-free salsa, fat-free flavored mustards or fat-free salad dressings instead of mayonnaise or cream sauces for sandwiches or salads.

EQUIVALENTS AND SUBSTITUTIONS

How many cups are there in a pint? How many tomatoes are needed to equal 2 cups chopped tomatoes? How many carrots are needed to equal 1 cup shredded carrots? If you are in the middle of baking your favorite sweet treat and do not have baking powder, what can you substitute to prevent a total failure? The answers to all your "equivalents and substitutes" questions nave been provided to make fat-free cooking a stress-free experience!

Basic Measurements:

pinch = $\frac{1}{16}$ teaspoon
dash = 6 drops or $\frac{1}{8}$ teaspoon
tablespoon = 3 teaspoons
$\frac{1}{8}$ cup = 1 fluid ounce = 2 tablespoons
$\frac{1}{4}$ cup = 2 fluid ounces = 4 tablespoons = $\frac{1}{8}$ pound
$\frac{1}{3}$ cup = 5$\frac{1}{3}$ tablespoons
$\frac{1}{2}$ cup = 4 fluid ounces = 8 tablespoons = $\frac{1}{4}$ pound
$\frac{2}{3}$ cup = 10$\frac{2}{3}$ tablespoons
$\frac{3}{4}$ cup = 6 fluid ounces = 12 tablespoons
1 cup = 8 fluid ounces = 16 tablespoons = $\frac{1}{2}$ pint = $\frac{1}{2}$ pound
2 cups = 16 fluid ounces = 1 pint = 1 pound
4 cups = 32 fluid ounces = 2 pints = 1 quart = 2 pounds
16 cups = 4 quarts = 1 gallon
1 liter = 4 quarts + 3 ounces
1 pound = 16 ounces

Baking Pans:

8 x 8 x 2 inches = 6 cups
9 x 9 x $\frac{1}{2}$ inches = 8 cups
9 x 9 x 2 inches = 10 cups
8 x 1$\frac{1}{2}$ inch round = 4 cups
9 x 1$\frac{1}{2}$ inch round = 6 cups
8 x 1$\frac{1}{4}$ inch pie plate = 3 cups
9 x 1$\frac{1}{2}$ inch pie plate = 4 cups
8$\frac{1}{2}$ x 4$\frac{1}{2}$ x 2$\frac{1}{2}$ inch loaf pan = 6 cups
9 x 5 x 3 inch loaf pan = 8 cups

8 x 1½ inch round = 10 x 6 x 2 inch pan = 9 x 1½ inch pan = 8 x
4 x 2 inch loaf pan = 9 inch pie plate
8 x 8 x 2 inch pan = 9 x 5 x 3 inch loaf pan = 2–8 x 1½ inch
round pans
13 x 9 x 2 inch pan = 14 x 11 x 2 inch pan = 2–9 x 1½ inch round
pans = 3–8 x 1½ inch round pans

Baking Equivalents and Substitutions:

1 lb. flour = 3½ - 4 cups white flour
      = 4 - 4½ cups cake flour
      = 3 cups sifted whole wheat flour
      = 4 cups graham flour

1 lb. white all-purpose flour = 3½ cups unsifted = 4 cups sifted

1 cup white all-purpose flour = ½ cup barley flour = 1⅛ cups cake flour = 1 cup cornmeal = 1½ cups rye flour = 1½ cups oat flour

1 lb. rye flour = 4½ cups

1 lb. whole wheat flour = 3⅓ - 3¾ cups

1 cup self-rising flour = 1 cup flour + 1½ teaspoons baking powder + ¼ teaspoon salt

1 cup all-purpose flour = 1 cup self-rising flour (baking powder and salt in recipe)

1 cup cake flour = ⅞ cup all-purpose flour

1⅓ cups oat flour = 1 cup whole wheat flour

¾ cup oat flour = 1 cup white all-purpose flour

oat flour = processed oatmeal in food processor or blender

1 lb. sugar = 2 cups granulated sugar
      = 3½ - 4 cups powdered sugar
      = 2¼ cups brown sugar

1 lb. brown sugar = 2¼ cups

1 cup brown sugar = 1 cup granulated sugar + 2 tablespoons molasses or corn syrup

1 cup granulated sugar = 1½ cups corn syrup

1 cup corn syrup = 1 cup sugar + ¼ cup water (Boil mixture 3 minutes and cool to room temperature.)

1 cup granulated sugar   = 1 cup brown sugar
                      = 1 cup corn syrup less ¼ cup liquid in recipe
                      = ¾ cup honey less ¼ cup liquid in recipe

1 lb. powdered sugar = 4½ cups unsifted

1¾ cup powdered sugar = 1 cup granulated

1 cup powdered sugar = 1 cup granulated sugar + 2 tbsp. cornstarch (process in blender)

1 lb. honey = 1⅓ cups = 1⅔ cups granulated sugar

1 tsp. vanilla = ¼ tsp. maple flavoring

1 tbsp. baking powder = 1½ tsp. cream of tartar + 1 tsp. baking soda

8 oz. unsweetened cocoa powder = 2 cups cocoa

¼ oz. unflavored gelatin = 1 tbsp. gelatin

Fruit Equivalents and Substitutions:

1 lb. apples = 3 medium apples = 3 cups sliced or diced apples

1 lb. fresh apricots = 10 medium apricots = 3 cups cooked apricots

1 lb. dried apricots = 3 cups dried apricots = 4½ cups cooked apricots

1 lb. bananas = 3-4 medium bananas = 2 cups sliced bananas = 1½ cups mashed bananas

1 pint berries = 2 cups berries (strawberries, blueberries, raspberries, etc.)

2¼ cups whole dates = 1½ - 2 cups chopped dates

1 lb. seedless grapes = 2½ cups grapes

1 whole lemon = 1½ - 2 tbsp. lemon juice = 2 tsp. grated rind

1 whole lime = 1½ - 2 tbsp. lime juice = 1½ tsp. grated rind

1 medium orange = 6 tbsp. juice = 2 tbsp. grated rind

1 lb. peaches = 4-6 peaches = 2 cups sliced peaches

1 lb. pears = 3-5 pears = 2 cups sliced pears

2 lb. fresh pineapple = 3 cups cubed pineapple

1 lb. raisins = 2¾ - 3 cups raisins

1 cup fresh fruit = 10 oz. package frozen fruit
= 1 cup canned fruit, drained

Vegetable Equivalents and Substitutions:

1 lb. asparagus = 3½ - 4 cups cooked asparagus

1 lb. green beans = 2½ - 3 cups cooked beans

1 lb. head broccoli = 2 cups cooked broccoli florets

1 lb. cabbage = 6 cups shredded cabbage
= 2-3 cups cooked cabbage

1 lb. carrots = 3 cups sliced carrots = 2½ cups shredded carrots

4 cups shredded carrots = 6-7 whole carrots
= 3 cups cooked carrots
1 lb. cauliflower = 1½ - 2 cups cooked cauliflower
1¼ lb. celery = 3 cups diced celery = 2 cups cooked celery
2 medium stalks celery = ¾ - 1 cup sliced celery
4 medium ears of corn = 1 cup corn kernels
10 oz. frozen corn kernels = 2 cups corn kernels
1 lb. eggplant = 15—⅓ inch slices eggplant
= 4½ cups raw diced eggplant
= 1¾ cup cooked diced eggplant
= 3 cups raw chopped eggplant
1 large head garlic = 10 - 15 cloves garlic
1 small clove garlic = ½ tsp. minced garlic = ⅛ tsp. garlic powder
1 medium clove garlic = ¾ tsp. minced garlic
= ¼ tsp. garlic powder
1 large clove garlic = 1 tsp. minced garlic =½ tsp. garlic power
1 lb. mushrooms = 5-6 cups sliced mushrooms
= 6 oz. canned mushrooms
= 3 oz. dried mushrooms
1 lb. onion = 3 large onions
1 large onion = 1 cup diced onion
1 medium onion = ½ - ⅔ cup diced onions
= 1 tbsp. dried minced onion
= 1 tbsp. onion powder
1 small onion = ¼ - ⅓ cup diced onions
10 oz. frozen peas = 2 cups peas
1 medium pepper (red, green, or yellow) = 1 cup diced peppers
1 lb. potatoes = 3 medium potatoes
= 3 cups sliced potatoes
= 2½ cups diced potatoes
= 2 cups mashed potatoes
= 2 cups french fries
= 3 servings potato salad
3 medium potatoes = 2½ cups cooked and diced potatoes
= 1¾ cups mashed potatoes
6 scallions = ¾ cup minced or sliced scallions
1 lb. fresh spinach= 4-8 cups raw spinach leaves
= 1½ - 2 cups cooked spinach
= 10 oz. frozen chopped spinach
10 oz. frozen chopped spinach = 1¼ cups cooked spinach
= 1 cup cooked and drained
spinach

1 lb. fresh tomatoes = 2 large or 4 small tomatoes
= 2 cups diced tomatoes
2 medium tomatoes = 1 cup chopped tomatoes
= 8 oz. canned tomatoes
16 oz. can tomatoes, drained = 1¼ cups tomatoes
28 oz. can tomatoes, drained = 2 cups tomatoes
2 cups fresh cooked vegetables = 16 oz. can vegetables, drained
= 2 cups frozen vegetables
1¼ cups fresh vegetables = 10 oz. package frozen vegetables

Spice Equivalents and Substitutions:

1 tsp. allspice = ½ tsp. cinnamon + ⅛ tsp. cloves
1 tsp. anise = 1 tsp. cardamom
1 bay leaf = 1 tsp. marjoram, oregano, rosemary, sage, or thyme
caraway seeds = poppy or sesame seeds
dash cayenne pepper = 1 tsp. chili powder
⅛ tsp. cayenne pepper = 4 drops hot pepper sauce
½ cup cinnamon-sugar = ½ cup sugar + 1½ tsp. cinnamon
1 tbsp. Italian seasoning = ¼ tsp. each: oregano, basil, thyme, rosemary, cayenne pepper
1 tsp. dry mustard = 1 tsp. prepared mustard
1 tsp. pumpkin pie spice = ½ tsp. cinnamon, ¼ tsp. ginger, ⅛ tsp. cloves, ⅛ tsp. nutmeg
1 tsp. poultry seasoning = ½ tsp. rosemary + ½ tsp. thyme + ½ tsp. sage
1 cup soy sauce = 6 tbsp. Worcestershire sauce + 2 tbsp. water
1 tbsp. fresh herbs = 1 tsp. crushed dried herbs
= ½ tsp. ground herbs
1 tbsp. freshly grated horseradish = 2 tbsp. bottled horseradish

Dairy Produce Equivalents and Substitutions:

1 quart milk = 4 cups milk
1 - 1⅓ cups dry milk powder = 1 quart milk, reconstituted
¼ - ⅓ cup dry milk powder = 1 cup milk reconstituted
13 oz. evaporated skim milk = 1⅓ cups evaporated milk
1 cup skim milk = ½ cup evaporated skim milk + ½ cup water
= ⅓ cup instant nonfat dry milk + 7 tbsp. water
16 oz. fat-free cottage cheese = 2 cups cottage cheese
15 oz. fat-free ricotta cheese = 2 cups ricotta cheese

3 oz. fat-free Parmesan cheese (whole) = 1 cup grated Parmesan cheese

4 oz. fat-free whole cheese = 1 - 1⅓ cups shredded cheese

¼ cup shredded fat-free cheese = 1 oz. shredded cheese

2 cups fat-free shredded cheese = 8 oz. shredded cheese

1 cup fat-free sour cream = 1 cup undiluted evaporated skim milk + 4 tsp. vinegar or lemon juice = 1 cup fat-free yogurt

1 cup cream = 1 cup powdered fat-free nondairy creamer +1 cup hot water

1 cup light cream = 1 cup undiluted evaporated skim milk

1 cup buttermilk = 2 tbsp. lemon juice or vinegar + enough skim milk to equal 1 cup (let stand 5 minutes)= 1 cup fat-free yogurt = ¼ cup Buttermilk Blend + 1 cup water

Miscellaneous Equivalents and Substitutions:

1 lb. bread = 12-16 slices

1 slice fresh bread = ½ cup fresh bread crumbs

1 slice dried bread = ⅓ cup dry crumbs

1 cup bread crumbs = ¾ cup cracker or cereal crumbs

12 squares graham crackers = 1 cup graham cracker crumbs

1 graham cracker pie crust = 14 squares graham crackers

22 fat-free saltine crackers = 1 cup cracker crumbs

1 cup bread crumb substitutions = 4 cups cornflake crumbs
         = 3 cups fat-free potato chips, crushed
         = 22 fat-free saltines
         = 4 slices fat-free fresh bread

1 cup cornmeal = 4 cups cooked cornmeal

Substitute equal amounts of Malt-O-Meal cereal or Cream of Wheat for cornmeal in quick bread recipes, for breading, or flouring pans

1 lb. rolled oats = 5 cups uncooked oats

1 cup regular or quick-cooking oatmeal = 1¾ cups cooked oatmeal

1 lb. spaghetti = 6½ cups cooked spaghetti

2 oz. spaghetti = 1 cup cooked spaghetti

1 lb. macaroni = 5 cups uncooked macaroni
         = 8-10 cups cooked macaroni

1 cup small pasta = 1¾ cups cooked pasta

1 cup noodles = 1¾ cups cooked noodles

1 lb. rice (long-grain, white or brown) = 2½ cups uncooked rice

1 cup raw rice = 3 cups cooked rice

1 lb. large beans (i.e. kidney beans) = 2 cups uncooked beans
= 5½ cups cooked beans

1 cup dried beans (large or small) = 2-3 cups cooked beans

1 lb. dried small beans (i.e. navy beans)= 2⅓ cups uncooked beans
= 5½ cups cooked beans

1 cup lentils = 3 cups cooked lentils

1 cup uncooked barley = 3½ cups cooked barley

1 cup cracked wheat (bulgur) = 2½ - 3 cups cooked bulgur

1 package dry active yeast = 1 tbsp. yeast

1 cup marshmallows= 11 large marshmallows
= 77 miniature marshmallows

1 tsp. lemon juice = ½ tsp. vinegar (do not substitute vinegar if lemon-flavor is needed)

1 bouillon cube = 1 tbsp. instant bouillon granules
= 1 cup broth

Substitutions for nuts: toasted oatmeal, crushed cornflakes, Grape-Nuts cereal, fat-free granola

Substitutions for raisins: chopped dates, chopped prunes, dried apricots, apples, figs, dried mixed fruit

FAT FREE LIVING MADE SIMPLE

✦ ✦ ✦

Meal planning and preparation are important factors for fat-free living. Here are some suggestions for simple solutions to living fat-free:

- Stock your pantry with healthy staples and nutritious snacks to make fast fat-free foods.
- Try to stick to a grocery list when shopping, to prevent impulse buying.
- Do not shop when you are hungry.
- Do not cook when you are hungry.

Filling a Fat-free Kitchen:

- fat-free broth: chicken, oriental, beef, and vegetable
- fat-free sour cream
- fat-free yogurt
- fat-free cottage cheese
- fat-free buttermilk or Buttermilk Blend Mix
- skim milk
- nonfat dry milk powder
- fat-free yogurt: plain and flavored
- fat-free cheeses: cheddar, mozzarella, Monterey jack, Mexican mix, Pizza cheese, Parmesan, cream cheese
- fat-free mayonnaise
- baking needs: flour, sugar, brown sugar, honey, molasses, baking powder, baking soda
- fat-free margarine (Promise)
- apple butter
- unsweetened applesauce
- Lighter Bake (Sunsweet Growers, Inc. 1-800-447-5218), which is a fat and oil substitute made up of prunes. If you're unable to find Lighter Bake you may substitute with a mixture that is ½ apple butter and ½ "baby" prunes.
- fat-free grains (white rice, wild rice, couscous, barley, bulgur, etc.)
- assorted pastas

- assorted mustards: prepared, Dijon, deli-style, brown, etc.
- low-sodium teriyaki sauce
- low-sodium soy sauce
- low-sodium tomato sauce and tomato paste
- fat-free pasta sauce (any variety)
- fat-free black beans
- fat-free baked beans
- fat-free salsa
- low-calorie ketchup
- vinegars: cider, white wine, red wine, rice, fruit-flavored, etc.
- fresh lemons and limes or juice (great for fish, chicken, sodas, etc.)
- variety of spices: basil, rosemary, thyme, oregano, cumin, paprika, cinnamon, nutmeg, ginger, chili powder, garlic powder, onion powder, pepper
- minced garlic, minced onion flakes
- vanilla, almond extract
- assorted frozen vegetables
- unsweetened frozen fruit (blueberries, raspberries, strawberries, etc.)
- sun-dried tomatoes (not oil-packed)
- assorted fruit juices or frozen concentrates (orange, lemon, lime, etc.)
- potatoes: baking, preshredded packaged, presliced packaged
- assorted fat-free whole grain breads, pita pockets, bagels, fat-free crackers
- fat-free flour tortillas
- fat-free egg substitute
- fat-free chicken breasts, chicken or turkey tenders
- fat-free ground chicken or turkey
- fat-free Harvest Burgers for Recipes or Morningstar Farms beef crumbles (1-800-243-1810)
- fat-free roast beef, corned beef, pastrami - Ember Foods, Inc. (1-800-323-0639)
- fat-free frozen shrimp
- fat-free granola or Grape-Nuts cereal
- popcorn
- nonfat cooking spray
- fat-free Cool Whip (1-800-431-1001)
- calorie-free sparkling water

CONTENTS

AWESOME
APPETIZERS

✦ ✦ ✦

ARTICHOKE QUICHE APPETIZER SQUARES

EASY - DO AHEAD - FREEZE

INGREDIENTS:
½ cup egg substitute
3 tbsp. Cornflake crumbs
1 tbsp. fat-free mayonnaise
¼ tsp. garlic powder
1 tsp. onion powder
⅛ tsp. cayenne pepper
10 oz. frozen artichoke hearts, thawed and chopped
¾ cup fat-free Swiss cheese, shredded

DIRECTIONS:
Preheat oven to 350 degrees. Lightly spray 8 x 8-inch baking dish with nonfat cooking spray. In a large bowl, combine egg substitute, Cornflake crumbs, mayonnaise, garlic powder, onion powder, and cayenne pepper. Stir in artichokes and cheese and mix until blended. Spread misture into prepared pan and bake in preheated oven 25 to 30 minutes, until golden brown. Let cool at room temperature 5 minutes; cut into squares.

Serves: 8

Nutrition per Serving		Exchanges
Calories	69	1 starch
Carbohydrate	9 grams	3 vegetable
Cholesterol	0 milligrams	
Dietary Fiber	3 grams	
Protein	8 grams	
Sodium	250 milligrams	

SHOPPING LIST:
4 oz. egg substitute, Cornflake crumbs, fat-free mayonnaise, garlic powder, onion powder, cayenne pepper, 10 oz. frozen artichoke hearts, 3 oz. fat-free Swiss cheese

BASIL GARLIC SPREAD

EASY - DO AHEAD

✦ ✦ ✦

INGREDIENTS:

1 cup fat-free ricotta cheese
1 tsp. minced garlic
1 tsp. thyme
1 tbsp. dried basil

DIRECTIONS:

Combine all ingredients in a food processor or blender and
process until smooth.

Serves: 4

Nutrition per Serving		Exchanges
Calories	48	1 meat
Carbohydrate	4 grams	1 vegetable
Cholesterol	10 milligrams	
Dietary Fiber	< 1 gram	
Protein	9 grams	
Sodium	120 milligrams	

SHOPPING LIST:

8 oz. fat-free ricotta cheese, minced garlic, thyme, dried
basil

CHEESE CRAB DIP

EASY - DO AHEAD

INGREDIENTS:

6 oz. can fat-free crabmeat
8 oz. fat-free cream cheese
¼ cup fat-free mayonnaise
1 tsp. sugar
¼ tsp. garlic powder

DIRECTIONS:

Combine all ingredients in a medium saucepan over low heat and cook, stirring constantly, until cheese is melted and ingredients are blended.

Serves: 6

Nutrition per Serving

Calories	67
Carbohydrate	7 grams
Cholesterol	6 milligrams
Dietary Fiber	0 grams
Protein	8 grams
Sodium	545 milligrams

Exchanges

1 meat
½ starch

SHOPPING LIST:

6 oz. can fat-free crabmeat, 8 oz. fat-free cream cheese, 2 oz. fat-free mayonnaise, sugar, garlic powder

CRAB RANGOON SPREAD

EASY - DO AHEAD

◆ ◆ ◆

INGREDIENTS:

20 wonton wrappers
½ cup fat-free Parmesan cheese
1 cup fat-free cream cheese
2 tbsp. skim milk
1 tsp. onion powder
½ tsp. garlic powder
6 oz. can fat-free crabmeat
1 cup fat-free sweet and sour sauce

DIRECTIONS:

Preheat oven to 375 degrees. Lightly spray cookie sheets with nonfat cooking spray. Arrange wontons on cookie sheet in a single layer. Spray very lightly with nonfat cooking spray and immediately sprinkle with Parmesan cheese. Bake 5 to 7 minutes until lightly browned and crisp; remove from oven and cool. Place cream cheese, milk, onion powder, and garlic powder in medium bowl and blend until smooth. Fold in crabmeat and mix lightly. Spread crab mixture in shallow dish and top with sweet and sour sauce. Serve with wonton crisps.

Serves: 8

Nutrition per Serving		Exchanges
Calories	164	½ fruit
Carbohydrate	29 grams	½ starch
Cholesterol	4 milligrams	½ meat
Dietary Fiber	2 grams	1 milk
Protein	13 grams	
Sodium	730 milligrams	

SHOPPING LIST:

1 package wonton wrappers, 4 oz. fat-free Parmesan cheese, 8 oz. fat-free cream cheese, 1 oz. skim milk, onion powder, garlic powder, 6 oz. can fat-free crabmeat, 8 oz. fat-free sweet and sour sauce

CREAMY CHEESE DIP

EASY - DO AHEAD

INGREDIENTS:

½ cup fat-free cream cheese, softened
½ cup fat-free sour cream
½ cup fat-free cottage cheese
1 tbsp. fat-free mayonnaise
2 tsp. dried dill weed
½ tsp. onion powder
½ tsp. garlic powder

DIRECTIONS:

Combine all ingredients in a food processor or blender and process until smooth. Great with assorted vegetables or fat-free crackers.

Serves: 24 Yields: 1½ cups

Nutrition per Serving (1 tbsp.)		Exchanges
Calories	9	free
Carbohydrate	< 1 gram	
Cholesterol	< 1 milligram	
Dietary Fiber	0 grams	
Protein	1 gram	
Sodium	45 milligrams	

SHOPPING LIST:

4 oz. fat-free cream cheese, 4 oz. fat-free sour cream, 4 oz. fat-free cottage cheese, fat-free mayonnaise, dried dill weed, onion powder, garlic powder

CURRY DIP

EASY - DO AHEAD

INGREDIENTS:
1 cup fat-free mayonnaise
½ tsp. onion powder
1 tsp. horseradish
1 tsp. garlic powder
1 tsp. curry powder
1 tsp. vinegar

DIRECTIONS:
Combine all ingredients in a medium bowl and mix until blended. Refrigerate several hours before serving. Great vegetable dip!

Serves: 6

Nutrition per Serving	
Calories	30
Carbohydrate	6 grams
Cholesterol	0 milligrams
Dietary Fiber	0 grams
Protein	< 1 gram
Sodium	290 milligrams

Exchanges
½ fruit

SHOPPING LIST:
8 oz. fat-free mayonnaise, onion powder, horseradish, garlic powder, curry powder, vinegar

LOBSTER DIP

EASY - DO AHEAD

INGREDIENTS:
½ cup fat-free sour cream
1 cup fat-free cream cheese, softened
1 tbsp. freeze-dried chives
½ cup chili sauce
12 oz. fat-free imitation lobster flakes

DIRECTIONS:
Place sour cream, cream cheese, chives and chili sauce in food processor or blender and process until smooth. Place mixture in medium bowl; fold in lobster. Refrigerate overnight.

Serves: 6

Nutrition per Serving		Exchanges
Calories	112	1 starch
Carbohydrate	14 grams	1¼ meat
Cholesterol	6 milligrams	
Dietary Fiber	< 1 gram	
Protein	12 grams	
Sodium	831 milligrams	

SHOPPING LIST:
4 oz. fat-free sour cream, 8 oz. fat-free cream cheese, freeze-dried chives, 4 oz. chili sauce, 12 oz. fat-free imitation lobster flakes

NACHO CHEESE DIP

EASY - DO AHEAD

INGREDIENTS:
1 cup fat-free cream cheese
1 cup fat-free Mexican shredded cheese
2 tsp. skim milk
½ cup fat-free medium chunky-style salsa

DIRECTIONS:
In a small saucepan over low heat, combine cream cheese and Mexican cheese. Cook until cheese is melted. Add milk and salsa and continue cooking 10 minutes until thoroughly heated. Serve with fat-free chips.

Serves: 8

Nutrition per Serving		Exchanges
Calories	49	1 meat
Carbohydrate	4 grams	1 vegetable
Cholesterol	1 milligram	
Dietary Fiber	0 grams	
Protein	8 grams	
Sodium	333 milligrams	

SHOPPING LIST:
8 oz. fat-free cream cheese, 4 oz. fat-free shredded Mexican cheese, skim milk, 4 oz. fat-free medium chunky-style salsa

PICADILLO DIP

EASY - DO AHEAD

INGREDIENTS:
1 lb. fat-free ground turkey
1 tsp. cumin
½ tsp. garlic powder
¼ tsp. onion powder
¼ tsp. cayenne pepper
14½ oz. stewed tomatoes
¼ cup water
2 tbsp. tomato paste
½ cup raisins

DIRECTIONS:
Lightly spray medium nonstick skillet with nonfat cooking spray and heat over medium-high heat. Add turkey, cumin, garlic, onion, and cayenne pepper to skillet and cook until no longer pink and cooked through. Add tomatoes, water, tomato paste, and raisins to turkey and cook until mixture starts to boil. Reduce heat to low, cover, and simmer 10 minutes, until heated through. Serve with fat-free crackers, pita crisps or tortilla chips.

Serves: 8

Nutrition per Serving		Exchanges
Calories	97	2 meat
Carbohydrate	12 grams	⅔ fruit
Cholesterol	25 milligrams	
Dietary Fiber	1 gram	
Protein	13 grams	
Sodium	284 milligrams	

SHOPPING LIST:
1 lb. fat-free ground turkey, cumin, garlic powder, onion powder, cayenne pepper, 14½ oz. stewed tomatoes, 1 oz. tomato paste, 4 oz. raisins

PICKLED BEET VEGGIE DIP

EASY - DO AHEAD

INGREDIENTS:

8¼ oz. sliced pickled beets
½ cup minced red onion
½ cup fat-free sour cream
¼ tsp. pepper

DIRECTIONS:

Drain beets, reserving ¼ cup liquid. In a food processor or blender, combine beets and liquid and process until smooth. Place beets in a medium bowl; add onion, sour cream, and pepper and mix well. Refrigerate 2 to 4 hours before serving. Serve with assorted cut-up vegetables.

Serves: 6

Nutrition per Serving		Exchanges
Calories	44	2 vegetable
Carbohydrate	8 grams	
Cholesterol	0 milligrams	
Dietary Fiber	< 1 gram	
Protein	2 grams	
Sodium	117 milligrams	

SHOPPING LIST:

8¼ oz. can pickled beets, 1 small red onion, 4 oz. fat-free sour cream, pepper

ROASTED RED PEPPER SPREAD

EASY - DO AHEAD

INGREDIENTS:
16 oz. roasted red peppers, drained
2 tsp. minced garlic
1 tbsp. fresh parsley
1 tbsp. capers, drained

DIRECTIONS:
Combine all ingredients in a food processor or blender and process until smooth. Serve with fat-free crackers or toasted pita chips

Serves: 4

Nutrition per Serving		Exchanges
Calories	31	1 vegetable
Carbohydrate	7 grams	
Cholesterol	0 milligrams	
Dietary Fiber	2 grams	
Protein	1 gram	
Sodium	1,332 milligrams	

SHOPPING LIST:
16 oz. roasted red peppers, minced garlic, fresh parsley, capers

SHRIMP DIJON DIP

EASY - DO AHEAD

✦ ✦ ✦

INGREDIENTS:
1 cup fat-free cream cheese, softened
¼ cup Dijon mustard
¼ cup fat-free sour cream
½ cup fat-free frozen shrimp, cooked and chopped
1 tbsp. chopped scallions
1 tbsp. chopped celery

DIRECTIONS:
In a medium bowl, combine cream cheese, mustard, and sour cream and mix until blended smooth. Fold in shrimp, scallions, and celery; cover and refrigerate 2 to 4 hours before serving. Serve with fat-free crackers or assorted vegetables.

Serves: 6

Nutrition per Serving		Exchanges
Calories	65	1 meat
Carbohydrate	5 grams	1 vegetable
Cholesterol	2 milligrams	
Dietary Fiber	0 grams	
Protein	8 grams	
Sodium	619 milligrams	

SHOPPING LIST:
8 oz. fat-free cream cheese, 2 oz. Dijon mustard, 2 oz. fat-free sour cream, 4 oz. fat-free frozen shrimp, 1 scallion, 1 stalk celery

SPICY CHILI DIP

EASY - DO AHEAD

INGREDIENTS:
½ cup fat-free yogurt
½ cup fat-free sour cream
2 tbsp. chili sauce
1½ tsp. prepared horseradish

DIRECTIONS:
Combine all ingredients in a medium bowl and mix until blended. Refrigerate at least 1 to 2 hours before serving. Great with vegetables, fat-free crackers, or pita crisps.

Serves: 4

Nutrition per Serving		Exchanges
Calories	43	½ milk
Carbohydrate	4 grams	
Cholesterol	< 1 milligram	
Dietary Fiber	0 grams	
Protein	4 grams	
Sodium	161 milligrams	

SHOPPING LIST:
4 oz. fat-free yogurt, 4 oz. fat-free sour cream, 1 oz. chili sauce, prepared horseradish

SUN-DRIED TOMATO SPREAD

EASY - DO AHEAD

✦ ✦ ✦

INGREDIENTS:
¼ cup sun-dried tomatoes
¼ cup fat-free cottage cheese
¼ cup fat-free ricotta cheese
½ cup fat-free cream cheese, softened
2 tsp. dried basil
⅛ tsp. cayenne pepper
½ cup roasted red peppers, drained and dried

DIRECTIONS:
Place sun-dried tomatoes in a small bowl and cover with very hot water. Let stand at room temperature until tomatoes are soft and tender. Drain well and chop into small pieces. In a medium bowl, combine cottage cheese, ricotta cheese, cream cheese, basil, cayenne, and red peppers with tomatoes and mix until well blended. Serve with fat-free crackers, pita crisps, or bagel chips.

Serves: 6

Nutrition per Serving		Exchanges
Calories	47	2 vegetable
Carbohydrate	8 grams	
Cholesterol	2 milligrams	
Dietary Fiber	1 gram	
Protein	3 grams	
Sodium	180 milligrams	

SHOPPING LIST:
sun-dried tomatoes (not oil-packed), 2 oz. fat-free cottage cheese, 2 oz. fat-free ricotta cheese, 4 oz. fat-free cream cheese, dried basil, cayenne pepper, 7 oz. roasted red peppers

SWEET ONION CHEESE DIP

EASY - DO AHEAD

INGREDIENTS:

1½ tbsp. reconstituted butter-flavored
    granules
2 large Vidalia onions, coarsely chopped
1½ cups fat-free shredded Cheddar cheese
¾ cup fat-free mayonnaise
¼ tsp. cayenne pepper
½ tsp. garlic powder

DIRECTIONS:

Preheat oven to 375 degrees. Lightly spray large nonstick skillet with nonfat cooking spray. Lightly spray 1-2 quart casserole with nonfat cooking spray. Add liquid butter to skillet and heat over medium-high heat. Cook onions in butter until tender; stir in cheese, mayonnaise, cayenne pepper, and garlic and mix until blended. Spread mixture into prepared casserole and bake in preheated oven 20 to 25 minutes until golden brown and heated through. Great with pita crisps, bagel chips, fat-free tortilla chips, or fat-free crackers.

Serves: 8

Nutrition per Serving		Exchanges
Calories	66	½ meat
Carbohydrate	8 grams	2 vegetable
Cholesterol	0 milligrams	
Dietary Fiber	1 gram	
Protein	7 grams	
Sodium	369 milligrams	

SHOPPING LIST:

butter-flavored granules, 2 large Vidalia onions, 6 oz. fat-free shredded Cheddar cheese, 6 oz. fat-free mayonnaise, cayenne pepper, garlic powder

TUNA SPREAD

EASY - DO AHEAD

✦ ✦ ✦

INGREDIENTS:
12 oz. fat-free tuna
½ cup fat-free cottage cheese
3 tbsp. lemon juice
½ tsp. pepper

DIRECTIONS:
Combine all ingredients in a food processor and process until smooth. Serve with fat-free crackers or assorted vegetables.

Serves: 4

Nutrition per Serving		Exchanges
Calories	120	3½ meat
Carbohydrate	1 gram	
Cholesterol	16 milligrams	
Dietary Fiber	< 1 gram	
Protein	26 grams	
Sodium	327 milligrams	

SHOPPING LIST:
12 oz. fat-free tuna, 4 oz. fat-free cottage cheese, 1½ oz. lemon juice, pepper

TURKEY CHEESE LAYER DIP

EASY - DO AHEAD

INGREDIENTS:

1 cup fat-free cream cheese, softened
½ cup pepperoncini peppers, stemmed
1½ cups shredded lettuce
1 cup fat-free sour cream
½ cup chopped onions
¼ lb. fat-free deli-style turkey, chopped
2 cups chopped tomatoes

DIRECTIONS:

Place cream cheese and peppers in a food processor or blender and process until blended and smooth. Spread cheese mixture onto serving platter. Sprinkle lettuce on top of cheese. In a small bowl, combine sour cream and onions; mix well. Spread sour cream on top of lettuce. Sprinkle chopped turkey and tomatoes over sour cream. Serve with fat-free bread, crackers, pita chips, or bagel chips.

Serves: 8

Nutrition per Serving		Exchanges
Calories	72	1 vegetable
Carbohydrate	6 grams	1 meat
Cholesterol	5 milligrams	
Dietary Fiber	1 gram	
Protein	8 grams	
Sodium	577 milligrams	

SHOPPING LIST:

8 oz. fat-free cream cheese, pepperoncini peppers, prepackaged shredded lettuce, 8 oz. fat-free sour cream, 1 small onion, ¼ lb. fat-free deli-style turkey, 2 tomatoes

BARBECUE MEATBALLS

EASY - DO AHEAD - FREEZE

✦ ✦ ✦

INGREDIENTS:

1 cup low-calorie ketchup	1 tbsp. minced onion flakes
¼ cup brown sugar	¼ tsp. garlic powder
¼ cup red wine vinegar	½ cup skim milk
½ cup water	¾ cup multi-grain oatmeal
1½ lb. fat-free beef crumbles	⅛ of tsp. pepper to taste

DIRECTIONS:

In small bowl, combine ketchup, brown sugar, vinegar, and water; blend until smooth and set aside. Preheat oven to 350 degrees. Lightly spray 10-inch baking dish with nonfat cooking spray. In a medium bowl, combine beef crumbles, onion flakes, garlic powder, milk, pepper, and oatmeal; blend well and shape mixture into small balls. Lightly spray large nonstick skillet with nonfat cooking spray and heat over medium-high heat. Place meatballs in skillet and brown on all sides; turn carefully with slotted spoon. Place meatballs in prepared baking dish. Cover with barbecue sauce and bake in preheated oven 1 hour, until bubbly. Prepare meatballs and sauce ahead, if desired; bake just before serving.

Serves: 6

Nutrition per Serving		Exchanges
Calories	218	3 vegetable
Carbohydrate	29 grams	1 starch
Cholesterol	1 milligram	2 meat
Dietary Fiber	1 gram	
Protein	26 grams	
Sodium	672 milligrams	

SHOPPING LIST:

8 oz. low-calorie ketchup, brown sugar, 2 oz. red wine vinegar, 1½ lb. beef crumbles (Morningstar Farms), minced onion flakes, garlic powder, 4 oz. skim milk, Quaker multi-grain oatmeal, pepper

CHICKEN-VEGETABLE QUESADILLAS

EASY - DO AHEAD

INGREDIENTS:
8 fat-free flour tortillas
1 cup fat-free chicken tenders, cooked and diced
1 cup fat-free shredded Monterey Jack cheese
1 cup fat-free shredded Cheddar cheese
1 cup canned corn kernels
2 cups Mexican tomatoes and jalapeños, drained
12 oz. roasted peppers, drained

DIRECTIONS:
Preheat oven to 450 degrees. Line baking sheets with foil and lightly spray with nonfat cooking spray. Place tortillas in single layer on baking sheets. Sprinkle each tortilla with ¼ cup chopped chicken, ¼ cup Monterey Jack cheese, ¼ cup Cheddar cheese, ¼ cup corn kernels, ½ cup tomatoes, and several slices red pepper; top with remaining cheese and remaining tortillas. Bake in preheated oven 8 to 10 minutes, until cheese is melted and tortillas are lightly browned.

Serves: 8

Nutrition per Serving		Exchanges
Calories	217	1 starch
Carbohydrate	35 grams	4 vegetable
Cholesterol	14 milligrams	1 meat
Dietary Fiber	3 grams	
Protein	20 grams	
Sodium	1,388 milligrams	

SHOPPING LIST:
8 fat-free flour tortillas, ½ pound fat-free chicken tenders, 4 oz. fat-free shredded Monterey Jack cheese, 4 oz. fat-free shredded Cheddar cheese, 8 oz. corn kernels, 28 oz. Mexican tomatoes and jalapeños, 12 oz. roasted peppers

CORN CRABCAKES

EASY - DO AHEAD

✦ ✦ ✦

INGREDIENTS:
8 oz. can fat-free crabmeat
2 tbsp. egg substitute
¼ cup fat-free bread crumbs
¼ cup corn kernels
⅛ tsp. cayenne pepper
⅛ tsp. pepper
1½ tsp. lemon juice
1 tsp. white Worcestershire sauce
1 tbsp. Dijon mustard
1 tbsp. fat-free sour cream

DIRECTIONS:
Lightly spray baking sheet with nonfat cooking spray. In a large bowl, combine all ingredients and mix until blended. Roll mixture into 8 balls and place on baking sheet; flatten each ball onto sheet. Cover with plastic wrap and refrigerate 20 to 30 minutes until firm. Preheat oven to 450 degrees. Bake crabcakes in oven 15 minutes; turn over and cook 10 to 15 minutes, until lightly browned on both sides.

Serves: 4

Nutrition per Serving		Exchanges
Calories	83	⅓ starch
Carbohydrate	4 grams	1⅔ meat
Cholesterol	5 milligrams	
Dietary Fiber	< 1 gram	
Protein	13 grams	
Sodium	318 milligrams	

SHOPPING LIST:
8 oz. canned fat-free crabmeat, 1 oz. egg substitute, fat-free bread crumbs, corn kernels, cayenne pepper, pepper, lemon juice, white Worcestershire sauce, Dijon mustard, fat-free sour cream

CRAB CRISPS

EASY - DO AHEAD

INGREDIENTS:
8 oz. can fat-free crabmeat
½ cup diced red bell pepper
2⅔ tbsp. fat-free mayonnaise
2 tsp. dried parsley
1 tsp. freeze-dried chives
1 tbsp. Dijon mustard
1 tbsp. lime juice
1 tbsp. fat-free Parmesan cheese
⅛ tsp. cayenne pepper
12 slices fat-free bread

DIRECTIONS:
Preheat the broiler on high. Line a baking sheet with foil and lightly spray with nonfat cooking spray. In a medium bowl, combine crabmeat, red pepper, mayonnaise, parsley, chives, mustard, lime juice, Parmesan cheese, and cayenne pepper; mix until blended. Spread 1 to 2 tablespoons crab mixture onto each bread slice. Place on prepared baking sheet and broil 4 inches from heat 5-7 minutes, until lightly browned.

Serves: 12

Nutrition per Serving		Exchanges
Calories	111	1⅓ starch
Carbohydrate	20 grams	⅓ meat
Cholesterol	7 milligrams	
Dietary Fiber	1 gram	
Protein	6 grams	
Sodium	346 milligrams	

SHOPPING LIST:
8 oz. can fat-free crabmeat, 1 red bell pepper, fat-free mayonnaise, dried parsley, freeze-dried chives, Dijon mustard, lime juice, fat-free Parmesan cheese, cayenne pepper, ¾ lb. fat-free bread

CRAB RANGOON

AVERAGE - DO AHEAD

✦ ✦ ✦

INGREDIENTS:
1 cup fat-free cream cheese, softened
8 oz. can fat-free crabmeat
1 tsp. sugar
3 green onions, sliced
1 tsp. fat-free ranch salad dressing
1 package wonton wrappers

DIRECTIONS:
Preheat oven to 375 degrees. Lightly spray baking sheet with nonfat cooking spray. In a medium bowl, combine cream cheese, crabmeat, sugar, onion, and salad dressing and mix well. To keep wonton skins moist, keep covered with damp paper towel during preparation. Place 1 teaspoon mixture in the center of each wonton skin. Moisten the edges with water and bring the corners together to form a triangle; fold in the side edges to form a packet. Place wontons on prepared baking sheet. Bake in preheated oven 10 to 15 minutes, until golden brown and crisp.

Serves: 10

Nutrition per Serving

Calories	47
Carbohydrate	7 grams
Cholesterol	3 milligrams
Dietary Fiber	0 grams
Protein	4 grams
Sodium	243 milligrams

Exchanges
½ meat
½ starch

SHOPPING LIST:
8 oz. fat-free cream cheese, 8 oz. can fat-free crabmeat, sugar, 3 green onions, fat-free ranch salad dressing, 1 package wonton wrappers

MOZZARELLA STICKS

EASY - DO AHEAD - FREEZE

INGREDIENTS:

1 lb. fat-free mozzarella cheese, whole
¾ cup egg substitute
1½ cups cornflake crumbs
1 tsp. onion powder
1 tsp. garlic powder
1 tbsp. dried parsley

DIRECTIONS:

Preheat oven to 400 degrees. Lightly spray foil-lined baking sheet with nonfat cooking spray. Cut cheese into 3 x ¾-inch sticks. Place egg substitute in a small bowl. In a separate bowl, combine cornflake crumbs, onion powder, garlic powder, and parsley and mix well. Dip each cheese stick into egg substitute; roll in cornflake crumbs and coat well. Place on prepared sheet in a single layer. Bake in preheated oven 10 to 15 minutes, until outside is lightly browned and crisp. Great served with fat-free pasta sauce.

Serves: 8

Nutrition per Serving		Exchanges
Calories	163	1 starch
Carbohydrate	13 grams	2½ meat
Cholesterol	0 milligrams	
Dietary Fiber	< 1 gram	
Protein	22 grams	
Sodium	615 milligrams	

SHOPPING LIST:

1 lb. fat-free mozzarella cheese (whole), 6 oz. egg substitute, cornflake crumbs, onion powder, garlic powder, dried parsley

SPINACH CHEESE SQUARES

EASY - DO AHEAD - FREEZE

INGREDIENTS:
½ cup egg substitute
6 tbsp. flour
10 oz. frozen chopped spinach, thawed and
    drained
2 cups fat-free cottage cheese
2 cups fat-free shredded Cheddar cheese
½ tsp. pepper
½ tsp. onion powder

DIRECTIONS:
Preheat oven to 350 degrees. Lightly spray a 9x13-inch baking dish with nonfat cooking spray. In a large bowl, combine egg substitute and flour and mix until smooth. Add spinach, cottage cheese, Cheddar cheese, pepper, and onion powder and mix well. Pour into prepared pan and bake in preheated oven 45 minutes. Let stand 10 minutes before cutting. This can be made ahead of time, refrigerated or frozen and reheated in oven before serving.

Serves: 16

Nutrition per Serving		Exchanges
Calories	47	⅓ starch
Carbohydrate	5 grams	⅔ meat
Cholesterol	< 1 milligram	
Dietary Fiber	< 1 gram	
Protein	6 grams	
Sodium	188 milligrams	

SHOPPING LIST:
4 oz. egg substitute, flour, 10 oz. frozen chopped spinach, 16 oz. fat-free cottage cheese, 8 oz. fat-free shredded Cheddar cheese, pepper, onion powder

WONTON SHELLS

EASY - DO AHEAD

INGREDIENTS:

12 oz. wonton wrappers
¼ cup reconstituted butter-flavored granules

DIRECTIONS:

Preheat oven to 400 degrees. Lightly spray regular-size muffin cups with nonfat cooking spray. Brush each wonton with liquid butter and press into muffin cups. Bake in preheated oven 3 to 4 minutes until lightly browned. Store in tightly-sealed container until ready to serve. Fill with chicken, crab, shrimp, or tuna filling.

Serves: 24

Nutrition per Serving		Exchanges
Calories	41	½ starch
Carbohydrate	9 grams	
Cholesterol	0 milligrams	
Dietary Fiber	0 grams	
Protein	1 gram	
Sodium	65 milligrams	

SHOPPING LIST:

12 oz. wonton wrappers (50 wraps), butter-flavored granules

CHICKEN FILLING FOR WONTON SHELLS

EASY - DO AHEAD

INGREDIENTS:
- ¼ cup fat-free mayonnaise
- ¼ cup chopped celery
- ½ cup canned, chopped water chestnuts
- 1 tsp. curry powder
- ¼ tsp. pepper
- 2 cups fat-free chicken tenders, cooked and chopped
- ¾ cup chopped apple

DIRECTIONS:

In a medium bowl, combine mayonnaise, celery, water chestnuts, curry powder, and pepper and mix until blended. Fold in chopped chicken and apple. Store in refrigerator until ready to serve. Divide filling among Wonton Shells (page 26).

Serves: 12

Nutrition per Serving		Exchanges
Calories	43	1 meat
Carbohydrate	2 grams	½ vegetable
Cholesterol	23 milligrams	
Dietary Fiber	2 grams	
Protein	8 grams	
Sodium	129 milligrams	

SHOPPING LIST:

2 oz. fat-free mayonnaise, 1 stalk celery, canned water chestnuts, curry powder, pepper, 1 lb. fat-free chicken tenders, 1 small apple

CRAB FILLING FOR WONTON SHELLS

EASY - DO AHEAD

INGREDIENTS:

8 oz. can fat-free crabmeat
¼ cup mayonnaise
2 tbsp. fat-free sour cream
¼ cup canned water chestnuts, chopped fine
¼ tsp. garlic powder
½ tsp. onion powder
¼ tsp. pepper

DIRECTIONS:

Combine all ingredients in a medium bowl and mix until blended. Store in refrigerator until ready to serve. Divide filling among Wonton Shells (page 26).

Serves: 12

Nutrition per Serving		Exchanges
Calories	26	½ meat
Carbohydrate	3 grams	½ vegetable
Cholesterol	4 milligrams	
Dietary Fiber	0 grams	
Protein	2 grams	
Sodium	196 milligrams	

SHOPPING LIST:

8 oz. can fat-free crabmeat, 2 oz. fat-free mayonnaise, 1 oz. fat-free sour cream, canned water chestnuts, garlic powder, onion powder, pepper

SHRIMP FILLING FOR WONTON SHELLS

EASY - DO AHEAD

INGREDIENTS:

8 oz. fat-free frozen cooked shrimp, thawed and chopped
¼ cup fat-free mayonnaise
2 tbsp. fat-free sour cream
¼ cup chopped celery
¼ cup chopped green onions
¼ tsp. garlic powder
¼ tsp. pepper

DIRECTIONS:

Combine all ingredients in a medium bowl and mix until blended. Store in refrigerator until ready to serve. Divide filling among Wonton Shells (page 26).

Serves: 12

Nutrition per Serving		Exchanges
Calories	25	½ meat
Carbohydrate	3 grams	½ vegetable
Cholesterol	2 milligrams	
Dietary Fiber	0 grams	
Protein	2 grams	
Sodium	163 milligrams	

SHOPPING LIST:

8 oz. fat-free frozen cooked shrimp, 2 oz. fat-free mayonnaise, 1 oz. fat-free sour cream, 1 stalk celery, 2 green onions, garlic powder, pepper

PINEAPPLE-CHEESE BAGEL SNACKS

EASY - DO AHEAD

INGREDIENTS:
1 cup fat-free cream cheese, softened
8 oz. crushed pineapple in juice, drained
12 fat-free baked bagel chips
¾ cup Grape-Nuts cereal

DIRECTIONS:
In a small bowl, combine cream cheese and pineapple and mix until blended. Refrigerate at least 1 hour. Spread bagel chips with cheese mixture and sprinkle with Grape-Nuts cereal.

Serves: 6

Nutrition per Serving		Exchanges
Calories	129	1 meat
Carbohydrate	25 grams	⅔ starch
Cholesterol	0 milligrams	1 fruit
Dietary Fiber	1 gram	
Protein	8 grams	
Sodium	369 milligrams	

SHOPPING LIST:
8 oz. fat-free cream cheese, 8 oz. crushed pineapple in juice, fat-free bagels or precut bagel chips, Grape-Nuts cereal

SHRIMP BALLS

EASY - DO AHEAD

INGREDIENTS:
1 cup fat-free cream cheese, softened
1 tsp. dry mustard
½ tsp. onion powder
1½ tsp. lemon juice
⅛ tsp. cayenne pepper
1½ cups fat-free frozen, cooked small shrimp, thawed and drained

DIRECTIONS:
In a medium bowl, combine cream cheese with mustard, onion powder, lemon juice, and cayenne pepper; blend well. Fold in shrimp. Refrigerate 1 to 2 hours until slightly firm. Roll mixture into 1-inch balls and place on serving platter. Refrigerate 45 to 60 minutes. Serve with toothpicks and dip in cocktail sauce, if desired.

Serves: 4

Nutrition per Serving		Exchanges
Calories	105	¾ starch
Carbohydrate	12 grams	1⅓ meat
Cholesterol	4 milligrams	
Dietary Fiber	0 grams	
Protein	13 grams	
Sodium	828 milligrams	

SHOPPING LIST:
8 oz. fat-free cream cheese, dry mustard, onion powder, lemon juice, cayenne pepper, 10 oz. fat-free frozen cooked shrimp

SPINACH TORTILLA ROLLS

AVERAGE - DO AHEAD

INGREDIENTS:

1 cup fat-free cream cheese, softened
2 tbsp. sliced green onions
4 fat-free flour tortillas
1 cup fresh spinach, chopped
½ cup shredded fat-free Monterey Jack cheese
¼ cup chopped green chilies
1 cup chopped red bell pepper

DIRECTIONS:

In a small bowl, combine cream cheese and green onions; mix until blended. Spread ¼ cup cream cheese mixture on each tortilla. Top each tortilla with ¼ cup chopped spinach, 2 tablespoons shredded cheese, 1 tablespoon green chilies, and ¼ cup chopped red pepper. Roll tortillas up from narrow end and wrap in plastic wrap; refrigerate 1 hour before serving. Remove tortilla rolls from wrap and place on serving platter. Cut each tortilla into 6 to 8 pieces, securing each piece with toothpick. Serve with fat-free salsa, if desired.

Serves: 8

Nutrition per Serving		Exchanges
Calories	105	½ meat
Carbohydrate	16 grams	⅔ starch
Cholesterol	0 milligrams	1 vegetable
Dietary Fiber	1 gram	
Protein	10 grams	
Sodium	537 milligrams	

SHOPPING LIST:

8 oz. fat-free cream cheese, 2 green onions, 4 fat-free flour tortillas, ¼ pound fresh spinach, 2 oz. fat-free shredded Monterey Jack cheese, 2 oz. chopped green chilies, 1 small red bell pepper

TORTILLA CHEESE WRAPS

AVERAGE - DO AHEAD

✦ ✦ ✦

INGREDIENTS:
¼ cup fat-free cream cheese, softened
3 tbsp. fat-free mayonnaise
3 tbsp. Dijon mustard
4 fat-free flour tortillas
¼ cup chopped green chilies
1 cup chopped cucumbers
1 cup chopped tomatoes

DIRECTIONS:
In a small bowl, combine cream cheese, mayonnaise, and mustard and mix until blended. Spread 1½ tablespoons cheese mixture down the center of each tortilla. Sprinkle with 1 tablespoon green chilies, ¼ cup cucumbers, and ¼ cup tomatoes. Roll tortillas up burrito-style and slice into 4 to 6 pieces; hold secure with a toothpick if necessary. Cover with plastic wrap and refrigerate several hours before serving.

Serves: 4

Nutrition per Serving

Calories	160
Carbohydrate	31 grams
Cholesterol	0 milligrams
Dietary Fiber	3 grams
Protein	7 grams
Sodium	988 milligrams

Exchanges
1 starch
3 vegetable

SHOPPING LIST:
2 oz. fat-free cream cheese, 1½ oz. fat-free mayonnaise, 1½ oz. Dijon mustard, 4 fat-free flour tortillas, 2 oz. chopped green chiles, 1 cucumber, 1 tomato

BEAUTIFUL BRUNCH, BREADS, AND MUFFINS

✦ ✦ ✦

BROWN SUGAR-CINNAMON PANCAKES

EASY - DO AHEAD - FREEZE

INGREDIENTS:
2 cups fat-free pancake mix
1½ cups water
2½ tbsp. brown sugar
1 tsp. cinnamon

DIRECTIONS:
Lightly spray large nonstick skillet with nonfat cooking spray. In a large bowl, combine all ingredients and mix until blended. (Do not overmix batter.) Heat skillet over medium heat; pour ¼ cup batter for each pancake into hot skillet and cook about 2 minutes per side, until golden brown.

Serves: 6

Nutrition per Serving		Exchanges
Calories	149	1 starch
Carbohydrate	37 grams	1⅓ fruit
Cholesterol	0 milligrams	
Dietary Fiber	4 grams	
Protein	3 grams	
Sodium	295 milligrams	

SHOPPING LIST:
fat-free pancake mix (Krusteaz or Pioneer), brown sugar, cinnamon

CINNAMON-FRENCH TOAST

EASY - DO AHEAD

♦ ♦ ♦

INGREDIENTS:
¼ cup brown sugar
1 tsp. cinnamon
3 tbsp. fat-free margarine, melted
¾ cup egg substitute
2 tbsp. skim milk
½ tsp. vanilla
2 tsp. sugar
8 slices fat-free French bread
powdered sugar, lite syrup, or preserves

DIRECTIONS:
Preheat oven to 400 degrees. Lightly spray a 10x15-inch baking dish with nonfat cooking spray. In a small bowl, combine brown sugar and cinnamon and mix well. Spread brown sugar mixture in bottom of dish; drizzle margarine over sugar and mix well. In a medium bowl, combine egg substitute, milk, vanilla and sugar; blend until smooth. Dip bread slices in egg mixture and coat well on both sides. Arrange slices in baking dish; pour remaining egg mixture on top and refrigerate until ready to bake. Bake in preheated oven 20 minutes. Serve with powdered sugar, lite syrup, or preserves.

Serves: 4

Nutrition per Serving		Exchanges
Calories	257	3⅓ starch
Carbohydrate	51 grams	
Cholesterol	< 1 milligram	
Dietary Fiber	2 grams	
Protein	10 grams	
Sodium	440 milligrams	

SHOPPING LIST:
brown sugar, cinnamon, fat-free margarine, 6 oz. egg substitute, 1 oz. skim milk, vanilla, sugar, ½ lb. fat-free French bread (8 slices). For topping, powdered sugar, lite syrup, or preserves.

FRENCH TOAST STICKS

EASY - DO AHEAD - FREEZE

INGREDIENTS:
8 slices fat-free French bread
4 large egg whites
½ cup egg substitute
1 tsp. vanilla
⅓ cup skim milk
1½ tsp. cinnamon
1½ tbsp. fat-free margarine
½ tbsp. low-fat margarine

DIRECTIONS:
Lightly spray large nonstick skillet with nonfat cooking spray. Cut bread slices into sticks, about 4 inches long. In a medium bowl, combine egg whites, egg substitute, vanilla, milk and cinnamon; mix until blended. Add 1 teaspoon fat-free margarine and ¾ teaspoon low-fat margarine to skillet and cook until melted over medium-high heat. Dip bread sticks into egg mixture and coat on all sides; place in hot skillet and cook until lightly browned on all sides. Respray skillet and add margarines as needed. Wrap sticks in foil and keep warm in 300 degree oven. Serve with powdered sugar or syrup, if desired.

Serves: 4

Nutrition per Serving		Exchanges
Calories	217	2⅓ starch
Carbohydrate	37 grams	1 meat
Cholesterol	< 1 milligram	
Dietary Fiber	2 grams	
Protein	13 grams	
Sodium	457 milligrams	

SHOPPING LIST:
½ lb. fat-free French bread, 4 eggs, 4 oz. egg substitute, vanilla, skim milk, cinnamon, fat-free margarine, low-fat margarine (Weight Watchers)

POTATO WAFFLES

EASY - DO AHEAD - FREEZE

✦ ✦ ✦

INGREDIENTS:
1 cup flour
⅓ cup potato flakes
2 tsp. sugar
2 tsp. baking powder
½ cup egg substitute
1½ cups skim milk
1 tbsp. Lighter Bake

DIRECTIONS:
In a large bowl, combine flour, potato flakes, sugar, baking powder. In a separate bowl, combine egg substitute, milk and Lighter Bake and mix until smooth. Add to flour mixture and mix just until dry ingredients are moistened and blended. Pour batter onto waffle iron following directions suggested by the manufacturer and bake until golden brown.

Serves: 8

Nutrition per Serving		Exchanges
Calories	98	1⅓ starch
Carbohydrate	19 grams	
Cholesterol	< 1 milligram	
Dietary Fiber	1 gram	
Protein	5 grams	
Sodium	129 milligrams	

SHOPPING LIST:
flour, instant potato flakes, sugar, baking powder, 4 ounces egg substitute, 12 oz. skim milk, Lighter Bake

SPICED APPLE PANCAKES

EASY - DO AHEAD - FREEZE

INGREDIENTS:
2 cups fat-free pancake mix
1½ cups water
½ cup chunky-style applesauce
1 tsp. cinnamon

DIRECTIONS:
Lightly spray large nonstick skillet with nonfat cooking spray. In a large bowl, combine all ingredients and mix until blended. (Do not overmix batter.) Heat skillet over medium heat; pour ¼ cup batter for each pancake into hot skillet and cook about 2 minutes per side, until golden brown. Great with Apple Raisin Pancake Sauce (page 126)!

Serves: 6

Nutrition per Serving		Exchanges
Calories	136	1 starch
Carbohydrate	34 grams	1 fruit
Cholesterol	0 milligrams	
Dietary Fiber	4 grams	
Protein	3 grams	
Sodium	294 milligrams	

SHOPPING LIST:
fat-free pancake mix (Krusteaz or Pioneer), 4 oz. chunky-style applesauce, cinnamon

RICE AND FRUIT BREAKFAST

AVERAGE

✦ ✦ ✦

INGREDIENTS:
1 cup wild rice
1 cup water
1 cup fat-free chicken broth
2 tbsp. reconstituted butter-flavored granules
¼ cup brown sugar
1½ tsp. cinnamon
1 cup apple, peeled and sliced
1 medium banana, peeled and sliced
1½ cups skim milk, warmed
cinnamon-sugar, optional

DIRECTIONS:
Combine rice with water and chicken broth in a medium saucepan; bring to a boil over high heat. Reduce heat to low, cover and simmer until rice is cooked through, about 35 to 40 minutes. Lightly spray a large nonstick skillet with nonfat cooking spray; add liquid butter, brown sugar and cinnamon, and mix well. Stir in apple and cook 3 to 5 minutes until tender. Add banana and cook over medium heat until heated through. To serve, spoon rice into bowls and top with milk and warmed fruit. Sprinkle with cinnamon-sugar, if desired.

Serves: 6

Nutrition per Serving		Exchanges
Calories	188	2 starch
Carbohydrate	41 grams	⅔ fruit
Cholesterol	1 milligram	
Dietary Fiber	2 grams	
Protein	6 grams	
Sodium	187 milligrams	

SHOPPING LIST:
wild rice, 8 oz. fat-free chicken broth, butter-flavored granules, brown sugar, cinnamon, 1 medium apple, 1 medium banana, 12 oz. skim milk, cinnamon-sugar (optional)

WARM APPLE GRANOLA

EASY

INGREDIENTS:

1½ cups canned apple slices
3 cups fat-free granola
1½ cups frozen apple juice concentrate,
  thawed
¼ cup chopped dates
¼ cup raisins
¼ cup water
1 tsp. cinnamon
1½ tbsp. lemon juice

DIRECTIONS:

Combine all ingredients in a medium saucepan and heat over high heat until mixture comes to a boil. Reduce heat to low, cover, and simmer 3 to 5 minutes, until heated through. Serve immediately.

Serves: 6

Nutrition per Serving		Exchanges
Calories	326	1 starch
Carbohydrate	82 grams	4¼ fruit
Cholesterol	0 milligrams	
Dietary Fiber	2 grams	
Protein	3 grams	
Sodium	8 milligrams	

SHOPPING LIST:

20 oz. canned apple slices, Health Valley fat-free granola, 12 oz. frozen apple juice concentrate, chopped dates, raisins, cinnamon, lemon juice

CARROT-ZUCCHINI QUICHE

AVERAGE - DO AHEAD

INGREDIENTS:

1 cup chopped zucchini	⅛ tsp. cayenne pepper
1 cup grated carrots	2 large egg whites
1 cup chopped mushrooms	¾ cup egg substitute
1 tsp. onion powder	⅔ cup fat-free cottage cheese
1 tsp. garlic powder	¼ cup skim milk
½ cup chopped tomatoes	½ cup fat-free Parmesan
2 cups fat-free rice, cooked	cheese
½ tsp. basil	

DIRECTIONS:

Preheat oven to 350 degrees. Lightly spray a 9 or 10-inch pie plate with nonfat cooking spray. Lightly spray a medium saucepan with nonfat cooking spray and heat over medium-high heat. Add zucchini, carrots, mushrooms, onion powder and garlic powder; cook until vegetables are soft and tender. Remove pan from heat; stir in tomatoes, rice, basil, and cayenne pepper and mix well. In a separate small bowl, combine egg whites, egg substitute, cottage cheese, milk and 3 tablespoons Parmesan cheese; blend until smooth. Fold into vegetable mixture; mix well. Pour in prepared pan; sprinkle with remaining Parmesan cheese. Bake in preheated oven 30 minutes; let stand at room temperature 10 minutes, until set in center.

Serves: 6

Nutrition per Serving		Exchanges
Calories	121	1 starch
Carbohydrate	20 grams	1 vegetable
Cholesterol	< 1 milligram	½ meat
Dietary Fiber	2 grams	
Protein	10 grams	
Sodium	186 milligrams	

SHOPPING LIST:

½ lb. zucchini, ½ lb. carrots, ¼ lb. mushrooms, onion powder, garlic powder, 1 small tomato, ¾ cup fat-free raw rice, basil, cayenne pepper, 2 large eggs, 6 oz. egg substitute, 5 to 6 oz. fat-free cottage cheese, 2 oz. skim milk, 4 oz. fat-free Parmesan cheese

MEXICAN FRITTATA UNDER WRAP

EASY

INGREDIENTS:

½ cup chopped red bell pepper

1½ cups egg substitute

¼ tsp. garlic powder

½ cup fat-free chunky-style salsa

¾ cup corn kernels, drained

4 oz. chopped green chilies

½ cup fat-free shredded Cheddar cheese

4 whole fat-free flour tortillas

DIRECTIONS:

Lightly spray large nonstick skillet with nonfat cooking spray; heat over medium-high heat. Add chopped peppers to skillet; cook until tender, about 5 minutes. In medium bowl, combine egg substitute, garlic powder and salsa; mix until blended. Stir in corn, green chilies and cheese; mix well. Pour mixture over peppers; stir lightly. Reduce heat to low, cover skillet; cook over low heat (without stirring) about 10 minutes, until eggs are set. Wrap tortillas in paper towels; heat in microwave on high 1 minute, just until warm and soft. (Tortillas can be wrapped in foil and heated in 350 degree oven 2 to 3 minutes, just until soft.) Divide egg mixture among tortillas; roll up and serve immediately. Serve with extra salsa, if desired.

Serves: 4

Nutrition per Serving		Exchanges
Calories	214	1 starch
Carbohydrate	37 grams	4 vegetable
Cholesterol	0 milligrams	1 meat
Dietary Fiber	3 grams	
Protein	17 grams	
Sodium	823 milligrams	

SHOPPING LIST:

small red bell pepper, 12 oz. egg substitute, garlic powder, 4 oz. chunky-style salsa, small corn kernels, 4 oz. can chopped green chilies, 2 oz. fat-free shredded Cheddar cheese, fat-free flour tortillas (large)

MUSHROOM-CHEESE EGG CASSEROLE

EASY - DO AHEAD

✦ ✦ ✦

INGREDIENTS:

3 cups fat-free shredded
  Cheddar cheese
3 cups fat-free shredded
  mozzarella cheese
½ cup sliced mushrooms
⅓ cup sliced green onions

½ cup chopped red and
  green peppers
½ cup flour
1¾ cups skim milk
2 cups egg substitute,
  beaten
pepper, to taste

DIRECTIONS:

Preheat oven to 350 degrees. Lightly spray a 9x13-inch baking dish with nonfat cooking spray. In large bowl, combine Cheddar and mozzarella cheese and toss to mix. Sprinkle half the cheese mixture on bottom of prepared dish. Lightly spray nonstick skillet with nonfat cooking spray; heat over medium-high heat. Add mushrooms, green onion, and red and green peppers; cook until vegetables are tender and soft, about 5 to 8 minutes. Spread vegetable mixture over cheese; top with remaining cheese. In large bowl, combine flour, milk, egg substitute and pepper. Pour over top of cheese in baking dish. Bake in preheated oven 35 to 40 minutes, until mixture is set and lightly browned. Let stand at room temperature 10 to 15 minutes before cutting into squares.

Serves: 8

Nutrition per Serving

Calories	279
Carbohydrate	13 grams
Cholesterol	1 milligram
Dietary Fiber	< 1 gram
Protein	47 grams
Sodium	1,136 milligrams

Exchanges

¾ milk
1 vegetable
5½ meat

SHOPPING LIST:

flour, 14 oz. skim milk, 16 oz. egg substitute, pepper, 12 oz. fat-free shredded Cheddar cheese, 12 oz. fat-free shredded mozzarella cheese, 3 oz. mushrooms, 2 to 3 green onions, 1 small green pepper, 1 small red pepper

· ·

SPINACH-CRAB FRITTATA

AVERAGE

INGREDIENTS:
1½ cups egg substitute
2½ tbsp. skim milk
¼ tsp. onion powder
3 cups frozen chopped spinach, thawed and drained
½ cup canned sliced water chestnuts
6 oz. imitation crab flakes
¼ cup fat-free shredded Swiss cheese

DIRECTIONS:
Lightly spray large nonstick skillet with nonfat cooking spray and heat over low heat. In a medium bowl, combine egg substitute, milk, and onion powder and blend well. In a separate bowl, combine well-drained spinach, water chestnuts and crab flakes and mix well. Pour egg mixture into hot skillet and top with spinach mixture. Cover skillet and cook, lifting edges of eggs occasionally, about 8 to 10 minutes, until eggs are set. Sprinkle cheese over top of frittata, cover, and cook until cheese is melted, about 1 minute.

Serves: 4

Nutrition per Serving		Exchanges
Calories	147	3 vegetable
Carbohydrate	17 grams	2 meat
Cholesterol	9 milligrams	
Dietary Fiber	3 grams	
Protein	19 grams	
Sodium	672 milligrams	

SHOPPING LIST:
12 oz. egg substitute, skim milk, onion powder, 16 oz. frozen chopped spinach, 4 oz. canned sliced water chestnuts, 6 oz. imitation crab flakes, 1 oz. fat-free shredded Swiss cheese (can substitute Cheddar or mozzarella cheese)

SPINACH FRITTATA

EASY - DO AHEAD

✦ ✦ ✦

INGREDIENTS:

2 10-oz. packages frozen, chopped spinach, thawed and
drained
1½ cups fat-free ricotta cheese
1 cup fat-free bread crumbs
¾ cup fat-free Parmesan cheese
1 cup + 2 tbsp. egg substitute

DIRECTIONS:

Preheat oven to 350 degrees. Lightly spray 9-inch baking
dish with nonfat cooking spray. In a large bowl, combine
spinach, ricotta cheese, ¾ cup bread crumbs, and ½ cup
Parmesan cheese and mix well. Add ½ cup + 2 tablespoons
egg substitute to spinach mixture and mix until ingredients
are blended. Sprinkle remaining bread crumbs; in the bottom of prepared pan and bake in preheated oven 5 minutes,
until lightly browned. Spread spinach mixture on top of
bread crumbs, pour remaining egg substitute on top and
sprinkle with remaining Parmesan cheese. Bake 40 to 45
minutes until lightly browned; let cool at room temperature
5 to 10 minutes, so mixture sets. Cut into squares and serve.

Serves: 8

Nutrition per Serving		Exchanges
Calories	104	1⅔ meat
Carbohydrates	12 grams	½ starch
Cholesterol	7 milligrams	1 vegetable
Dietary Fiber	2 grams	
Protein	15 grams	
Sodium	290 milligrams	

SHOPPING LIST:

2 10-oz. packages frozen chopped spinach, 12 oz. fat-free ricotta cheese, 1 cup bread crumbs (2 slices bread crushed), 6
oz. fat-free Parmesan cheese, 9 oz. egg substitute

VEGETABLE-CHEESE STRATA

AVERAGE - DO AHEAD

INGREDIENTS:

2 slices fat-free bread, cubed
3 tbsp. fat-free shredded
   Swiss cheese
3 tbsp. fat-free shredded
   Cheddar cheese
½ cup sliced mushrooms
½ cup sliced carrots
½ cup broccoli florets
1 tbsp. onion flakes
¼ tsp. minced garlic
½ cup chopped tomatoes
¾ cup egg substitute
2 large egg whites
¾ cup skim milk

DIRECTIONS:

Preheat oven to 375 degrees. Lightly spray 1½-quart casserole dish with nonfat cooking spray. Place bread cubes on bottom of casserole dish and top with Swiss and Cheddar cheeses. Lightly spray a large nonstick skillet with nonfat cooking spray; heat over medium-high heat. Add mushrooms, carrots, broccoli, onion flakes and garlic; cook about 5 minutes, until tender. Stir in tomatoes and heat 1 to 2 minutes. Pour vegetable mixture over cheese. In a small bowl, combine egg substitute, egg whites, and milk; mix until blended. Pour over vegetable mixture; bake in preheated oven 45 to 50 minutes, until knife inserted in center comes out clean. Let casserole sit at room temperature 5 to 10 minutes before serving, so eggs and cheese set.

Serves: 4

Nutrition per Serving		Exchanges
Calories	124	3½ vegetable
Carbohydrate	17 grams	1 meat
Cholesterol	< 1 milligram	
Dietary Fiber	2 grams	
Protein	13 grams	
Sodium	349 milligrams	

SHOPPING LIST:

fat-free bread, 1 oz. fat-free shredded Swiss cheese, 1 oz. fat-free shredded Cheddar cheese, 3 to 4 mushrooms, 1 to 2 carrots, ¼ lb. broccoli, onion flakes, minced garlic, 1 small tomato, 6 oz. egg substitute, 2 eggs, 6 oz. skim milk

VEGGIE EGG WHITE OMELET

EASY

✦ ✦ ✦

INGREDIENTS:
- 2 tbsp. scallions, chopped
- 2 tbsp. tomatoes, chopped
- 1 tbsp. green pepper, chopped
- 1 tbsp. red pepper, chopped
- 8 large egg whites
- ¼ cup fat-free shredded Cheddar cheese

DIRECTIONS:
Lightly spray nonstick skillet with nonfat cooking spray and heat over medium-high heat. Add scallions, tomatoes, green pepper and red pepper; cook until vegetables are tender. Remove vegetables from skillet and drain well. Lightly respray skillet and heat over medium-high heat until hot. Add egg whites and let set (do not scramble). Top egg whites with vegetables; sprinkle with cheese. Cover skillet and cook over medium heat until eggs are set and cheese is melted. Serve immediately.

Serves: 2

Nutrition per Serving

		Exchanges
Calories	121	⅓ starch
Carbohydrate	6 grams	3 meat
Cholesterol	0 milligrams	
Dietary Fiber	1 gram	
Protein	22 grams	
Sodium	488 milligrams	

SHOPPING LIST:
2 scallions, 1 small tomato, 1 small green pepper, 1 small red pepper, 8 eggs, 1 oz. fat-free shredded Cheddar cheese

APPLESAUCE MUFFINS

EASY - DO AHEAD - FREEZE

INGREDIENTS:
1¼ cups chunky applesauce
1 tbsp. apple butter
¼ cup egg substitute
¼ cup sugar
2 tbsp. brown sugar
2 cups flour
2 tsp. baking powder
¾ tsp. baking soda
¾ tsp. cinnamon
¼ tsp. nutmeg
¾ cup raisins

DIRECTIONS:
Preheat oven to 375 degrees. Lightly spray muffin cups with nonfat cooking spray. In a large bowl, combine applesauce, apple butter, egg substitute, sugar and brown sugar; blend until smooth. Add flour, baking powder, baking soda, cinnamon and nutmeg and mix until dry ingredients are moistened and blended. Fold in raisins. Fill muffin cups ¾ full and bake in preheated oven 20 minutes.

Serves: 12

Nutrition per Serving		Exchanges
Calories	153	1 starch
Carbohydrate	36 grams	1⅓ fruit
Cholesterol	0 milligrams	
Dietary Fiber	1 gram	
Protein	3 grams	
Sodium	116 milligrams	

SHOPPING LIST:
10 oz. chunky applesauce, apple butter, 2 oz. egg substitute, sugar, brown sugar, ¾ lb. flour, baking powder, baking soda, cinnamon, nutmeg, 6 oz. raisins

BREAKFAST MUFFINS

EASY - DO AHEAD - FREEZE

✦ ✦ ✦

INGREDIENTS:
¼ cup egg substitute
2 tbsp. apple butter
2 tbsp. lite applesauce
¼ cup sugar
¼ cup brown sugar
¾ cup skim milk
1 tsp. vanilla
2 cups flour
¾ cup Malt-O-Meal cereal
3 tsp. baking powder
1 tsp. cinnamon
¾ cup raisins (optional)

DIRECTIONS:
Preheat oven to 375 degrees. Lightly spray muffin cups with nonfat cooking spray. In a large bowl, combine egg substitute, apple butter, applesauce, sugar, brown sugar, milk and vanilla and blend until smooth. Add flour, Malt-O-Meal, baking powder and cinnamon; mix until dry ingredients are moistened. Fold in raisins, if desired. Fill muffin cups ¾ full and bake in preheated oven 20 minutes, until toothpick inserted in center comes out clean.

Serves: 12

Nutrition per Serving		Exchanges
Calories	168	1⅓ starch
Carbohydrate	38 grams	1 fruit
Cholesterol	0 milligrams	
Dietary Fiber	1 gram	
Protein	4 grams	
Sodium	100 milligrams	

SHOPPING LIST:
2 oz. egg substitute, 1 oz. apple butter, 1 oz. lite applesauce, sugar, brown sugar, 6 oz. skim milk, vanilla, flour, Malt-O-Meal cereal, baking powder, cinnamon, raisins (optional)

....

51

CINNAMON BERRY MUFFINS

EASY - DO AHEAD - FREEZE

INGREDIENTS:

2 cups flour
⅓ cup + 2 tbsp. sugar, divided
1 tbsp. baking powder
⅓ cup nonfat dry milk powder
⅔ cup water
¼ cup egg substitute
¼ cup raspberry applesauce
2 tbsp. Lighter Bake
1 tsp. vanilla
½ cup frozen cranberries
½ tsp. cinnamon

DIRECTIONS:

Preheat oven to 375 degrees. Lightly spray muffin cups with nonfat cooking spray. In a large bowl, combine flour, ⅓ cup sugar, baking powder, and nonfat dry milk powder and mix well. In a separate bowl, combine water, egg substitute, applesauce, Lighter Bake, and vanilla; blend until smooth. Pour egg mixture into flour mixture and mix until dry ingredients are moistened. Fold in cranberries. In a small bowl, combine 2 tablespoons sugar with cinnamon and mix well. Sprinkle over tops of muffins and bake in preheated oven 20 to 25 minutes, until lightly browned and knife inserted in center comes out clean.

Serves: 12

Nutrition per Serving		Exchanges
Calories	118	1 starch
Carbohydrate	26 grams	⅔ fruit
Cholesterol	< 1 milligram	
Dietary Fiber	1 gram	
Protein	3 grams	
Sodium	100 milligrams	

SHOPPING LIST:

flour, sugar, baking powder, nonfat dry milk powder, 2 oz. egg substitute, 2 oz. raspberry applesauce, Lighter Bake, vanilla, frozen cranberries, cinnamon

CORNBREAD AND CHEESE MUFFINS

EASY - DO AHEAD - FREEZE

✦ ✦ ✦

INGREDIENTS:
- 1 cup yellow cornmeal
- 1 cup whole wheat flour
- 1 tbsp. baking powder
- 1 tbsp. sugar
- ½ tsp. salt
- ¾ cup egg substitute
- 1 cup fat-free creamer
- 1 cup fat-free cottage cheese
- ¾ cup nonfat shredded Cheddar cheese

DIRECTIONS:
Preheat oven to 400 degrees. Lightly spray muffin cups with nonfat cooking spray. In a large bowl, combine cornmeal, flour, baking powder, sugar, and salt; mix well. In a separate bowl, combine egg substitute, creamer, and cottage cheese; blend until smooth. Using electric mixer, add egg mixture to flour mixture and blend until smooth. Fold in shredded cheese and let stand 5 minutes at room temperature. Fill muffin cups ¾ full and bake in preheated oven 25 to 30 minutes, until toothpick inserted in center comes out clean.

Serves: 12

Nutrition per Serving		Exchanges
Calories	135	1⅔ starch
Carbohydrate	26 grams	
Cholesterol	< 1 milligram	
Dietary Fiber	2 grams	
Protein	6 grams	
Sodium	309 milligrams	

SHOPPING LIST:
yellow cornmeal, whole wheat flour, baking powder, sugar, salt, 6 oz. egg substitute, 8 oz. fat-free creamer, 8 oz. fat-free cottage cheese, 3 oz. nonfat shredded Cheddar cheese

· · · · · · · · · · · · · · · · · · · ·

CRUNCHY SWEET POTATO MUFFINS

EASY - DO AHEAD - FREEZE

INGREDIENTS:

½ cup canned sweet pota-
toes, mashed
¼ cup sugar
¼ cup brown sugar
2 tbsp. Lighter Bake
2 tbsp. lite applesauce
¼ cup egg substitute

½ tsp. vanilla
½ cup skim milk
1½ cups flour
2 tsp. baking powder
¾ tsp. cinnamon
½ tsp. nutmeg
½ cup fat-free granola

DIRECTIONS:

Preheat oven to 400 degrees. Lightly spray muffin cups with
nonfat cooking spray. In large bowl, combine sweet potatoes, sugar, brown sugar, Lighter Bake, applesauce, egg substitute, vanilla and skim milk; blend until smooth. Stir in
flour, baking powder, cinnamon and nutmeg; mix until dry
ingredients are moistened. Fold in granola and mix lightly.
Bake in preheated oven 20 to 25 minutes, until lightly
browned and cooked through. Great with holiday dinners!

Serves: 12

Nutrition per Serving		Exchanges
Calories	126	1 starch
Carbohydrate	28 grams	¾ fruit
Cholesterol	< 1 milligram	
Dietary Fiber	1 gram	
Protein	3 grams	
Sodium	78 milligrams	

SHOPPING LIST:

4 oz. canned sweet potatoes, sugar, brown sugar, 1 oz.
Lighter Bake, 1 oz. lite applesauce, 2 oz. egg substitute,
vanilla, 4 oz. skim milk, flour, baking powder, cinnamon,
nutmeg, Health Valley fat-free granola (any flavor)

DATE-BRAN MUFFINS

EASY - DO AHEAD - FREEZE

INGREDIENTS:

3 cups All-Bran cereal
¼ cup + 2 tbsp. Lighter Bake
1 cup boiling water
½ cup egg substitute
1 cup fat-free vanilla yogurt
1 cup skim milk
1½ tsp. vanilla

½ cup brown sugar
1 cup whole wheat flour
1¼ cups flour
1 tsp. cinnamon
1½ tsp. baking powder
1 tsp. baking soda
1 cup chopped dates

DIRECTIONS:

Preheat oven to 400 degrees. Lightly spray muffin cups with nonfat cooking spray. In a large bowl, combine cereal, Lighter Bake and boiling water; let mixture stand 5 minutes until cereal is moistened. In small bowl, combine egg substitute, yogurt, milk, vanilla and sugar; blend until smooth. Add this mixture to cereal mixture and blend ingredients. Stir in whole wheat flour, flour, cinnamon, baking powder and baking soda and mix until dry ingredients are moistened and blended. Fold in dates. Bake in preheated oven 20 to 25 minutes; cool slightly before removing from muffin cups.

Nutrition per Serving		Exchanges
Calories	126	1⅓ starch
Carbohydrate	30 grams	½ fruit
Cholesterol	< 1 milligram	
Dietary Fiber	5 grams	
Protein	4 grams	
Sodium	197 milligrams	

SHOPPING LIST:

All-Bran cereal, 3 oz. Lighter Bake, 4 oz. egg substitute, 8 oz. fat-free yogurt, 8 oz. skim milk, vanilla, brown sugar, whole wheat flour, flour, cinnamon, baking powder, baking soda, 6 oz. chopped dates

LEMON-GINGER MUFFINS

EASY - DO AHEAD - FREEZE

INGREDIENTS:
1 cup lemon-flavored fat-free yogurt
⅓ cup apple butter
½ cup egg substitute
1 cup sugar
1 tbsp. grated lemon peel
2⅛ cups flour
1½ tsp. ginger
½ tsp. baking soda
¼ tsp. baking powder
lemon-flavored powdered sugar

DIRECTIONS:
Preheat oven to 350 degrees. In a large bowl, combine lemon yogurt, apple butter, egg substitute, sugar and lemon peel and mix until blended smooth. Add flour, ginger, baking soda and baking powder; mix until dry ingredients are moistened. Fill muffin cups ¾ full and bake in preheated oven 15 to 20 minutes, until toothpick inserted in center comes out clean. Cool 15 minutes and sprinkle tops with lemon-flavored powdered sugar.

Serves: 12

Nutrition per Serving		Exchanges
Calories	170	1⅓ starch
Carbohydrate	39 grams	1 fruit
Cholesterol	< 1 gram	
Dietary Fiber	1 gram	
Protein	4 grams	
Sodium	675 milligrams	

SHOPPING LIST:
8 oz. fat-free lemon yogurt, 3 oz. apple butter, 4 oz. egg substitute, ½ lb. sugar, grated lemon peel, ½ lb. flour, ginger, baking soda, baking powder, lemon-flavored powdered sugar

OATMEAL RAISIN MUFFINS

EASY - DO AHEAD - FREEZE

INGREDIENTS:
- 3 tbsp. Lighter Bake
- ¼ cup egg substitute
- 1 cup skim milk
- 1 tsp. vanilla
- ⅓ cup sugar
- 2 cups flour
- 1 cup multi-grain oatmeal
- 3 tsp. baking powder
- ¾ cup raisins

DIRECTIONS:

Preheat oven to 350 degrees. Lightly spray muffin cups with nonfat cooking spray. In a large bowl, combine Lighter Bake, egg substitute, skim milk, vanilla and sugar; mix until blended smooth. Add flour, oatmeal and baking powder; mix until all ingredients are blended. Fold in raisins. Fill muffin cups ¾ full and bake in preheated oven 15 to 20 minutes.

Serves: 12

Nutrition per Serving		Exchanges
Calories	126	1 starch
Carbohydrate	29 grams	1 fruit
Cholesterol	< 1 milligram	
Dietary Fiber	2 grams	
Protein	3 grams	
Sodium	104 milligrams	

SHOPPING LIST:

3 oz. Lighter Bake, 2 oz. egg substitute, 8 oz. skim milk, vanilla, sugar, flour, Quaker multi-grain oatmeal, baking powder, 6 oz. raisins

ORANGE-BERRY CORN MUFFINS

EASY - DO AHEAD

INGREDIENTS:

1½ cups frozen orange juice concentrate, thawed
½ cup apple butter
⅓ cup fat-free vanilla yogurt
¾ cup egg substitute
2½ cups flour
½ cup cornmeal
1 tsp. baking soda
½ tsp. baking powder
2 tsp. grated orange peel
2 cups frozen blueberries, divided

DIRECTIONS:

Preheat oven to 375 degrees. Lightly spray muffin cups with nonfat cooking spray. In large bowl, combine orange juice, apple butter, yogurt and egg substitute; mix until blended. Add flour, cornmeal, baking soda, baking powder and orange peel to liquid mixture; mix until dry ingredients are moistened. Fold 1½ cups blueberries into batter and mix lightly. Spoon batter into prepared muffin cups; sprinkle with remaining blueberries. Bake in preheated oven 20 minutes, until toothpick inserted in center comes out clean. Best served warm.

Serves: 12

Nutrition per Serving		Exchanges
Calories	227	1⅔ starch
Carbohydrate	50 grams	1½ fruit
Cholesterol	< 1 gram	
Dietary Fiber	2 grams	
Protein	5 grams	
Sodium	108 milligrams	

SHOPPING LIST:

12 oz. frozen orange juice concentrate, 4 oz. apple butter, 3 oz. fat-free yogurt, 6 oz. egg substitute, ½ to ¾ lb. flour, cornmeal, baking soda, baking powder, orange peel, 10 oz. frozen blueberries

ORANGE CARROT MUFFINS

EASY - DO AHEAD - FREEZE

INGREDIENTS:

2½ cups flour
1 cup whole wheat flour
2 tbsp. baking powder
1½ tsp. cinnamon
1 tsp. nutmeg
½ cup brown sugar
½ cup egg substitute

½ tsp. vanilla
½ tsp. orange extract
¾ cup + 2 tbsp. skim milk
¼ cup orange juice
2 tbsp. Lighter Bake
1¼ cups grated carrots

DIRECTIONS:

Preheat oven to 350 degrees. Lightly spray muffin cups with nonfat cooking spray. In large bowl, combine flour, whole wheat flour, baking powder, cinnamon, nutmeg, and brown sugar; mix well. In separate medium bowl, combine egg substitute, vanilla, orange extract, milk, orange juice, and Lighter Bake; blend until smooth. Gradually pour liquid mixture in flour mixture; blend until all dry ingredients are moistened. Fold in carrots; mix lightly. Bake in preheated oven 20 to 25 minutes, until lightly browned.

Serves: 12

Nutrition per Serving		Exchanges
Calories	191	2 starch
Carbohydrate	41 grams	⅔ fruit
Cholesterol	< 1 milligram	
Dietary Fiber	2 grams	
Protein	6 grams	
Sodium	196 milligrams	

SHOPPING LIST:

⅔ lb. flour, ⅓ lb. whole wheat flour, baking powder, cinnamon, nutmeg, ¼ lb. brown sugar, 4 oz. egg substitute, vanilla, orange extract, 8 oz. skim milk, 2 oz. orange juice, 2 oz. Lighter Bake, ½ lb. carrots

ORANGE-CRUNCH MUFFINS

EASY - DO AHEAD - FREEZE

INGREDIENTS:

2½ tbsp. Lighter Bake, divided
1 tbsp. lite applesauce
1 cup orange juice
¼ cup sugar
¼ cup egg substitute

2½ cups flour, divided
3 tsp. baking powder
2 tsp. orange peel, grated
¼ cup Grape-Nuts
¼ cup brown sugar
½ tsp. cinnamon

DIRECTIONS:

Preheat oven to 400 degrees. Lightly spray muffin cups with nonfat cooking spray. In a large bowl, combine 2 tablespoons Lighter Bake, lite applesauce, orange juice, sugar, and egg substitute and blend until smooth. Add 2 cups flour, baking powder, and orange peel; blend until dry ingredients are moistened. Fill muffin cups ¾ full with batter. In a small bowl, combine ½ cup flour, Grape-Nuts, brown sugar and cinnamon. Stir in 2 teaspoons Lighter Bake until mixture becomes crumbly. Sprinkle topping over batter and bake in preheated oven 18 to 20 minutes, until knife inserted in center comes out clean.

Serves: 12

Nutrition per Serving		Exchanges
Calories	160	1⅓ starch
Carbohydrate	36 grams	1 fruit
Cholesterol	0 milligrams	
Dietary Fiber	1 gram	
Protein	4 grams	
Sodium	109 milligrams	

SHOPPING LIST:

3 oz. Lighter Bake, lite applesauce, 8 oz. orange juice, sugar, 2 oz. egg substitute, flour, baking powder, grated orange peel, Grape-Nuts, brown sugar, cinnamon

ORANGE-RAISIN MUFFINS

EASY - DO AHEAD - FREEZE

INGREDIENTS:
2 tbsp. apple butter
2 tbsp. lite applesauce
¼ cup egg substitute
1½ cups orange juice
½ tsp. orange extract
½ tsp. vanilla
1 cup whole wheat flour
1 cup flour
2 tsp. baking powder
½ tsp. baking soda
½ cup raisins

DIRECTIONS:
Preheat oven to 400 degrees. Lightly spray muffin cups with nonfat cooking spray. In a large bowl, combine apple butter, applesauce, egg substitute, orange juice, orange extract, and vanilla; blend until smooth. In a medium bowl, combine whole wheat flour, flour, baking powder, and baking soda and mix until ingredients are blended. Add flour mixture to applesauce mixture and blend until dry ingredients are moistened. Fold in raisins. Fill muffin cups ¾ full and bake in preheated oven 20 to 25 minutes.

Serves: 12

Nutrition per Serving		Exchanges
Calories	114	1 starch
Carbohydrate	25 grams	⅔ fruit
Cholesterol	0 milligrams	
Dietary Fiber	2 grams	
Protein	3 grams	
Sodium	97 milligrams	

SHOPPING LIST:
1 oz. apple butter, 1 oz. lite applesauce, 2 oz. egg substitute, 12 oz. orange juice, orange extract, vanilla, whole wheat flour, flour, baking powder, baking soda, 4 oz. raisins

STREUSEL OATMEAL MUFFINS

EASY - DO AHEAD - FREEZE

INGREDIENTS:
1⅓ cups multi-grain oatmeal, divided
1¾ cups flour, divided
½ cup sugar
1 tbsp. baking powder
1 cup skim milk
⅜ cup apple butter, divided
¼ cup egg substitute
¼ cup brown sugar

DIRECTIONS:
Preheat oven to 375 degrees. Lightly spray muffin cups with nonfat cooking spray. In a large bowl, combine 1 cup oatmeal, 1½ cups flour, sugar and baking powder and mix well. Stir in milk, ¼ cup apple butter, and egg substitute and mix until dry ingredients are moistened. Spoon batter into muffin cups. In a small bowl, combine ⅓ cup oatmeal, ¼ cup flour, ¼ cup brown sugar and 2 tablespoons apple butter; mix until crumbly. Sprinkle crumb mixture over batter and bake in preheated oven 15 to 20 minutes.

Serves: 12

Nutrition per Serving		Exchanges
Calories	175	1⅓ starch
Carbohydrate	39 grams	1⅓ fruit
Cholesterol	< 1 milligram	
Dietary Fiber	2 grams	
Protein	4 grams	
Sodium	103 milligrams	

SHOPPING LIST:
Quaker multi-grain oatmeal, flour, sugar, baking powder, 8 oz. skim milk, 4 oz. apple butter, 2 oz. egg substitute, brown sugar

SUGARLESS BERRY MUFFINS

EASY - DO AHEAD - FREEZE

✦ ✦ ✦

INGREDIENTS:
2 tbsp. lite applesauce
2 tbsp. apple butter
½ cup egg substitute
¾ cup orange juice
1 tsp. vanilla
1¾ cups + 2 tsp. flour, divided
1 tbsp. baking powder
½ tsp. cinnamon
¼ tsp. nutmeg
1 cup berries (blueberries, strawberries, raspberries, or any
  combination)

DIRECTIONS:
Preheat oven to 400 degrees. Lightly spray muffin cups with
nonfat cooking spray. In a large bowl, combine applesauce,
apple butter, egg substitute, orange juice, and vanilla; blend
until smooth. In a medium bowl, combine 1¾ cups flour,
baking powder, cinnamon, and nutmeg and mix until
blended. Add flour mixture to applesauce mixture and mix
until all dry ingredients are blended. In a small bowl, toss
berries with 2 teaspoons flour; fold berries into batter and
mix gently. Fill muffin cups ¾ full and bake in preheated
oven 20 to 25 minutes.

Serves: 12

Nutrition per Serving		Exchanges
Calories	92	1 starch
Carbohydrate	19 grams	⅓ fruit
Cholesterol	0 milligrams	
Dietary Fiber	1 gram	
Protein	3 grams	
Sodium	96 milligrams	

SHOPPING LIST:
1 oz. lite applesauce, 1 oz. apple butter, 4 oz. egg substitute,
6 oz. orange juice, vanilla, flour, baking powder, cinnamon,
nutmeg, ½ pint berries

....

BUTTERMILK BANANA BREAD

EASY - DO AHEAD - FREEZE

INGREDIENTS:
½ cup apple butter
¾ cup sugar
¼ cup brown sugar
¾ cup water
½ tsp. banana extract
½ tsp. vanilla
2½ cups flour
1 tbsp. Buttermilk Blend Mix
1 tsp. baking powder
½ tsp. baking soda
1¼ cups mashed bananas

DIRECTIONS:
Preheat oven to 350 degrees. Lightly spray a 9x5-inch loaf pan with nonfat cooking spray. In large bowl, combine apple butter, sugar, brown sugar, water, banana extract, and vanilla; mix until blended. In a medium bowl, combine flour, Buttermilk Blend, baking powder, and baking soda; mix well. Stir into butter mixture; mix until dry ingredients are moistened. Fold in bananas and mix lightly. Spread batter into prepared pan; bake in preheated oven 60 to 75 minutes, until knife inserted in center comes out clean. Cool completely before slicing.

Serves: 12

Nutrition per Serving		Exchanges
Calories	211	1 starch
Carbohydrate	49 grams	2⅓ fruit
Cholesterol	0 milligrams	
Dietary Fiber	1 gram	
Protein	3 grams	
Sodium	67 milligrams	

SHOPPING LIST:
4 oz. apple butter, sugar, brown sugar, banana extract, vanilla, ½ lb. flour, Buttermilk Blend Mix, baking powder, baking soda, 3 to 4 bananas

••••••••••••••••••••

CARROT-ZUCCHINI FRUIT BREAD

EASY - DO AHEAD - FREEZE

INGREDIENTS:

¼ cup apple butter
1 cup sugar
⅓ cup brown sugar
1 cup water
½ cup grated zucchini
½ cup shredded carrots
1 tsp. vanilla

2½ cups flour
2 tsp. cinnamon
1 tsp. baking soda
1 tsp. baking powder
¾ cup pitted prunes,
   chopped
½ cup Grape-Nuts cereal

DIRECTIONS:

Preheat oven to 350 degrees. Lightly spray a 9x5-inch loaf pan with nonfat cooking spray. In a large bowl, combine apple butter, sugar, brown sugar, water, zucchini, carrots, and vanilla; mix until well blended. Add flour, cinnamon, baking soda and baking powder to butter mixture and mix until dry ingredients are moistened. Fold in prunes and Grape-Nuts; mix lightly. Spoon batter into prepared pan; bake in preheated oven 1 hour, until knife inserted in center comes out clean. Cool completely before slicing.

Serves: 16

Nutrition per Serving		Exchanges
Calories	177	1 starch
Carbohydrate	42 grams	1⅔ fruit
Cholesterol	0 milligrams	
Dietary Fiber	1 gram	
Protein	3 grams	
Sodium	100 milligrams	

SHOPPING LIST:

2 oz. apple butter, ½ lb. sugar, brown sugar, 1 zucchini, 1 carrot, vanilla, ½ lb. flour, cinnamon, baking soda, baking powder, pitted prunes, Grape-Nuts cereal

CINNAMON RAISIN SCONES

AVERAGE - DO AHEAD

INGREDIENTS:

2¼ cups Pioneer baking mix
½ cup raisins
¼ cup brown sugar
2 tbsp. egg substitute
½ cup skim milk
2 tbsp. sugar
½ tsp. cinnamon

DIRECTIONS:

Preheat oven to 400 degrees. Lightly spray baking sheet
with nonfat cooking spray. In a large bowl, combine baking
mix, raisins, and brown sugar and mix well. In a small
bowl, combine egg substitute and milk; mix until blended.
Pour egg mixture into dry mixture and stir until dry ingredients are moistened. Turn dough onto lightly floured surface and roll into ½-inch-thick circle or rectangle. Cut dough
with cookie cutter, knife, or glass dipped in sugar; place
scones on baking sheet. In a small bowl, combine sugar and
cinnamon; mix well. Sprinkle over scones and bake in preheated oven 10 to 15 minutes, until lightly browned.

Serves: 12

Nutrition per Serving		Exchanges
Calories	160	1 starch
Carbohydrate	42 grams	1 ⅔ fruit
Cholesterol	0 milligrams	
Dietary Fiber	1 gram	
Protein	3 grams	
Sodium	393 milligrams	

SHOPPING LIST:

Pioneer baking mix (or comparable low-fat or fat-free baking mix), raisins, brown sugar, 1 oz. egg substitute, 4 oz.
skim milk, sugar, cinnamon

CRAISIN PUMPKIN BREAD

EASY - DO AHEAD - FREEZE

INGREDIENTS:

16 oz. canned pumpkin
1 cup egg substitute
1⅓ cups sugar
1⅓ cups brown sugar
⅔ cup water
⅓ cup Lighter Bake
⅓ cup lite applesauce

3⅓ cups flour
1 tsp. baking powder
1½ tsp. baking soda
1½ tsp. cinnamon
½ tsp. pumpkin pie spice
⅔ cup Craisins

DIRECTIONS:

Preheat oven to 350 degrees. Lightly spray two 5x9-inch loaf pans with nonfat cooking spray. In a large bowl, combine pumpkin, egg substitute, sugar, brown sugar, water, Lighter Bake, and applesauce and blend until smooth. Add flour, baking powder, baking soda, cinnamon, and pumpkin pie spice and blend until dry ingredients are moistened. Fold in Craisins. Divide batter between loaf pans. Bake in preheated oven 1 hour and 15 minutes, until knife inserted in center comes out clean. Cool several minutes before removing from pans; cool completely before slicing.

Serves: 24

Nutrition per Serving		Exchanges
Calories	180	1 starch
Carbohydrate	43 grams	1⅔ fruit
Cholesterol	0 milligrams	
Dietary Fiber	1 gram	
Protein	3 grams	
Sodium	85 milligrams	

SHOPPING LIST:

16 oz. canned pumpkin, 8 oz. egg substitute, ½ lb. sugar, ½ lb. brown sugar, Lighter Bake, lite applesauce, flour, baking powder, baking soda, cinnamon, pumpkin pie spice, Craisins

DOUBLE ORANGE BREAD

EASY - DO AHEAD - FREEZE

INGREDIENTS:
¼ cup apple butter
2 tbsp. sugar
¼ cup brown sugar
¾ cup orange juice
½ cup orange marmalade
2 cups flour
½ tsp. baking soda
1½ tsp. baking powder
¼ cup Grape-Nuts cereal
6 oz. Craisins

DIRECTIONS:
Preheat oven to 350 degrees. Lightly spray a 5x9-inch loaf pan with nonfat cooking spray. In a large bowl, combine apple butter, sugar, brown sugar, orange juice, and orange marmalade and mix until smooth. Add flour, baking soda, and baking powder to butter mixture and mix until dry ingredients are moistened. Stir in Grape-Nuts and Craisins. Spoon batter into prepared pan and bake in preheated oven 1 hour, until knife inserted in center comes out clean. Cool completely before slicing.

Serves: 12

Nutrition per Serving		Exchanges
Calories	211	1 starch
Carbohydrate	50 grams	2⅓ fruit
Cholesterol	0 milligrams	
Dietary Fiber	2 grams	
Protein	3 grams	
Sodium	95 milligrams	

SHOPPING LIST:
2 oz. apple butter, sugar, brown sugar, 6 oz. orange juice, 4 oz. orange marmalade, ½ lb. flour, baking soda, baking powder, Grape-Nuts cereal, 6 oz. Craisins

LEMON APPLE BREAD

EASY - DO AHEAD - FREEZE

INGREDIENTS:
2 cups flour
¾ cup sugar
3 tsp. baking powder
½ tsp. baking soda
1 tsp. cinnamon
¼ cup egg substitute
1½ cups chunky applesauce
2 tbsp. apple butter
¼ tsp. lemon extract

DIRECTIONS:
Preheat oven to 350 degrees. Lightly spray 9x5-inch loaf pan with nonfat cooking spray. In a large bowl, combine flour, sugar, baking powder, baking soda, and cinnamon; mix well. In a medium bowl, combine egg substitute, applesauce, apple butter, and lemon extract; stir until blended. Add egg mixture to flour mixture and mix until dry ingredients are well moistened. Spread batter into prepared pan and bake in preheated oven 1 hour, until knife inserted in center comes out clean.

Serves: 12

Nutrition per Serving		Exchanges
Calories	155	1 starch
Carbohydrate	36 grams	1⅓ fruit
Cholesterol	0 milligrams	
Dietary Fiber	1 gram	
Protein	3 grams	
Sodium	125 milligrams	

SHOPPING LIST:
flour, ½ lb. sugar, baking powder, baking soda, cinnamon, 2 oz. egg substitute, 12 oz. chunky applesauce, 1 oz. apple butter, lemon extract

QUICK BLUEBERRY CORNBREAD

EASY - DO AHEAD

INGREDIENTS:
1⅓ cups flour
1 cup yellow cornmeal
1 tbsp. baking powder
⅓ cup nonfat dry milk powder
⅔ cup water
¼ cup egg substitute
¼ cup lite applesauce
¼ cup frozen blueberries
1 tbsp. sugar

DIRECTIONS:
Preheat oven to 425 degrees. Lightly spray 8-inch baking pan with nonfat cooking spray. In a large bowl, combine flour, cornmeal, baking powder, and dry milk and mix well. In a separate bowl, combine water, egg substitute, and lite applesauce and blend until smooth. Pour into flour mixture and stir just until dry ingredients are moistened. Fold in blueberries and sprinkle with sugar. Pour batter into prepared pan and bake in preheated oven 20 to 25 minutes. Cool 5 to 10 minutes before cutting into squares. Great with honey!

Serves: 8

Nutrition per Serving		Exchanges
Calories	212	2 starch
Carbohydrate	44 grams	1 fruit
Cholesterol	< 1 milligram	
Dietary Fiber	1 gram	
Protein	6 grams	
Sodium	150 milligrams	

SHOPPING LIST:
flour, yellow cornmeal, baking powder, nonfat dry milk powder, 2 oz. egg substitute, 2 oz. lite applesauce, 4 oz. frozen blueberries, sugar

CHEESE POLENTA

EASY - DO AHEAD

✦ ✦ ✦

INGREDIENTS:

2¾ cups water
1 cup yellow cornmeal
1 drop hot pepper sauce
1 cup cold water
1 cup fat-free shredded
  mozzarella cheese

2½ tbsp. grated Parmesan
  cheese, divided
⅓ cup chopped green pepper
⅓ cup chopped red pepper
1 cup fat-free pasta sauce

DIRECTIONS:

Preheat oven to 400 degrees. Lightly spray 9-inch pie plate with nonfat cooking spray. Pour 2¾ cups water into large saucepan; bring to a boil over high heat. In a small bowl, combine cornmeal, pepper sauce, and 1 cup cold water and mix until blended. Slowly add cornmeal mixture to boiling water, stirring constantly. Cook over medium heat until mixture returns to boiling. Reduce heat to low and cook 10 to 15 minutes, until mixture thickens, stirring occasionally. Pour half the mixture into prepared pan and spread evenly. Sprinkle mozzarella and 2 tablespoons Parmesan cheese on top. Spread red and green peppers over cheese. Top with remaining cornmeal mixture and spread evenly. Sprinkle remaining Parmesan cheese on top. Cover and chill several hours, or until firm. Bake in preheated oven 30 to 35 minutes, until golden brown and heated through. Heat pasta sauce in saucepan or microwave until warm. Cut baked polenta into four wedges and serve with pasta sauce.

Serves: 4

Nutrition per Serving		Exchanges
Calories	242	2⅓ meat
Carbohydrate	32 grams	2 starch
Cholesterol	0 milligrams	
Dietary Fiber	2 grams	
Protein	22 grams	
Sodium	582 milligrams	

SHOPPING LIST:

1 cup yellow cornmeal, hot pepper sauce, 4 oz. fat-free shredded mozzarella cheese, grated Parmesan cheese, 1 small green pepper, 1 small red pepper, 8 oz. fat-free pasta sauce

• •

CINNAMON RAISIN COFFEECAKE

EASY - DO AHEAD - FREEZE

INGREDIENTS:

1 tbsp. instant coffee powder	1¾ cups flour
2 tbsp. hot water	2 tsp. baking powder
½ cup egg substitute	¾ cup sugar
¼ cup skim milk	¼ cup brown sugar
1 cup fat-free sour cream	1½ tsp. cinnamon
¼ cup cinnamon applesauce	½ cup raisins
1½ tsp. vanilla	

DIRECTIONS:

Preheat oven to 350 degrees. Lightly spray 9-inch baking pan with nonfat cooking spray. In a medium bowl, combine coffee powder with hot water and stir until powder is completely dissolved. Stir in egg substitute, milk, sour cream, applesauce, and vanilla; blend well. In a large bowl, combine flour, baking powder, sugar, brown sugar, and cinnamon; mix until ingredients are blended. Add egg mixture and mix until dry ingredients are moistened. Fold in ¼ cup raisins and sprinkle remaining raisins on top. Bake in preheated oven 35 to 40 minutes, until knife inserted in center comes out clean.

Serves: 8

Nutrition per Serving		Exchanges
Calories	261	2⅓ starch
Carbohydrate	56 grams	1⅓ fruit
Cholesterol	< 1 milligram	
Dietary Fiber	1 gram	
Protein	7 grams	
Sodium	131 milligrams	

SHOPPING LIST:

instant coffee powder, 4 oz. egg substitute, 2 oz. skim milk, 8 oz. fat-free sour cream, 2 oz. cinnamon applesauce, vanilla, flour, baking powder, sugar, brown sugar, cinnamon, 4 oz. raisins

FULL OF BERRIES BREAKFAST CAKE

AVERAGE - DO AHEAD - FREEZE

◆ ◆ ◆

INGREDIENTS:

½ cup + 2 tbsp. apple butter
¾ cup sugar
¾ cup brown sugar, divided
½ cup egg substitute
1 cup fat-free sour cream
1½ tsp. vanilla
1¼ cup multi-grain oatmeal, divided

1¾ cups flour, divided
2 tsp. baking powder
½ tsp. baking soda
⅓ cup strawberry preserves
½ cup raspberries
¼ cup blueberries
¼ tsp. cinnamon

DIRECTIONS:

Preheat oven to 350 degrees. Lightly spray 10-inch baking dish with nonfat cooking spray. In large bowl, combine ½ cup apple butter, sugar, ½ cup brown sugar, egg substitute, sour cream, and vanilla; blend until smooth. Stir in ¾ cup oatmeal, 1½ cups flour, baking powder, and baking soda; mix until all dry ingredients are moistened. Drop preserves by tablespoons on batter; swirl with knife. Top with raspberries. In small bowl, combine ½ cup oatmeal, ¼ cup flour, cinnamon, and ¼ cup brown sugar; stir in 2 tablespoons apple butter until mixture is crumbly. Sprinkle over raspberries; bake in preheated oven 50 to 55 minutes, until knife inserted in center comes out clean.

Serves: 12

Nutrition per Serving		Exchanges
Calories	249	1⅔ starch
Carbohydrate	56 grams	2 fruit
Cholesterol	0 milligrams	
Dietary Fiber	1 gram	
Protein	5 grams	
Sodium	123 milligrams	

SHOPPING LIST:

5 oz. apple butter, sugar, brown sugar, 4 oz. egg substitute, 8 oz. fat-free sour cream, vanilla, Quaker multi-grain oatmeal, flour, baking powder, baking soda, 3 oz. strawberry preserves, ¼ pint raspberries, ⅛ pint blueberries, cinnamon

FULL 'O FRUIT BREAKFAST CRISP

EASY - DO AHEAD

INGREDIENTS:
4 cups canned apple slices
1 cup frozen blueberries
1 cup frozen raspberries
¾ cup brown sugar, divided
¼ cup frozen orange juice concentrate, thawed
¼ cup flour, divided
1½ tsp. cinnamon
1 cup multi-grain oatmeal
¼ cup Lighter Bake

DIRECTIONS:
Preheat oven to 350 degrees. Lightly spray 9x13-inch baking dish with nonfat cooking spray. In a large bowl, combine apple slices, blueberries, raspberries, ¼ cup brown sugar, orange juice concentrate, 2 tablespoons flour, and cinnamon; mix well. Spoon mixture into prepared dish. In a small bowl, combine oatmeal, ½ cup brown sugar, and 2 tablespoons flour and mix well; stir in Lighter Bake with fork until mixture becomes crumbly. Sprinkle topping over fruit and bake in preheated oven 30 to 40 minutes, until fruit is tender and topping is lightly browned.

Serves: 16

Nutrition per Serving		Exchanges
Calories	107	⅓ starch
Carbohydrate	26 grams	1⅓ fruit
Cholesterol	0 milligrams	
Dietary Fiber	2 grams	
Protein	1 gram	
Sodium	6 milligrams	

SHOPPING LIST:
2 20-oz. cans apple slices, 8 oz. frozen blueberries, 8 oz. frozen raspberries, brown sugar, frozen orange juice concentrate, flour, cinnamon, Quaker multi-grain oatmeal, 2 oz. Lighter Bake

MINI CHERRY COFFEECAKES

EASY - DO AHEAD - FREEZE

✦ ✦ ✦

INGREDIENTS:

1 cup + 2 tbsp. sugar
5 tbsp. + 1 tsp. Lighter Bake, divided
1 cup fat-free sour cream
½ cup egg substitute
1½ tsp. vanilla

2¼ cups flour, divided
1½ tsp. baking powder
½ tsp. baking soda
20 oz. light cherry pie filling
2 tbsp. powdered sugar
1½ tbsp. fat-free margarine

DIRECTIONS:

Preheat oven to 325 degrees. Lightly spray muffin-cup pan with nonfat cooking spray. In a large bowl, combine 1 cup sugar, 5 tablespoons Lighter Bake, sour cream, egg substitute, and vanilla; mix until smooth. Gradually add 2 cups flour, baking powder, and baking soda; mix well. Fill muffin cups ½ full; top each muffin with 1 tablespoon cherry pie filling. Spread 2 tablespoons batter on to pie filler to fill muffin cup. In small bowl, combine ¼ cup flour, 2 tablespoons sugar and 2 tablespoons powdered sugar; mix well. Using fork, stir in margarine until mixture becomes crumbly. Sprinkle on top of mini cakes and bake in preheated oven 30 minutes, or until knife inserted in center comes out clean. Repeat with remaining batter, pie filling, and topping.

Serves: 12 (½ cake per serving)

Nutrition per Serving		Exchanges
Calories	243	1⅔ starch
Carbohydrate	54 grams	2 fruit
Cholesterol	0 milligrams	
Dietary Fiber	1 gram	
Protein	5 grams	
Sodium	155 milligrams	

SHOPPING LIST:

½ lb. sugar, 5 oz. Lighter Bake, 8 oz. fat-free sour cream, 4 oz. egg substitute, vanilla, ½ lb. flour, baking powder, baking soda, 20 oz. light cherry pie filling, powdered sugar, fat-free margarine

SENSATIONAL SALAD, SOUP, AND SANDWICHES

✦ ✦ ✦

BEEF TACO SALAD

AVERAGE - DO AHEAD

INGREDIENTS:

1½ lbs. fat-free beef crumbles
1½ tsp. minced garlic
1 15 oz. can fat-free chili
   beans
2 tsp. chili powder
1½ tsp. onion powder
1 tsp. cumin
¼ tsp.pepper
8 cups chopped lettuce
1 small cucumber, chopped

¾ cup chopped red onion
½ cup chopped green bell
   pepper
2 large tomatoes, chopped
¾ cup fat-free shredded
   Cheddar cheese
1 cup fat-free chunky-style
   salsa
¾ cup fat-free French salad
   dressing

DIRECTIONS:

Lightly spray large nonstick skillet with nonfat cooking spray and heat over medium-high heat. Add beef to skillet and cook over medium heat until cooked through. Stir in garlic, beans, chili powder, onion powder, cumin, and pepper; cook until ingredients are blended and heated through. Place lettuce on plates or fill taco salad shells with lettuce. Top with beef mixture, cucumbers, red onions, green peppers, tomatoes, and cheese. In small bowl, combine chunky salsa with French salad dressing; mix well. Pour over salad; toss lightly to mix.

Serves: 6

Nutrition per Serving		Exchanges
Calories	345	4 vegetable
Carbohydrate	50 grams	2 starch
Cholesterol	50 milligrams	2½ meat
Dietary Fiber	10 grams	
Protein	34 grams	
Sodium	1,041 milligrams	

SHOPPING LIST::

1½ lb. fat-free beef crumbles (Morningstar Farms), minced garlic, 15 oz. can fat-free chili beans, chili powder, onion powder, cumin, pepper, 1½ lb. lettuce (or prepackaged shredded lettuce to equal 8 cups), 1 small cucumber, 1 red onion, 1 small green bell pepper, 2 large tomatoes, 3 oz. fat-free shredded Cheddar cheese, 8 oz. fat-free chunky-style salsa, fat-free French salad dressing (Western Valley)

CHICKEN-RASPBERRY SALAD

EASY - DO AHEAD

INGREDIENTS:
1½ cups rotini, uncooked
6 cups mixed salad greens
1½ cups fresh raspberries
2 cups fat-free chicken tenders, cooked and cubed
¾ cup shredded carrots
¾ cup chopped celery
1½ cups fat-free raspberry vinaigrette dressing

DIRECTIONS:
Cook rotini according to package directions; drain and rinse under cold water. In a large bowl, combine salad greens, raspberries, chicken, carrots, and celery; toss until mixed. Stir pasta into salad; pour dressing over salad and toss lightly.

Serves: 6

Nutrition per Serving		Exchanges
Calories	195	1 starch
Carbohydrate	25 grams	2 vegetable
Cholesterol	37 milligrams	2 meat
Dietary Fiber	3 grams	
Protein	20 grams	
Sodium	410 milligrams	

SHOPPING LIST:
8 oz. rotini pasta, 6 cups mixed salad greens (romaine, leaf lettuce, endive, etc.), ¾ pint raspberries, 1 lb. fat-free chicken tenders, prepackaged shredded carrots or 1 to 2 carrots, 2 to 3 stalks celery, 12 oz. fat-free raspberry vinaigrette dressing

CHINESE CHICKEN SALAD

EASY - DO AHEAD

INGREDIENTS:

½ cup low-sodium teriyaki
  sauce
¼ cup rice vinegar
½ tsp. pepper
½ tsp. sesame seeds
1½ lbs. fat-free chicken
  breasts
4 cups shredded lettuce

4 cups shredded cabbage
¼ cup canned water chest-
  nuts, chopped
1 cup shredded carrots
1 cup sliced red bell pepper
1 cup frozen sugar snap
  peas, thawed and drained

DIRECTIONS:

Preheat broiler on high heat. Lightly spray broiler pan or foil-lined baking sheet with nonfat cooking spray. In a medium bowl, combine teriyaki sauce, vinegar, pepper, and sesame seeds and mix well; remove ½ cup dressing from bowl and set aside. Add chicken to marinade; turn to coat on all sides; let chicken marinate at room temperature 15 minutes. Remove chicken; place on prepared pan; discard any remaining marinade. Broil chicken 10 to 15 minutes, until no longer pink and cooked through. In large bowl, combine lettuce, cabbage, water chestnuts, carrots, red peppers, and snap peas; add reserved dressing and toss until well mixed and coated. Add chicken to salad; toss lightly to mix.

Serves: 4

Nutrition per Serving		Exchanges
Calories	271	5 vegetable
Carbohydrate	24 grams	4⅓ meat
Cholesterol	106 milligrams	
Dietary Fiber	4 grams	
Protein	40 grams	
Sodium	1,646 milligrams	

SHOPPING LIST:

4 oz. low-sodium teriyaki sauce, 2 oz. rice vinegar, pepper, sesame seeds, 1½ lb. fat-free chicken breasts, packaged shredded lettuce or ¾ lb. head lettuce, packaged shredded cabbage or ¾ lb. cabbage, 6 oz. sliced water chestnuts, ½ lb. carrots or packaged shredded carrots, 1 medium red bell pepper, 10 oz. frozen sugar snap peas

COLESLAW

EASY - DO AHEAD

INGREDIENTS:
4 cups shredded cabbage
1 cup chopped green pepper
1 medium carrot, shredded
1 cup chopped onion
2 tbsp. pickle relish
½ tsp. vinegar
½ tsp. sugar
¼ cup fat-free mayonnaise

DIRECTIONS:
Combine all ingredients in a large bowl. Toss until ingredients are blended. Refrigerate several hours before serving.

Serves: 8

Nutrition per Serving		Exchanges
Calories	34	1 vegetable
Carbohydrate	8 grams	1⅔ vegetable
Cholesterol	0 milligrams	
Dietary Fiber	2 grams	
Protein	1 gram	
Sodium	69 milligrams	

SHOPPING LIST:
¾ lb. cabbage (or packaged preshredded cabbage), 1 green pepper, 1 medium carrot, 1 large onion, 1 oz. pickle relish, vinegar, sugar, 2 oz. fat-free mayonnaise

COLORFUL COLESLAW

EASY - DO AHEAD

INGREDIENTS:

4 cups shredded cabbage mix
½ cup shredded carrot
1 large red bell pepper, sliced thin
1 large yellow bell pepper, sliced thin
2 tsp. onion powder
2 tbsp. Dijon mustard
3 tbsp. balsamic vinegar
5 tbsp. cider vinegar
1 tbsp. low-sodium soy sauce
2 tsp. sugar
¼ tsp. pepper

DIRECTIONS:

In a large bowl, combine cabbage, carrot, peppers, and onion powder and toss to mix. In a small jar, combine mustard, vinegars, soy sauce, sugar, and pepper; cover and shake until all ingredients are blended. Pour mixture over cabbage mixture and toss well. Refrigerate 1 to 2 hours before serving.

Serves: 4

Nutrition per Serving		Exchanges
Calories	64	2½ vegetable
Carbohydrate	14 grams	
Cholesterol	0 milligrams	
Dietary Fiber	3 grams	
Protein	2 grams	
Sodium	357 milligrams	

SHOPPING LIST:

1 lb. prepackaged shredded mixed cabbage, 1 carrot (or prepackaged shredded carrots), 1 large red bell pepper, 1 large yellow bell pepper (red, yellow, orange, or green peppers can be substituted), onion powder, 1 oz. Dijon mustard, 1½ oz. balsamic vinegar, 2½ oz. cider vinegar, low-sodium soy sauce, sugar, pepper

CREAMY VEGETABLE SALAD

EASY - DO AHEAD

✦ ✦ ✦

INGREDIENTS:
2½ cups broccoli florets
2½ cups cauliflower florets
1 cup red onion, sliced
1 cup fat-free mayonnaise
⅓ cup fat-free Parmesan cheese
¼ cup sugar
pepper to taste

DIRECTIONS:
Combine broccoli, cauliflower, and onion in a large bowl; toss to mix vegetables. In a small bowl, combine mayonnaise, Parmesan cheese, sugar, and pepper; blend until smooth. Pour dressing over vegetables, cover, and refrigerate several hours or overnight.

Serves: 8

Nutrition per Serving		Exchanges
Calories	75	2 vegetable
Carbohydrate	16 grams	⅓ starch
Cholesterol	0 milligrams	
Dietary Fiber	2 grams	
Protein	3 grams	
Sodium	253 milligrams	

SHOPPING LIST:
1½ lb. broccoli, 1 to 2 lb. cauliflower, 1 large red onion, 8 oz. fat-free mayonnaise, 1½ oz. fat-free Parmesan cheese, sugar, pepper

CURRY CHICKEN SALAD

EASY - DO AHEAD

INGREDIENTS:

¼ cup fat-free sour cream
¼ cup fat-free mayonnaise
1 tsp. curry powder
pepper to taste
2 cups fat-free chicken tenders, cooked and diced
1 cup canned water chestnuts, chopped

DIRECTIONS:

In a medium bowl, combine sour cream, mayonnaise, curry powder, and pepper; mix until blended. Fold in chicken and water chestnuts. Serve with fat-free crackers, bagel chips, fat-free pita pockets, or fat-free flour tortillas.

Serves: 4

Nutrition per Serving		Exchanges
Calories	156	3 meat
Carbohydrate	10 grams	1 vegetable
Cholesterol	71 milligrams	⅓ starch
Dietary Fiber	< 1 gram	
Protein	25 grams	
Sodium	393 milligrams	

SHOPPING LIST:

2 oz. fat-free sour cream, 2 oz. fat-free mayonnaise, curry powder, pepper, 1 lb. fat-free chicken tenders, 8 oz. can sliced water chestnuts

MACARONI SALAD

EASY - DO AHEAD

✦ ✦ ✦

INGREDIENTS:

8 oz. macaroni, cooked and drained
½ cup fat-free mayonnaise
½ cup fat-free sour cream
2 tbsp. white vinegar
2 tsp. Dijon mustard
¾ tsp. onion powder
2 tbsp. dried parsley
pepper to taste
1½ cups chopped celery
¼ cup sweet pickle relish
10 oz. frozen peas, thawed and drained
½ cup chopped red bell pepper

DIRECTIONS:

Drain cooked macaroni in a colander and rinse with cold water; drain well. In a large bowl, combine mayonnaise, sour cream, vinegar, mustard, onion powder, parsley, and pepper; mix until blended smooth. Add macaroni and coat well. Fold in celery, pickle relish, peas, and red peppers and mix lightly until blended. Cover with plastic wrap and refrigerate at least 2 hours before serving.

Serves: 6

Nutrition per Serving		Exchanges
Calories	95	1 starch
Carbohydrate	16 grams	½ vegetable
Cholesterol	0 milligrams	
Dietary Fiber	1 gram	
Protein	4 grams	
Sodium	204 milligrams	

SHOPPING LIST:

8 oz. macaroni, 4 oz. fat-free mayonnaise, 4 oz. fat-free sour cream, 1 oz. white vinegar, Dijon mustard, onion powder, dried parsley, pepper, 4 medium stalks celery, 2 oz. sweet pickle relish, 10 oz. frozen peas, 1 small red bell pepper

MUSHROOM COUSCOUS

AVERAGE - DO AHEAD

INGREDIENTS:
1¼ cups couscous
1½ cups boiling water
1 tbsp. fat-free chicken broth
2 cups button mushrooms, sliced
2 cups shiitake mushrooms, sliced
½ cup sliced green onion
1 cup chopped red bell pepper
1 cup chopped yellow bell pepper
1 cup chopped green bell pepper
1½ cups fat-free red wine vinegar salad dressing

DIRECTIONS:
Place couscous in a large bowl; pour boiling water over couscous, cover and let stand 5 to 7 minutes, until water is absorbed. Fluff couscous with a fork. Lightly spray a large nonstick skillet with nonfat cooking spray. Pour chicken broth into skillet and heat over medium-high heat. Add mushrooms to skillet and cook 5 minutes, until tender. Add mushrooms to couscous; stir in green onions and peppers and mix well. Cover salad and refrigerate several hours. Pour salad dressing over couscous just before serving.

Serves: 6

Nutrition per Serving		Exchanges
Calories	237	1 starch
Carbohydrate	50 grams	2 vegetable
Cholesterol	0 milligrams	1 ⅔ fruit
Dietary Fiber	7 grams	
Protein	7 grams	
Sodium	256 milligrams	

SHOPPING LIST:
couscous, fat-free chicken broth, ½ lb. button mushrooms, ½ lb. shiitake mushrooms, 4 to 5 green onions, 1 medium red bell pepper, 1 medium yellow bell pepper, 1 green bell pepper, 12 oz. fat-free red wine vinegar salad dressing

PASTA SALAD BOWL

EASY - DO AHEAD

✦ ✦ ✦

INGREDIENTS:
2 cups uncooked pasta
¼ cup frozen broccoli florets, thawed and drained
¼ cup frozen cauliflower florets, thawed and drained
10 oz. frozen snow peas, thawed and drained
½ cup frozen carrot slices, thawed and drained
¼ pound sliced mushrooms
½ cup cherry tomatoes, halved
1 green onion, chopped
⅓ cup fat-free Italian salad dressing
pepper to taste

DIRECTIONS:
Cook pasta according to package directions; rinse under cold water and drain well. In a large bowl, combine pasta, thawed and drained vegetables, mushrooms, tomatoes, and onions; pour dressing over mixture and toss to mix all ingredients. Add pepper to taste. Refrigerate at least 2 hours before serving.

Serves: 6

Nutrition per Serving		Exchanges
Calories	172	1 starch
Carbohydrate	35 grams	4 vegetable
Cholesterol	0 milligrams	
Dietary Fiber	1 gram	
Protein	6 grams	
Sodium	101 milligrams	

SHOPPING LIST:
8 oz. package pasta (rotini, shells, etc.), 10 oz. frozen broccoli florets, 10 oz. frozen cauliflower florets, 10 oz. frozen snow peas, 10 oz. frozen sliced carrots, ¼ lb. mushrooms, ¼ pint cherry tomatoes, green onion, 3 oz. fat-free Italian salad dressing, pepper

PINEAPPLE-CHICKEN SALAD

EASY - DO AHEAD

INGREDIENTS:
2 cups fat-free chicken tenders, cooked and cubed
1 cup chopped celery
1 cup chopped red onion
½ cup chopped red bell pepper
8 oz. crushed pineapple in juice, drained
¼ cup raisins
¼ cup chopped dates
½ cup fat-free mayonnaise
½ cup fat-free sour cream
¼ tsp. mustard
½ tsp. lemon juice
¼ tsp. pepper

DIRECTIONS:
In large bowl, combine chopped chicken, celery, red onion, bell pepper, pineapple, raisins, and dates; mix well. Refrigerate several hours before serving. In a medium bowl, combine mayonnaise, sour cream, mustard, lemon juice, and pepper; blend until smooth. Refrigerate several hours before serving. Toss salad and dressing; serve immediately.

Serves: 4

Nutrition per Serving		Exchanges
Calories	240	3 meat
Carbohydrate	29 grams	3 vegetable
Cholesterol	71 milligrams	1 fruit
Dietary Fiber	3 grams	
Protein	27 grams	
Sodium	537 milligrams	

SHOPPING LIST:
1 lb. fat-free chicken tenders, 2 to 3 stalks celery, 1 medium red onion, 1 small red bell pepper, 8 oz. crushed pineapple in juice, raisins, chopped dates, 4 oz. fat-free mayonnaise, 4 oz. fat-free sour cream, mustard, lemon juice, pepper

SENSATIONAL SALAD, SOUP, & SANDWICHES

SEAFOOD SALAD

EASY- DO AHEAD

INGREDIENTS:

6 oz. imitation crab flakes
4 oz. fat-free frozen shrimp, cooked and diced
¼ cup chopped green onion
¼ cup chopped celery
¼ cup fat-free mayonnaise
2 tbsp. fat-free sour cream
⅛ tsp. garlic powder
½ tsp. Dijon mustard
pepper to taste

DIRECTIONS:

In a medium bowl, combine all ingredients and mix well.
Refrigerate several hours before serving. Great with fat-free
crackers, bagels, or fat-free pita pockets.

Serves: 4

Nutrition per Serving		Exchanges
Calories	84	1 meat
Carbohydrate	11 grams	⅔ starch
Cholesterol	8 milligrams	
Dietary Fiber	< 1 gram	
Protein	8 grams	
Sodium	504 milligrams	

SHOPPING LIST:

6 oz. imitation crab flakes, 4 oz. fat-free frozen shrimp, 2 to
3 green onions, 1 stalk celery, 2 oz. fat-free mayonnaise, 1 oz.
fat-free sour cream, garlic powder, Dijon mustard, pepper

SHRIMP PASTA SALAD

EASY - DO AHEAD

INGREDIENTS:
½ lb. rotini, cooked and drained
1 lb. fat-free frozen cooked shrimp, thawed and drained
10 oz. frozen peas, thawed and drained
½ c. chopped green bell pepper
½ cup chopped red bell pepper
½ cup chopped celery
½ cup canned, sliced water chestnuts
¼ cup chopped red onion
½ cup fat-free sour cream
2 tbsp. fat-free mayonnaise
1 tbsp. horseradish
1 tbsp. white wine vinegar
1 tsp. Dijon mustard
1 tsp. dried basil

DIRECTIONS:
In large bowl, combine pasta, shrimp, peas, peppers, celery, water chestnuts, and onion; mix well. In separate bowl, combine sour cream, mayonnaise, horseradish, white wine vinegar, mustard, and basil; mix until blended smooth. Refrigerate salad and dressing until ready to serve. Toss pasta salad with dressing just before serving.

Serves: 6

Nutrition per Serving		Exchanges
Calories	196	1 meat
Carbohydrate	32 grams	1 starch
Cholesterol	9 milligrams	3 vegetable
Dietary Fiber	2 grams	
Protein	14 grams	
Sodium	646 milligrams	

SHOPPING LIST:
8 oz. rotini pasta, ½ lb. fat-free frozen cooked shrimp, 10 oz. frozen peas, 1 small green bell pepper, 1 small red bell pepper, 1 stalk celery, 4 oz. sliced water chestnuts, 1 small red onion, 4 oz. fat-free sour cream, 1 oz. fat-free mayonnaise, horseradish, white wine vinegar, Dijon mustard, dried basil

SHRIMP SPINACH SALAD

EASY - DO AHEAD

INGREDIENTS:

12 cups fresh chopped spinach
1 cup sliced red bell pepper
½ cup chopped red onions
1 cup mandarin oranges in juice, drained
1 lb. fat-free frozen cooked shrimp, thawed and drained

DIRECTIONS:

Combine spinach, red pepper, onion, oranges, and cooked shrimp in a large bowl. Toss with Mango Salad Dressing (page 148) or Hot Orange Dressing (page 147) and serve.

Serves: 4

Nutrition per Serving		Exchanges
Calories	180	1⅓ fruit
Carbohydrate	29 grams	2 vegetable
Cholesterol	13 milligrams	2 meat
Dietary Fiber	6 grams	
Protein	18 grams	
Sodium	881 milligrams	

SHOPPING LIST:

1½ lb. fresh spinach, 1 medium red bell pepper, 1 small red onion, 8 oz. can mandarin oranges in juice, 1 lb. fat-free frozen cooked shrimp

TACO SALAD SHELL

EASY - DO AHEAD

INGREDIENTS:
1 large fat-free flour tortilla

DIRECTIONS:
Preheat oven to 450 degrees. Place a glass bowl upside-down on a baking sheet; lightly spray the outside of the bowl with nonfat cooking spray. Quickly dip the tortilla in water to soften and immediately spray lightly with nonfat cooking spray. Drape tortilla over bowl and bake in pre-heated oven 5 minutes, until lightly browned and firm. Carefully lift tortilla off the bowl; turn shell right-side-up and place on baking sheet. Return to oven and bake until crisp, about 2 to 3 minutes. Cool to room temperature and fill with favorite salad. Store in an airtight container for up to 1 week.

Serves: 1

Nutrition per Serving		Exchanges
Calories	165	2 starch
Carbohydrate	36 grams	
Cholesterol	0 milligrams	
Dietary Fiber	3 grams	
Protein	6 grams	
Sodium	510 milligrams	

SHOPPING LIST:
fat-free flour tortilla, nonfat cooking spray

TART 'N TANGY CARROT SALAD

EASY - DO AHEAD

INGREDIENTS:

2 cups shredded carrots
2 cups shredded apples
1 cup pineapple chunks in juice
2 tbsp. fat-free sour cream
2 tbsp. fat-free plain yogurt
½ tsp. cinnamon

DIRECTIONS:

Combine all ingredients in a large bowl and toss to mix. Refrigerate several hours before serving.

Serves: 4

Nutrition per Serving	
Calories	103
Carbohydrate	25 grams
Cholesterol	< 1 milligram
Dietary Fiber	3 grams
Protein	2 grams
Sodium	31 milligrams

Exchanges

1 vegetable
1⅓ fruit

SHOPPING LIST:

1 lb. carrots (or packaged preshredded carrots), 2 apples, 8 oz. pineapple chunks in juice, 1 oz. fat-free sour cream, 1 oz. fat-free yogurt, cinnamon

TORTILLA SALAD

EASY

INGREDIENTS:

2 fat-free corn tortillas, sliced into strips
1 tbsp. fresh ginger root, minced
¼ cup chopped green bell pepper
¼ cup chopped red bell pepper
½ cup chopped tomatoes
1 tbsp. fresh basil, chopped
2 tbsp. red wine vinegar
4 cups assorted greens (arugula, red leaf lettuce, radicchio)

DIRECTIONS:

Preheat oven to 350 degrees. Lightly spray baking sheet with nonfat cooking spray. Place tortilla strips in a single layer on baking sheet and bake 5 minutes in preheated oven to crisp. In a large salad bowl, combine ginger root, peppers, tomato, basil, and vinegar; mix well. Add assorted greens and toss. Top with crisp tortilla strips.

Serves: 4

Nutrition per Serving		Exchanges
Calories	56	2 vegetable
Carbohydrate	13 grams	
Cholesterol	0 milligrams	
Dietary Fiber	2 grams	
Protein	2 grams	
Sodium	54 milligrams	

SHOPPING LIST:

2 fat-free corn tortillas, fresh ginger root, 1 small green bell pepper, 1 small red bell pepper, 2 small tomatoes, fresh basil, red wine vinegar, 4 cups mixed salad greens

TURKEY-RICE SALAD

EASY - DO AHEAD

✦ ✦ ✦

INGREDIENTS:

1 cup cooked brown rice
2 cups fat-free cooked rice
2 cups fat-free turkey tenders, cooked and diced
½ cup canned, sliced water chestnuts
¾ cup pineapple tidbits in juice, drained
¼ cup raisins
¼ cup chopped red onion
½ cup mandarin oranges in juice, drained
½ cup fat-free mayonnaise
½ cup fat-free sour cream
1 tsp. lemon juice
½ tsp. curry powder
Romaine lettuce leaves

DIRECTIONS:

In a large bowl, combine rice, turkey, water chestnuts, pineapple, raisins, onions, and oranges; toss until mixed. In a small bowl, combine mayonnaise, sour cream, lemon juice, and curry powder; mix until blended smooth. Pour dressing over rice mixture and toss until well coated. To serve, line plates with lettuce leaves and top with turkey-rice salad.

Serves: 6

Nutrition per Serving		Exchanges
Calories	322	3 meat
Carbohydrate	46 grams	2 starch
Cholesterol	54 milligrams	1 fruit
Dietary Fiber	2 grams	
Protein	26 grams	
Sodium	1,831 milligrams	

SHOPPING LIST:

⅓ cup brown rice, ⅔ cup fat-free white rice, ½ lb. fat-free turkey tenders, canned sliced water chestnuts, 8 oz. pineapple tidbits in juice, 2 oz. raisins, small red onion, 6 oz. mandarin oranges in juice, 4 oz. fat-free mayonnaise, 4 oz. fat-free sour cream, lemon juice, curry powder, Romaine lettuce

TUNA PASTA SALAD

AVERAGE

INGREDIENTS:

6 oz. rotini
2 cups frozen broccoli florets, thawed and drained
¾ cup frozen carrot slices, thawed and drained
¾ cup frozen cauliflower florets, thawed and drained
¾ cup low-fat cream of celery soup
1¼ cups evaporated skim milk
½ tsp. garlic powder
6 oz. fat-free tuna, drained
3 tbsp. fat-free Parmesan cheese

DIRECTIONS:

Prepare pasta according to package directions. Add broccoli, carrots, and cauliflower during last 2 to 3 minutes of cooking time; drain well and keep warm. In a small saucepan over medium heat, combine soup, milk, and garlic powder; cook until ingredients are blended smooth. Add tuna and cheese to soup mixture and cook over medium-low heat 10 to 15 minutes, until heated through. Combine pasta with tuna mixture and toss lightly; serve immediately.

Serves: 8

Nutrition per Serving		Exchanges
Calories	179	1 starch
Carbohydrate	29 grams	3 vegetable
Cholesterol	7 milligrams	1 meat
Dietary Fiber	3 grams	
Protein	15 grams	
Sodium	331 milligrams	

SHOPPING LIST:

6 oz. rotini, 10 oz. frozen broccoli florets, 10 oz. frozen carrot slices, 10 oz. frozen cauliflower florets, 10½ oz. can low-fat cream of celery soup, 8 oz. evaporated skim milk, garlic powder, 6 oz. fat-free tuna, 3 oz. fat-free Parmesan cheese

WALDORF SALAD

EASY - DO AHEAD

INGREDIENTS:
1 cup fat-free sour cream
1 cup fat-free mayonnaise
2 tbsp. honey
3 cups chopped apples
2 cups chopped celery
2 cups red seedless grapes
½ cup Grape-Nuts cereal (optional)

DIRECTIONS:
Combine all ingredients in a large bowl and refrigerate several hours before serving.

Serves: 4

Nutrition per Serving		Exchanges
Calories	251	2 starch
Carbohydrate	51 grams	1½ fruit
Cholesterol	0 milligrams	
Dietary Fiber	4 grams	
Protein	7 grams	
Sodium	612 milligrams	

SHOPPING LIST:
8 oz. fat-free sour cream, 8 oz. fat-free mayonnaise, honey, 3 medium apples, 1 lb. celery, 1 lb. red seedless grapes, Grape-Nuts cereal (optional)

WILD RICE SALAD

EASY - DO AHEAD

INGREDIENTS:
2 cups cooked wild rice
2 tbsp. chopped green onion
½ cup corn kernels
½ cup diced red bell pepper
⅛ tsp. garlic powder
⅛ tsp. pepper
2 tbsp. white wine vinegar
2 tbsp. lemon juice
2 tsp. Dijon mustard
2 tsp. horseradish

DIRECTIONS:
Combine rice, green onions, corn, and red pepper in a medium bowl. Sprinkle with garlic powder and pepper and toss lightly. In a small bowl, combine vinegar, lemon juice, mustard, and horseradish; mix until blended smooth. Just before serving, pour dressing over rice salad and toss until coated.

Serves: 4

Nutrition per Serving		Exchanges
Calories	113	1¼ starch
Carbohydrate	25 grams	1 vegetable
Cholesterol	0 milligrams	
Dietary Fiber	2 grams	
Protein	4 grams	
Sodium	95 milligrams	

SHOPPING LIST:
wild rice, 1 to 2 green onions, canned corn kernels, 1 red bell pepper, garlic powder, pepper, 1 oz. white wine vinegar, 1 oz. lemon juice, Dijon mustard, horseradish

BLACK BEAN SOUP

EASY - DO AHEAD - FREEZE

INGREDIENTS:
6 cups fat-free chicken broth
15 oz. fat-free black beans, drained and dried
¾ cup diced carrots
1¼ cups chopped onions
⅔ cup diced celery
½ tsp. oregano
½ tsp. pepper
½ tsp. garlic powder
1 cup diced potato

DIRECTIONS:
Pour chicken broth into a large soup pot and heat over high heat; add beans, carrots, onions, celery, oregano, pepper, and garlic powder and heat to almost boiling. Reduce temperature to low; cover and simmer 1 hour. Add diced potatoes and simmer until potatoes are tender, about 15 to 20 minutes.

Serves: 6

Nutrition per Serving

Calories	151	
Carbohydrate	29 grams	
Cholesterol	0 milligrams	
Dietary Fiber	5 grams	
Protein	8 grams	
Sodium	927 milligrams	

Exchanges
1 starch
3 vegetable

SHOPPING LIST:
4 15½-oz. cans fat-free chicken broth, 15 oz. can fat-free black beans, ¼ lb. carrots, 2 medium onions, 2 stalks celery, oregano, pepper, garlic powder, 1 medium potato

CHICKEN VEGETABLE NOODLE SOUP

EASY - DO AHEAD - FREEZE

INGREDIENTS:
8¼ cups fat-free chicken broth
1 cup chopped onions
3 large carrots, peeled and sliced
2 stalks celery, sliced
1 large red bell pepper, chopped
1 lb. fat-free chicken tenders, cubed
2 cups yolk-free noodles, uncooked
¼ tsp. pepper
¼ tsp. garlic powder

DIRECTIONS:
Lightly spray a large soup pot with nonfat cooking spray. Pour 2 tablespoons chicken broth into pot and heat over medium-high heat. Add onions, carrots, celery, and red pepper and cook 3 to 5 minutes, just until tender-crisp. Pour remaining chicken broth into pot; increase heat to high and bring soup to a boil. Add chicken pieces, noodles, pepper, and garlic powder to pot; reduce heat to medium-low, cover, and cook 25 to 30 minutes, until vegetables are tender and chicken is cooked through.

Serves: 6

Nutrition per Serving		Exchanges
Calories	161	1 starch
Carbohydrate	20 grams	1 vegetable
Cholesterol	47 milligrams	2 meat
Dietary Fiber	3 grams	
Protein	18 grams	
Sodium	1,643 milligrams	

SHOPPING LIST:
6 15½-oz. cans fat-free chicken broth (or 8 chicken bouillon cubes plus water), 1 large onion, 3 large carrots, 2 stalks celery, 1 red bell pepper, 1 lb. fat-free chicken tenders, 12 oz. yolk-free noodles, pepper, garlic powder

CHILLED MELON SOUP

EASY - DO AHEAD

INGREDIENTS:
4 cups cantaloupe balls
1 cup orange juice
½ tsp. cinnamon
½ tsp. sugar
1 tbsp. lime juice

DIRECTIONS:
Combine all ingredients in a food processor or blender and process until smooth. Refrigerate several hours before serving.

Serves: 4

Nutrition per Serving

Calories	87
Carbohydrate	21 grams
Cholesterol	0 milligrams
Dietary Fiber	2 grams
Protein	2 grams
Sodium	15 milligrams

Exchanges
1⅓ fruit

SHOPPING LIST:
1 large cantaloupe, 8 oz. orange juice, cinnamon, sugar, lime juice (or 1 small lime)

CHILLED PEACH SOUP

EASY - DO AHEAD

INGREDIENTS:

2 cups peeled and sliced peaches
⅛ tsp. cinnamon
¼ tsp. sugar
12 oz. peach nectar
1 tsp. lime juice
½ cup fat-free peach yogurt
1 cup sliced strawberries

DIRECTIONS:

Combine peaches, cinnamon, sugar, peach nectar, and lime juice in food processor or blender and process until smooth. Pour peach mixture into a medium bowl; fold in yogurt and mix lightly. Refrigerate overnight before serving. Pour into bowls and top with ¼ cup sliced strawberries.

Serves: 4

Nutrition per Serving		Exchanges
Calories	106	1⅔ fruit
Carbohydrate	26 grams	
Cholesterol	1 milligram	
Dietary Fiber	2 grams	
Protein	2 grams	
Sodium	24 milligrams	

SHOPPING LIST:

4 to 6 peaches, cinnamon, sugar, 12 oz. peach nectar, lime juice, 4 oz. fat-free peach yogurt, ½ pint strawberries

CHILLED YOGURT SOUP

EASY - DO AHEAD

✦ ✦ ✦

INGREDIENTS:
- 2 large cucumbers, peeled and chopped
- 2 large tomatoes, seeded and chopped
- 1 small Vidalia onion, chopped fine
- ¼ cup chopped chives
- 2 cups fat-free plain yogurt
- 1 tsp. cumin
- 3 drops hot pepper sauce

DIRECTIONS:
Place cucumber, tomato, onion, and chives in food processor or blender and process until chopped fine. Add yogurt, cumin and hot pepper sauce and blend until smooth. Refrigerate several hours before serving.

Serves: 4

Nutrition per Serving		Exchanges
Calories	126	½ milk
Carbohydrate	22 grams	3 vegetable
Cholesterol	2 milligrams	
Dietary Fiber	4 grams	
Protein	9 grams	
Sodium	105 milligrams	

SHOPPING LIST:
2 large cucumbers, 2 large tomatoes, 1 small Vidalia onion, chives, 16 oz. fat-free yogurt, cumin, hot pepper sauce

CLAM CHOWDER

AVERAGE - DO AHEAD

INGREDIENTS:

14½ oz. can fat-free chicken broth
½ cup low-fat cream of celery soup
⅛ tsp. pepper
3 cups diced potatoes
½ cup chopped celery
1 tbsp. onion powder
1 cup skim milk
2 tbsp. flour
2 6½-oz. cans fat-free minced clams

DIRECTIONS:

Lightly spray a medium saucepan with nonfat cooking spray and heat over medium-high heat. Add chicken broth, cream of celery soup, pepper, potatoes, celery, and onion powder to saucepan and bring to a boil over high heat. Cover saucepan, reduce heat to low, and simmer 15 to 20 minutes, until vegetables are tender. In a small bowl, combine milk with flour and mix until smooth. Gradually add to broth and cook until mixture starts to become thick. Stir in clams; increase heat to medium-high and bring to boil. Reduce heat to medium and cook, stirring constantly, until soup is thick and heated through.

Serves: 6

Nutrition per Serving		Exchanges
Calories	124	1⅓ starch
Carbohydrate	21 grams	½ meat
Cholesterol	13 milligrams	
Dietary Fiber	1 gram	
Protein	8 grams	
Sodium	736 milligrams	

SHOPPING LIST:

14½ oz. can fat-free chicken broth, 10½ oz. can low-fat cream of celery soup, pepper, 3 medium potatoes, 1 to 2 stalks celery, onion powder, 8 oz. skim milk, flour, 2 6½-oz. cans fat-free minced clams

COLD BEET BORSCHT SOUP

EASY - DO AHEAD

INGREDIENTS:

16 oz. canned beets, drained
2 cups tomato juice without salt
1½ cups fat-free chicken or vegetable broth
1½ tsp. onion powder
2 tsp. dried dill weed
2 drops hot pepper sauce
1 tsp. minced garlic
¼ tsp. pepper
2½ tbsp. lemon juice
¼ cup fat-free sour cream

DIRECTIONS:

Combine all ingredients, except sour cream, in a food processor or blender and process until smooth. Refrigerate 2 to 3 hours before serving. Pour into bowls and top with 1 tablespoon sour cream.

Serves: 4

Nutrition per Serving		Exchanges
Calories	66	2½ vegetable
Carbohydrate	13 grams	
Cholesterol	0 milligrams	
Dietary Fiber	3 grams	
Protein	3 grams	
Sodium	483 milligrams	

SHOPPING LIST:

16 oz. canned beets, 16 oz. tomato juice without salt, 13½ oz. can fat-free chicken or vegetable broth, onion powder, dried dill weed, hot pepper sauce, minced garlic, pepper, 1¼ oz. lemon juice, 2 oz. fat-free sour cream

COLD CUCUMBER SOUP

EASY - DO AHEAD

INGREDIENTS:

6 tbsp. cultured buttermilk mix
1½ cups water
4 cups peeled and chopped cucumbers
1 tbsp. red wine vinegar
¾ tsp. minced garlic
2 ice cubes
Salt and pepper to taste

DIRECTIONS:

In a small bowl, combine buttermilk mix with water and mix until blended. In a food processor or blender, combine 3½ cups cucumbers, buttermilk mixture, vinegar, minced garlic, and 2 ice cubes and blend until smooth. Season with salt and pepper to taste. Pour soup into a large bowl; add remaining cucumbers to garnish. Refrigerate several hours before serving.

Serves: 4

Nutrition per Serving		Exchanges
Calories	23	1 vegetable
Carbohydrate	4 grams	
Cholesterol	1 milligram	
Dietary Fiber	1 gram	
Protein	1 gram	
Sodium	26 milligrams	

SHOPPING LIST:

cultured buttermilk mix, 3 to 4 cucumbers, red wine vinegar, minced garlic, salt, and pepper

CREAM OF POTATO SOUP

AVERAGE - DO AHEAD - FREEZE

◆ ◆ ◆

INGREDIENTS:

14½ oz. fat-free chicken broth
½ cup low-fat cream of celery soup
½ cup chopped celery
3 medium potatoes, peeled and sliced
1½ tsp. onion powder
1 cup skim milk

DIRECTIONS:

In a medium saucepan over high heat, combine chicken broth, cream of celery soup, celery, potatoes, and onion powder. Bring to a boil; reduce heat to low, cover, and simmer 15 to 20 minutes, until vegetables are tender. Remove saucepan from heat. In a food processor or blender, combine half the broth mixture with ½ cup milk and process until smooth. Repeat with remaining broth and milk; return to pan and heat over medium heat 5 to 8 minutes, until heated through.

Serves: 4

Nutrition per Serving		Exchanges
Calories	135	1⅔ starch
Carbohydrate	27 grams	
Cholesterol	2 milligrams	
Dietary Fiber	3 grams	
Protein	5 grams	
Sodium	504 milligrams	

SHOPPING LIST:

14½ oz. can fat-free chicken broth, 10½ oz. can low-fat cream of celery soup, 1-2 stalks celery, 3 medium potatoes, onion powder, 8 oz. skim milk

LENTIL SOUP

EASY - DO AHEAD - FREEZE

INGREDIENTS:

2 cups chopped onions
3 medium carrots, shredded
1 tsp. garlic powder
¾ tsp. crushed thyme leaves
28 oz. low-sodium crushed tomatoes
3½ cups fat-free chicken broth
3½ cups water
1 cup dried lentils, rinsed and drained
pepper to taste
¾ cup dry white wine
2 tbsp. dried parsley
½ cup fat-free shredded Cheddar cheese (optional)

DIRECTIONS:

Lightly spray a large soup pot or Dutch oven with nonfat cooking spray and heat over medium-high heat. Add onions, carrots, garlic powder, and thyme; cook until vegetables are tender-crisp, about 5 minutes. Add tomatoes with liquid, chicken broth, water, and lentils. Bring soup to a boil over high heat; immediately reduce heat to low, cover pot and simmer 1½ hours, until lentils are tender. Add pepper, wine, and parsley and cook an additional 15 minutes. Top with shredded cheese before serving, if desired.

Serves: 6

Nutrition per Serving		Exchanges
Calories	182	1 starch
Carbohydrate	29 grams	3 vegetable
Cholesterol	0 milligrams	½ meat
Dietary Fiber	6 grams	
Protein	11 grams	
Sodium	654 milligrams	

SHOPPING LIST:

2 large onions, 3 medium carrots, garlic powder, crushed thyme, 28 oz. can low-sodium crushed tomatoes, 2 15½-oz. cans fat-free chicken broth (or 4 chicken bouillon cubes plus water), 1 cup lentils, pepper, 6 oz. dry white wine, dried parsley, 2 oz. fat-free shredded Cheddar cheese (optional)

SEAFOOD CHOWDER

AVERAGE - DO AHEAD

♦ ♦ ♦

INGREDIENTS:

2½ cups peeled and diced
   potatoes
10 oz. frozen corn kernels
1 cup carrots, peeled and
   chopped
1 tsp. minced garlic
2½ cups fat-free chicken broth
2½ cups broccoli florets

3 tbsp. flour
¼ tsp. pepper
2 cups skim milk
6 oz. fat-free frozen shrimp
6 oz. imitation fat-free crab
   flakes
1 cup fat-free shredded
   Cheddar cheese

DIRECTIONS:

In a large soup pot or Dutch oven, combine potato, 1 cup corn, carrot, garlic, and chicken broth; bring to a boil over high heat. Reduce heat to low and simmer, stirring frequently, until potatoes are tender, about 15 to 20 minutes. Pour potato mixture into food processor or blender and process until smooth. Return mixture to soup pot and add remaining corn and broccoli. Cover pot and cook over medium-high heat about 10 minutes. In a small bowl, combine flour and pepper. Gradually blend in skim milk, stirring constantly, until mixture is smooth. Stir into soup. Add shrimp and crab and cook over medium heat, stirring constantly, until thickened, about 10 to 15 minutes. Remove soup from heat and stir in cheese until melted.

Serves: 8

Nutrition per Serving		Exchanges
Calories	191	2 starch
Carbohydrate	34 grams	½ vegetable
Cholesterol	6 milligrams	1 meat
Dietary Fiber	3 grams	
Protein	14 grams	
Sodium	745 milligrams	

SHOPPING LIST:

¾ lb. potatoes, 10 oz. frozen corn kernels, ½ lb. carrots, minced garlic, 24 oz. fat-free chicken broth, 1 lb. head broccoli, flour, pepper, 1 pint skim milk, 6 oz. fat-free frozen shrimp, 6 oz. fat-free crab flakes, 4 oz. fat-free shredded Cheddar cheese

....

SPICY BLACK BEAN SOUP

EASY - DO AHEAD - FREEZE

INGREDIENTS:

1 tbsp. fat-free chicken broth
1 cup chopped onion
2 tsp. minced garlic
3 cups fat-free black beans
2½ tsp. chili powder
¾ tsp. cumin
28 oz. Mexican tomatoes and jalapeños
¾ tsp. lemon juice

DIRECTIONS:

Lightly spray large soup pot with nonfat cooking spray. Pour chicken broth into pot and heat over medium-high heat. Add onion and garlic to pot and cook until tender and soft, about 2 to 3 minutes. Add beans, chili powder, cumin, tomatoes with juice, and lemon juice and mix well. Bring soup to a boil; reduce heat to low, cover and simmer 15 minutes. If soup is too thick, add ¾ to 1 cup water as needed.

Serves: 6

Nutrition per Serving		Exchanges
Calories	187	2 starch
Carbohydrate	34 grams	1 vegetable
Cholesterol	0 milligrams	
Dietary Fiber	5 grams	
Protein	10 grams	
Sodium	1,157 milligrams	

SHOPPING LIST:

fat-free chicken broth, 1 large onion, minced garlic, 2 15-oz. cans fat-free black beans, chili powder, cumin, 2 14-oz. cans Mexican tomatoes and jalapeños, lemon juice

TURKEY CHILI

EASY - DO AHEAD - FREEZE

✦ ✦ ✦

INGREDIENTS:

1 cup chopped onion
1 tsp. minced garlic
1 large carrot, chopped
1 stalk celery, chopped
1 medium green bell pepper, chopped
2½ tbsp. chili powder
¾ tsp. cumin

14½ oz. Mexican tomatoes and jalapeños
13¾ oz. fat-free chicken broth
1¼ lb. fat-free turkey tenders, cubed
1¼ cups fat-free shredded Cheddar cheese

DIRECTIONS:

Lightly spray a large nonstick skillet with nonfat cooking spray and heat over medium-high heat. Add onion and garlic and cook 3 to 5 minutes, until soft. Add carrot, celery, and green pepper and cook 5 to 6 minutes, until vegetables are tender-crisp. Stir in chili powder and cumin; cook 1 minute, until ingredients are mixed. Pour Mexican tomatoes with juice and chicken broth into skillet; bring mixture to a boil. Reduce heat to medium; add turkey and cook, uncovered, 45 minutes, until turkey is cooked through. Top with shredded cheese just before serving.

Serves: 5

Nutrition per Serving

Calories	201	
Carbohydrate	18 grams	
Cholesterol	41 milligrams	
Dietary Fiber	3 grams	
Protein	26 grams	
Sodium	2,100 milligrams	

Exchanges

3 meat
1 starch
1 vegetable

SHOPPING LIST:

1 large onion, minced garlic (or 1 garlic clove), 1 large carrot, 1 stalk celery, 1 medium green bell pepper, chili powder, cumin, 14½ oz. can diced tomatoes and jalapeños with Mexican seasonings (S&W), 1 15-oz. can fat-free chicken broth (or 2 chicken bouillon cubes plus water), 1¼ lb. fat-free turkey tenders, 5 oz. fat-free Cheddar cheese

VEGETABLE-POTATO SOUP

AVERAGE - DO AHEAD - FREEZE

INGREDIENTS:

4 cups potatoes, peeled and cubed
3 large carrots, peeled and sliced
3 large celery stalks, sliced
2½ tsp. garlic powder
1½ tbsp. onion powder
8 cups fat-free chicken broth
½ cup canned chopped tomatoes, drained
1 cup frozen peas
1 cup frozen green beans
1 tsp. dried dill weed
½ tsp. pepper

DIRECTIONS:

Lightly spray large soup pot or Dutch oven with nonfat cooking spray and heat over medium-high heat. Add potatoes, carrots, and celery to pot; sprinkle vegetables with garlic and onion powder. Cook 2 to 3 minutes, until heated. Pour chicken broth into pan and bring to a boil over high heat. Reduce heat to medium-low, cover and simmer 20 to 30 minutes, until vegetables are tender and soft. Add tomatoes, peas, beans, dill weed, and pepper to vegetables and cook 5 to 7 minutes, until heated through.

Serves: 8

Nutrition per Serving		Exchanges
Calories	133	1 starch
Carbohydrate	29 grams	2 vegetable
Cholesterol	0 milligrams	
Dietary Fiber	3 grams	
Protein	4 grams	
Sodium	964 milligrams	

SHOPPING LIST:

4 medium russet potatoes, 3 large carrots, 3 celery stalks, garlic powder, onion powder, 64 oz. fat-free chicken broth, 4 oz. can chopped tomatoes, 8 oz. frozen peas, 8 oz. frozen green beans, dried dill weed, pepper

VEGETARIAN CHILI

EASY - DO AHEAD - FREEZE

✦ ✦ ✦

INGREDIENTS:

2 tbsp. fat-free vegetable broth
2 tbsp. water
2 cups chopped carrots
1 cup chopped onion
28 oz. Mexican tomatoes with jalapeños
24 oz. fat-free black beans
24 oz. fat-free kidney beans
3 tbsp. chili powder
dash cayenne pepper
1½ cups fat-free shredded Cheddar cheese (optional)

DIRECTIONS:

Combine vegetable broth, water, carrots, and onion in a large saucepan; bring to a boil over high heat and cook 8 to 10 minutes, until liquid is reduced and vegetables are tender. Add tomatoes with chilies, black beans, kidney beans, chili powder, and cayenne pepper to saucepan; bring to a boil over high heat. Reduce heat to low and simmer 15 to 20 minutes. Top each serving of chili with ¼ to ½ cup shredded cheese, if desired.

Serves: 6

Nutrition per Serving		Exchanges
Calories	282	2 starch
Carbohydrate	47 grams	3 vegetable
Cholesterol	0 milligrams	1½ meat
Dietary Fiber	13 grams	
Protein	24 grams	
Sodium	1,505 milligrams	

SHOPPING LIST:

1 can fat-free vegetable broth, 3 to 4 carrots, 1 medium onion, 28 oz. Mexican tomatoes with jalapeños, 24 oz. fat-free black beans, 24 oz. fat-free kidney beans, chili powder, cayenne pepper, 6 oz. fat-free shredded Cheddar cheese (optional)

CAESAR SALAD SANDWICHES

AVERAGE - DO AHEAD

INGREDIENTS:

2 cups diced tomatoes
½ cup diced cucumber
¼ cup diced red bell pepper
¼ cup diced green bell pepper
¼ cup chopped red onion
¾ cup fat-free Caesar Salad Dressing

16 slices fat-free bread
2 cups chopped romaine lettuce
1 cup fat-free shredded mozzarella cheese
1 lb. fat-free deli turkey, thinly sliced (optional)

DIRECTIONS:

In a large bowl, combine tomatoes, cucumbers, peppers, and onion. Toss with ½ cup salad dressing and marinate in the refrigerator 1 hour. Preheat broiler on high. Lightly spray baking sheet with nonfat cooking spray. Place bread slices on baking sheet and brush both sides with remaining salad dressing. Broil until lightly browned—watch closely! Remove bread from oven and turn slices, toasted-side down. Remove marinated vegetables from refrigerator; add lettuce and toss until mixed well. Top bread with lettuce mixture; sprinkle with shredded cheese. Place bread under broiler and cook just until cheese is melted. Serve immediately. If using turkey, place on bread before cheese.

Serves: 8

Nutrition per Serving		Exchanges
Calories	227	2 starch
Carbohydrate	41 grams	2 vegetable
Cholesterol	0 milligrams	½ meat
Dietary Fiber	3 grams	
Protein	12 grams	
Sodium	594 milligrams	

SHOPPING LIST:

2 large tomatoes, 1 small cucumber, 1 small red bell pepper, 1 small green bell pepper, 1 small red onion, 6 oz. fat-free Caesar Salad Dressing, 1 lb. fat-free French or sourdough bread, 1 large head romaine lettuce, 4 oz. fat-free shredded mozzarella cheese, 1 lb. fat-free deli turkey, thinly sliced (optional)

CAJUN CHICKEN SALAD SANDWICHES

EASY

INGREDIENTS:
1 tbsp. fat-free chicken broth
1½ lbs. fat-free chicken breasts
1½ tsp. Cajun seasoning
½ cup fat-free mayonnaise
1 tsp. grated lime peel
1 tsp. jalapeño sauce
¼ tsp. pepper
8 slices fat-free bread or 8 fat-free rolls
4 large lettuce leaves
1 large tomato, thinly sliced
1 small red onion, cut into rings

DIRECTIONS:
Lightly spray large nonstick skillet with nonfat cooking spray. Add chicken broth to skillet and heat over medium-high heat. Sprinkle both sides of chicken breasts with Cajun seasoning. Add chicken to skillet and cook 5 to 6 minutes per side, until no longer pink and cooked through. In a small bowl, combine mayonnaise, lime peel, jalapeño sauce, and pepper; blend until smooth. Spread mayonnaise mixture on both sides of bread; place 1 lettuce leaf, sliced tomato, and sliced red onion on half of bread slices. Place chicken on top and cover with remaining bread.

Serves: 4

Nutrition per Serving		Exchanges
Calories	366	2⅔ starch
Carbohydrate	43 grams	1 vegetable
Cholesterol	106 milligrams	4 meat
Dietary Fiber	3 grams	
Protein	41 grams	
Sodium	1,024 milligrams	

SHOPPING LIST:
fat-free chicken broth, 1½ lb. fat-free chicken breasts, Cajun seasoning blend, 4 oz. fat-free mayonnaise, lime peel, jalapeño sauce, pepper, ½ lb. fat-free bread (8 slices or 8 fat-free sandwich rolls), 1 small head lettuce, 1 large tomato, 1 small red onion

CREAMY TUNA MELTS

EASY

INGREDIENTS:

4 slices fat-free bread
1 cup skim milk
1½ tbsp. flour
½ tsp. onion powder
½ cup frozen peas, thawed and drained
½ cup frozen carrot slices, thawed and drained
1 cup fat-free tuna, drained
4 oz. fat-free American cheese slices

DIRECTIONS:

Toast bread slices in toaster, oven or broiler until lightly browned. In a medium saucepan, combine milk, flour, and onion powder; cook over medium heat, stirring constantly, until mixture thickens. Stir in peas and carrots; cook 5 minutes, until heated through. Stir in tuna and cook until heated through. Preheat broiler on high heat. Line baking sheet with foil and lightly spray with nonfat cooking spray. Place toasted bread slices on baking sheet. Pour ½ cup tuna mixture over each and top with 1 slice cheese. Place under broiler until cheese is melted (watch carefully).

Serves: 4

Nutrition per Serving		Exchanges
Calories	250	3 meat
Carbohydrate	27 grams	1 vegetable
Cholesterol	11 milligrams	1½ starch
Dietary Fiber	2 grams	
Protein	30 grams	
Sodium	624 milligrams	

SHOPPING LIST:

¼ lb. fat-free bread, 8 oz. skim milk, flour, onion powder, 10 oz. frozen peas and carrots, 12 oz. fat-free tuna, 4 oz. fat-free American cheese slices

CREAMY VEGETABLE PITA POCKETS

EASY - DO AHEAD

◆ ◆ ◆

INGREDIENTS:

2 cups fat-free cottage cheese
½ cup chopped red bell pepper
½ cup chopped green bell pepper
½ cup chopped red onion
½ cup chopped cucumber
1 tsp. dried basil
1 tsp. dried dill weed
1 tsp. curry powder
¼ tsp. pepper
2 tsp. rice vinegar
½ tsp. garlic powder
4 fat-free pita pockets
4 large lettuce leaves

DIRECTIONS:

Combine all ingredients, except pita pockets and lettuce leaves, in a large bowl and mix well. Place one lettuce leaf into each pita pocket and stuff with ½ to ¾ cup filling. Filling can be prepared ahead of time and stuffed into pitas just before serving.

Serves: 4

Nutrition per Serving		Exchanges
Calories	149	1 starch
Carbohydrate	27 grams	2 vegetable
Cholesterol	3 milligrams	½ meat
Dietary Fiber	2 grams	
Protein	9 grams	
Sodium	312 milligrams	

SHOPPING LIST:

16 oz. fat-free cottage cheese, 1 small red bell pepper, 1 small green bell pepper, 1 medium red onion, 1 small cucumber, dried basil, dried dill weed, curry powder, pepper, rice vinegar, garlic powder, 4 fat-free pita pockets, 1 small head lettuce

LOBSTER SALAD SANDWICHES

EASY - DO AHEAD

INGREDIENTS:
1 lb. imitation lobster flakes
¼ cup chopped celery
1 tbsp. fat-free mayonnaise
salt and pepper to taste
4 whole lettuce leaves
4 pita bread pockets
paprika

DIRECTIONS:
In a medium bowl, combine lobster, celery, mayonnaise, salt, and pepper and mix until blended. Place 1 lettuce leaf into each pita pocket and stuff with lobster salad. Sprinkle with paprika.

Serves: 4

Nutrition per Serving

		Exchanges
Calories	212	2 starch
Carbohydrate	34 grams	1½ meat
Cholesterol	13 milligrams	
Dietary Fiber	1 gram	
Protein	16 grams	
Sodium	880 milligrams	

SHOPPING LIST:
1 lb. imitation lobster flakes, 1 stalk celery, fat-free mayonnaise, salt, pepper, 1 small head lettuce, 4 pita pockets, paprika

REUBEN SANDWICH

EASY

INGREDIENTS:
- ½ cup fat-free mayonnaise
- 1 tbsp. chili sauce
- 8 slices fat-free bread (rye, pumpernickel, whole wheat, etc.)
- 4 oz. fat-free Swiss cheese slices, cut in half
- ½ lb. fat-free corned beef, thinly sliced
- 1 cup sauerkraut, drained

DIRECTIONS:

Combine mayonnaise and chili sauce in a small bowl and mix until blended. Spread 1 tablespoon mayonnaise sauce on each bread slice. Top with 1 slice cheese, ¼ corned beef, ¼ cup sauerkraut, and remaining cheese. Place remaining bread slice on top. Lightly spray large nonstick skillet with nonfat cooking spray and heat over medium heat. Place sandwiches into skillet and cook until browned on both sides and cheese is melted.

Serves: 4

Nutrition per Serving		Exchanges
Calories	291	3 starch
Carbohydrate	44 grams	1½ meat
Cholesterol	20 milligrams	
Dietary Fiber	3 grams	
Protein	19 grams	
Sodium	1,754 milligrams	

SHOPPING LIST:

4 oz. fat-free mayonnaise, chili sauce, ½ lb. fat-free bread, 4 oz. sliced fat-free Swiss cheese, ½ lb. fat-free corned beef, 8 oz. sauerkraut

ROAST BEEF SANDWICH WITH HORSERADISH SAUCE

EASY - DO AHEAD

INGREDIENTS:

¼ cup fat-free mayonnaise
2 tsp. skim milk
2 tbsp. prepared horseradish
8 slices fat-free bread
1 lb. fat-free deli roast beef, thinly sliced
½ cup roasted red pepper, drained and sliced
1 small cucumber, sliced thin
¼ red onion, sliced into rings

DIRECTIONS:

In a small bowl, combine mayonnaise, milk, and horseradish; mix until blended. Spread mayonnaise mixture on both sides of bread; top 1 slice bread with beef, red peppers, cucumbers, and red onion rings. Spoon extra sauce on top and cover with top half of bread.

Serves: 4

Nutrition per Serving		Exchanges
Calories	303	2 starch
Carbohydrate	45 grams	3 vegetable
Cholesterol	41 milligrams	2 meat
Dietary fiber	3 grams	
Protein	23 grams	
Sodium	1,909 milligrams	

SHOPPING LIST:

2 oz. fat-free mayonnaise, skim milk, prepared horseradish, ½ lb. fat-free bread, 1 lb. fat-free deli roast beef, 7 oz. roasted red peppers, 1 cucumber, 1 red onion

TOMATO BASIL ROAST BEEF SANDWICH

EASY - DO AHEAD

INGREDIENTS:
¼ cup fat-free mayonnaise
1½ tsp. tomato paste
2 tbsp. fresh basil leaves, chopped fine
8 slices fat-free bread
4 arugula leaves
1 medium tomato, sliced thin
1 small red onion, sliced into thin rings
1 lb. fat-free roast beef

DIRECTIONS:
In a small bowl, combine mayonnaise, tomato paste, and basil leaves; blend well and refrigerate at least 1 hour. Toast bread slices until lightly browned. Spread each bread slice with 1 teaspoon mayonnaise mixture. Place one arugula leaf on 4 slices of bread; top with tomato slices, red onion rings, and roast beef. Top with remaining bread slices.

Serves: 4

Nutrition per Serving		Exchanges
Calories	301	2 meat
Carbohydrate	44 grams	2⅔ starch
Cholesterol	41 milligrams	1 vegetable
Dietary Fiber	3 grams	
Protein	23 grams	
Sodium	1,645 milligrams	

SHOPPING LIST:
2 oz. fat-free mayonnaise, tomato paste, fresh basil leaves, ½ lb. fat-free bread, fresh arugula leaves (4), 1 medium tomato, 1 small red onion, 1 lb. fat-free roast beef

CRANBERRY APPLESAUCE

EASY - DO AHEAD

INGREDIENTS:

2 cups chunky applesauce
1 cup whole cranberry sauce
½ tsp. cinnamon

DIRECTIONS:

Combine all ingredients in a microwave-safe dish and heat on high for 2 minutes. Can be served hot or cold. Great side dish for holiday meals!

Serves: 4

Nutrition per Serving		Exchanges
Calories	202	3⅓ fruit
Carbohydrate	53 grams	
Cholesterol	0 milligrams	
Dietary Fiber	2 grams	
Protein	< 1 gram	
Sodium	24 milligrams	

SHOPPING LIST:

16 oz. chunky applesauce, 8 oz. whole cranberry sauce, cinnamon

SENSATIONAL
SALAD, SOUP, &
SANDWICHES

STRAWBERRY APPLESAUCE JELLO

EASY - DO AHEAD

INGREDIENTS:
    3 oz. strawberry Jell-O
    1 cup boiling water
    1½ cups lite applesauce
    1 tsp. lemon juice

DIRECTIONS:
    Dissolve Jell-O in boiling water. Stir in applesauce and lemon juice and mix until ingredients are blended. Pour into 4 individual dishes or 8-inch baking dish and refrigerate until firm.

Serves: 4

Nutrition per Serving
Calories	110
Carbohydrate	27 grams
Cholesterol	0 milligrams
Dietary fiber	1 gram
Protein	2 grams
Sodium	2 milligrams

Exchanges
⅔ starch
1 fruit

SHOPPING LIST:
    3 oz. strawberry Jell-O, 12 oz. lite applesauce, lemon juice

ITALIAN AND CHEESE CROUTONS

EASY - DO AHEAD

INGREDIENTS:
nonfat cooking spray
1 lb. fat-free Italian or French bread loaf, cut in 1-inch cubes
¾ tsp. Italian seasoning
¼ cup fat-free Parmesan cheese

DIRECTIONS:
Preheat oven to 300 degrees. Lightly spray baking sheet with nonfat cooking spray. Place bread cubes in a large bowl. Lightly spray with nonfat cooking spray and immediately sprinkle with Italian seasoning and cheese; toss lightly to mix. Place bread cubes on baking sheet; sprinkle with any seasoning left in bowl. Bake in preheated oven 20 to 25 minutes, until crisp. Cool completely and store in airtight container.

Serves: 4

Nutrition per Serving		Exchanges
Calories	121	1⅔ starch
Carbohydrate	23 grams	
Cholesterol	0 milligrams	
Dietary Fiber	1 gram	
Protein	6 grams	
Sodium	235 milligrams	

SHOPPING LIST:
nonfat cooking spray, 1 lb. loaf fat-free Italian or French bread, Italian seasoning, 1 oz. fat-free Parmesan cheese

SPECTACULAR SAUCES AND DRESSINGS

✦ ✦ ✦

APPLE RAISIN PANCAKE SAUCE

EASY - DO AHEAD

INGREDIENTS:
1 cup apple pie filling
¼ cup raisins
¾ tsp. cinnamon

DIRECTIONS:
Combine all ingredients in a small saucepan and heat over low heat until warm. Ingredients can be combined in microwave-safe bowl, covered with plastic wrap, and heated on high, about 1½ minutes. Great on Spiced Apple Pancakes (page 40)!

Serves: 6

Nutrition per Serving

		Exchanges
Calories	63	1 fruit
Carbohydrate	17 grams	
Cholesterol	0 milligrams	
Dietary Fiber	< 1 gram	
Protein	< 1 gram	
Sodium	20 milligrams	

SHOPPING LIST:
8 oz. apple pie filling, 2 oz. raisins, cinnamon

CHOCOLATE-ALMOND SAUCE

EASY - DO AHEAD

✦ ✦ ✦

INGREDIENTS:
- ½ cup sugar
- ¼ cup unsweetened cocoa powder
- 1 tbsp. cornstarch
- 12 oz. evaporated skim milk
- ½ tsp. vanilla
- ½ tsp. almond extract

DIRECTIONS:
Combine sugar, cocoa, and cornstarch in a medium saucepan; gradually add milk, stirring constantly, and heat over medium heat until mixture thickens and comes to a boil. Remove from heat and stir in vanilla and almond extract. Cover and refrigerate at least 1 hour before serving. Great with fresh fruit or over fat-free frozen yogurt!

Serves: 6

Nutrition per Serving		Exchanges
Calories	119	½ milk
Carbohydrate	26 grams	1⅓ fruit
Cholesterol	2 milligrams	
Dietary Fiber	0 grams	
Protein	5 grams	
Sodium	68 milligrams	

SHOPPING LIST:
¼ lb. sugar, unsweetened cocoa powder, cornstarch, 12 oz. evaporated skim milk, vanilla, almond extract

GARLIC MUSHROOM SAUCE

AVERAGE - DO AHEAD

INGREDIENTS:
½ cup + 3 tsp. fat-free chicken broth, divided
1 cup minced onions
1½ tbsp. minced garlic
4 cups sliced portabello mushrooms
4 cups sliced white mushrooms
½ cup red wine
¾ tsp. crushed rosemary
1 tsp. thyme
¼ tsp. pepper

DIRECTIONS:
Lightly spray a Dutch oven or large saucepan with nonfat cooking spray. Pour 3 teaspoons chicken broth into pan and heat over medium-high heat. Add onions and garlic to hot broth and cook until lightly browned, about 10 to 12 minutes. Add sliced mushrooms to onion mixture and cook until softened, about 5 to 8 minutes. Stir in wine, ½ cup chicken broth, rosemary, thyme, and pepper; bring mixture to a boil over high heat. Reduce temperature to medium-high and cook, uncovered, 15 to 20 minutes. Serve over rice, potatoes, or baked chicken.

Serves: 6

Nutrition per Serving		Exchanges
Calories	80	2 vegetable
Carbohydrate	11 grams	⅓ fruit
Cholesterol	0 milligrams	
Dietary Fiber	2 grams	
Protein	4 grams	
Sodium	118 milligrams	

SHOPPING LIST:
5 oz. fat-free chicken broth, 1 medium onion, minced garlic, ¾ lb. portabello mushrooms, ¾ lb. white mushrooms, 4 oz. red wine, rosemary, thyme, pepper

HERBED CREAM SANDWICH SAUCE

EASY - DO AHEAD

INGREDIENTS:
- ¼ cup fat-free sour cream
- ¼ cup fat-free plain yogurt
- 1 tbsp. onion flakes
- 1 tsp. cilantro
- 1½ tsp. mint leaves, chopped fine
- ¼ tsp. pepper

DIRECTIONS:
In a blender, food processor, or small bowl, combine all ingredients and mix until well blended. Great sauce for veggie, turkey, or chicken burgers.

Serves: 4

Nutrition per Serving		Exchanges
Calories	22	free
Carbohydrate	2 grams	
Cholesterol	< 1 milligram	
Dietary Fiber	0 grams	
Protein	2 grams	
Sodium	21 milligrams	

SHOPPING LIST:
2 oz. fat-free sour cream, 2 oz. fat-free yogurt, onion flakes, cilantro, fresh mint leaves, pepper

SPECTACULAR SAUCES AND DRESSINGS

HOMEMADE PIZZA SAUCE

EASY - DO AHEAD - FREEZE

INGREDIENTS:
1 cup low-sodium tomato sauce
¾ cup tomato paste
2 tbsp. water
1 tsp. minced garlic
1 tsp. oregano
½ tsp. sugar
⅛ tsp. crushed red pepper

DIRECTIONS:
Combine all ingredients in a medium saucepan and heat over medium-low heat, stirring frequently, about 20 minutes.

Serves: 8 Yields: 1½ to 2 cups sauce

Nutrition per Serving		Exchanges
Calories	34 grams	1½ vegetable
Carbohydrate	7 grams	
Cholesterol	0 milligrams	
Dietary Fiber	1 gram	
Protein	1 gram	
Sodium	203 milligrams	

SHOPPING LIST:
8 oz. low-sodium tomato sauce, 6 oz. tomato paste, minced garlic, oregano, sugar, crushed red pepper

HORSERADISH SAUCE

AVERAGE - DO AHEAD

INGREDIENTS:
½ cup fat-free plain yogurt
½ cup fat-free sour cream
¼ cup white horseradish
½ tsp. sugar
¼ tsp. pepper

DIRECTIONS:
Combine all ingredients in a small bowl and blend until smooth. Great sauce for potatoes (boiled, mashed, or baked) or fat-free roast beef sandwich.

Serves: 4

Nutrition per Serving		Exchanges
Calories	44	½ milk
Carbohydrate	4 grams	
Cholesterol	1 milligram	
Dietary Fiber	0 grams	
Protein	4 grams	
Sodium	207 milligrams	

SHOPPING LIST:
4 oz. fat-free yogurt, 4 oz. fat-free sour cream, 4 oz. white horseradish, sugar, pepper

HOT AND SPICY HONEY MUSTARD

EASY - DO AHEAD

INGREDIENTS:
    1½ tbsp. yellow mustard
    1½ tbsp. Dijon mustard
    ⅓ cup honey
    1½ tsp. hot pepper sauce

DIRECTIONS:
Combine all ingredients in a small bowl and blend well. Great dip with chicken fingers.

Serves: 6

Nutrition per Serving		Exchanges
Calories	66	1 fruit
Carbohydrate	15 grams	
Cholesterol	0 milligrams	
Dietary Fiber	0 grams	
Protein	< 1 gram	
Sodium	152 milligrams	

SHOPPING LIST:
yellow mustard, Dijon mustard, honey, hot pepper sauce

LEMON-PEPPER FISH SAUCE

EASY - DO AHEAD

✦ ✦ ✦

INGREDIENTS:
½ cup fat-free mayonnaise
½ cup fat-free sour cream
1 tbsp. chopped jalapeño peppers
1 tsp. lemon juice
1½ tbsp. skim milk
⅛ tsp. white pepper

DIRECTIONS:
Combine all ingredients in a small bowl and mix until blended smooth. Cover and refrigerate several hours or overnight before serving. Great fish sauce!

Serves: 4

Nutrition per Serving		Exchanges
Calories	43	½ milk
Carbohydrate	4 grams	
Cholesterol	0 milligrams	
Dietary Fiber	0 grams	
Protein	2 grams	
Sodium	264 milligrams	

SHOPPING LIST:
4 oz. fat-free mayonnaise, 4 oz. fat-free sour cream, 4 oz. can jalapeño peppers, lemon juice, skim milk, white pepper

SIMPLE SPAGHETTI SAUCE

EASY - DO AHEAD - FREEZE

INGREDIENTS:
16 oz. low-sodium tomatoes
6 oz. tomato paste
15 oz. low-sodium tomato sauce
1 tbsp. onion powder
½ cup chopped green bell pepper
½ tsp. garlic powder
1 tbsp. sugar
2 tsp. Italian seasoning
¼ tsp. pepper

DIRECTIONS:
Combine all ingredients in a food processor or blender and process until smooth. Pour sauce into microwave-safe bowl or small saucepan; cook on high in microwave 3 to 5 minutes, or 10 to 15 minutes over medium heat on stove top. Serve over cooked pasta.

Serves: 8

Nutrition per Serving		Exchanges
Calories	57	2 vegetable
Carbohydrate	13 grams	
Cholesterol	0 milligrams	
Dietary Fiber	2 grams	
Protein	2 grams	
Sodium	498 milligrams	

SHOPPING LIST:
16 oz. low-sodium tomatoes, 6 oz. tomato paste, 15 oz. low-sodium tomato sauce, onion powder, 1 small green pepper, garlic powder, sugar, Italian seasoning, pepper

SPICY BARBECUE SAUCE

EASY - DO AHEAD

INGREDIENTS:
1 cup low-calorie ketchup
2 tsp. onion powder
1 tsp. garlic powder
¼ cup brown sugar
2 tbsp. Worcestershire sauce
2 tbsp. lemon juice
2 tsp. dry mustard
1 tsp. prepared horseradish

DIRECTIONS:
Combine all ingredients in a food processor or blender and process until smooth. Use sauce to baste "beef" or chicken while cooking.

Serves: 6

Nutrition per Serving		Exchanges
Calories	66	1 fruit
Carbohydrate	17 grams	
Cholesterol	0 milligrams	
Dietary Fiber	0 grams	
Protein	1 gram	
Sodium	376 milligrams	

SHOPPING LIST:
8 oz. low-calorie ketchup (Healthy Choice), onion powder, garlic powder, brown sugar, 1 oz. Worcestershire sauce, 1 oz. lemon juice, dry mustard, prepared horseradish

SPECTACULAR SAUCES AND DRESSINGS

SPICY MUSTARD SAUCE

EASY - DO AHEAD

✦ ✦ ✦

INGREDIENTS:

½ cup fat-free mayonnaise
⅓ cup fat-free sour cream
½ cup Dijon mustard
¼ cup horseradish

DIRECTIONS:

Combine all ingredients in a medium bowl and blend until smooth. Great spread for sandwiches.

Serves: 12 Yields: 1½ cups

Nutrition per Serving		Exchanges
Calories	11	free
Carbohydrate	1 gram	
Cholesterol	0 milligrams	
Dietary Fiber	0 grams	
Protein	< 1 gram	
Sodium	133 milligrams	

SHOPPING LIST:

4 oz. fat-free mayonnaise, 3 oz. fat-free sour cream, 4 oz. Dijon mustard, 2 oz. horseradish

SWEET AND SOUR SAUCE

EASY - DO AHEAD

INGREDIENTS:
⅔ cup orange juice
2 tbsp. orange marmalade
¼ cup cider vinegar
1 small dried red chili
¾ tsp. ginger

SPECTACULAR
SAUCES AND
DRESSINGS

DIRECTIONS:
Combine all ingredients in a small saucepan over medium heat and cook, stirring constantly, until all ingredients are blended. Cool to room temperature before serving.

Serves: 16 Yields: 1 cup

Nutrition per Serving (1 tbsp.)		Exchanges
Calories	12	free
Carbohydrate	3 grams	
Cholesterol	0 milligrams	
Dietary Fiber	< 1 gram	
Protein	< 1 gram	
Sodium	2 milligrams	

SHOPPING LIST:
5 to 6 oz. orange juice, 1 oz. orange marmalade, 2 oz. cider vinegar, 1 small dried red chili, ground ginger

TARTAR SAUCE

EASY - DO AHEAD

INGREDIENTS:
½ cup fat-free mayonnaise
1 tsp. lemon juice
1 tsp. onion powder
2 small dill pickles, cut in 1-inch pieces
1 tsp. dried parsley

DIRECTIONS:
Combine all ingredients in food processor or blender and process until smooth. Serve with fish.

Serves: 6

Nutrition per Serving		Exchanges
Calories	19	free
Carbohydrates	4 grams	
Cholesterol	0 milligrams	
Dietary Fiber	0 grams	
Protein	< 1 gram	
Sodium	144 milligrams	

SHOPPING LIST:
4 oz. fat-free mayonnaise, lemon juice, onion powder, 2 small dill pickles, dried parsley

BUTTERMILK DRESSING

EASY - DO AHEAD

✦ ✦ ✦

INGREDIENTS:

¼ cup Cultured Buttermilk Blend Mix
1 cup water
⅓ cup fat-free mayonnaise
⅓ cup chopped green onion
1¼ tbsp. horseradish
3 tsp. dried dill weed
1 tsp. dried parsley
½ tsp. garlic powder
1¼ tbsp. lemon juice

DIRECTIONS:

Combine all ingredients in a blender or food processor and blend until smooth and creamy. Refrigerate several hours before serving. Dressing will keep in refrigerator 3 to 4 days.

Serves: 4 Yields: 1 cup

Nutrition per Serving (2 tbsp.)		Exchanges
Calories	45	½ starch
Carbohydrate	9 grams	
Cholesterol	1 milligram	
Dietary Fiber	< 1 gram	
Protein	2 grams	
Sodium	235 milligrams	

SHOPPING LIST:

Cultured Buttermilk Blend Mix, fat-free mayonnaise, 1 to 2 green onions, horseradish, dried dill weed, dried parsley, garlic powder, lemon juice

CREAMY CAESAR SALAD DRESSING

EASY - DO AHEAD

INGREDIENTS:
¼ cup fat-free sour cream
3 tbsp. lemon juice
3 tbsp. fat-free Parmesan cheese
1½ tsp. Worcestershire sauce
1½ tsp. Dijon mustard
¾ tsp. anchovy paste
1 tsp. garlic powder
pepper to taste

DIRECTIONS:
In a medium bowl or blender, combine all ingredients and mix until blended smooth. If dressing is too thick, add water 1 tablespoon at a time, mixing well after each addition.

Serves: 6

Nutrition per Serving		Exchanges
Calories	21	free
Carbohydrate	2 grams	
Cholesterol	< 1 milligram	
Dietary Fiber	0 grams	
Protein	2 grams	
Sodium	85 milligrams	

SHOPPING LIST:
2 oz. fat-free sour cream, 1½ oz. lemon juice, ¾ oz. fat-free Parmesan cheese, Worcestershire sauce, Dijon mustard, anchovy paste, garlic powder, pepper

CREAMY CUCUMBER DRESSING

EASY - DO AHEAD

INGREDIENTS:

1 cup fat-free sour cream
½ cup chopped cucumber
¼ cup fat-free mayonnaise
½ tsp. onion powder
½ tsp. dried dill weed
½ tsp. sugar
¼ tsp. pepper

DIRECTIONS:

In a medium bowl, combine all ingredients and blend well.
Chill several hours or overnight before serving.

Serves: 12 Yields: 1½ cups

Nutrition per Serving (2 tbsp.)		Exchanges
Calories	8	free
Carbohydrate	1 gram	
Cholesterol	0 milligrams	
Dietary Fiber	0 grams	
Protein	1 gram	
Sodium	23 milligrams	

SHOPPING LIST:

8 oz. fat-free sour cream, 1 cucumber, 2 oz. fat-free mayonnaise, onion powder, dried dill weed, sugar, pepper

CUCUMBER SALAD DRESSING

EASY - DO AHEAD

INGREDIENTS:
1 large cucumber, peeled and chopped
1 cup sliced green onion
1 cup fat-free plain yogurt
1 cup fat-free sour cream
½ tsp. garlic powder
½ tsp. dried basil
½ tsp. dried dill weed
2 tsp. dried parsley
½ tsp. pepper

DIRECTIONS:
Combine all ingredients in a food processor until smooth and creamy. Great as salad dressing, vegetable dip, or fish sauce.

Serves: 8

Nutrition per Serving		Exchanges
Calories	52	½ milk
Carbohydrate	6 grams	
Cholesterol	1 milligram	
Dietary Fiber	1 gram	
Protein	4 grams	
Sodium	44 milligrams	

SHOPPING LIST:
1 large cucumber, 1 bunch green onions (5 to 6), 8 oz. fat-free yogurt, 8 oz. fat-free sour cream, garlic powder, dried basil, dried dill weed, dried parsley, pepper

SPECTACULAR SAUCES AND DRESSINGS

DIJON RANCH DRESSING

EASY - DO AHEAD

✦ ✦ ✦

INGREDIENTS:
⅓ cup fat-free mayonnaise
⅓ cup fat-free sour cream
1 tbsp. white wine vinegar
1 tsp. Dijon mustard
½ tsp. crushed dried basil
½ tsp. onion powder
skim milk

DIRECTIONS:
In a small bowl, combine mayonnaise, sour cream, vinegar, mustard, basil, and onion powder; blend until smooth. Refrigerate up to 2 days. Just before serving, stir in enough skim milk to make the dressing the desired consistency. Great over mixed greens with sliced red onions, tomatoes, shredded carrots, and fat-free croutons.

Serves: 6

Nutrition per Serving		Exchanges
Calories	19	free
Carbohydrate	2 grams	
Cholesterol	0 milligrams	
Dietary Fiber	0 grams	
Protein	1 gram	
Sodium	114 milligrams	

SHOPPING LIST:
3 oz. fat-free mayonnaise, 3 oz. fat-free sour cream, white wine vinegar, Dijon mustard, dried basil, onion powder, skim milk

FRENCH DRESSING

EASY - DO AHEAD

INGREDIENTS:

½ cup fat-free sour cream
2½ tbsp. low-sodium ketchup
2 tbsp. water
1 tbsp. fat-free mayonnaise
1 tsp. minced garlic
¼ tsp. sugar

DIRECTIONS:

Combine all ingredients in food processor or blender and process until smooth.

Serves: 8 Yields: 1 cup

Nutrition per Serving (2 tbsp.)		Exchanges
Calories	7	free
Carbohydrate	1 gram	
Cholesterol	0 milligrams	
Dietary Fiber	0 grams	
Protein	1 gram	
Sodium	26 milligrams	

SHOPPING LIST:

4 oz. fat-free sour cream, low-sodium ketchup, fat-free mayonnaise, minced garlic, sugar

FRUIT SALAD DRESSING

INGREDIENTS:

3 tbsp. fat-free vanilla yogurt
2 tsp. fat-free mayonnaise
1 tbsp. pineapple juice
¼ tsp. cinnamon

DIRECTIONS:

Combine all ingredients in food processor or blender and process until smooth. Refrigerate several hours and serve over fruit salad.

Serves: 4

Nutrition per Serving		Exchanges
Calories	10	free
Carbohydrate	2 grams	
Cholesterol	0 milligrams	
Dietary Fiber	0 grams	
Protein	1 gram	
Sodium	26 milligrams	

SHOPPING LIST:

3 oz. fat-free yogurt, fat-free mayonnaise, ½ oz. pineapple juice, cinnamon

GREEN GODDESS SALAD DRESSING

EASY - DO AHEAD

INGREDIENTS:
¼ cup white wine vinegar
2 tbsp. fat-free sour cream
2 tbsp. lemon juice
1 tsp. minced garlic
¼ cup packed fresh basil leaves
14 oz. artichoke hearts, with liquid

DIRECTIONS:
Combine all ingredients in food processor or blender and process until smooth. Refrigerate several hours or overnight before serving, so dressing thickens. Dressing will keep in refrigerator 5 to 7 days.

Serves: 16

Nutrition per Serving (2 tbsp.)		Exchanges
Calories	15	free
Carbohydrate	3 grams	
Cholesterol	0 milligrams	
Dietary Fiber	0 grams	
Protein	1 gram	
Sodium	24 milligrams	

SHOPPING LIST:
2 oz. white wine vinegar, 1 oz. fat-free sour cream, 1 oz. lemon juice, minced garlic, fresh basil leaves, 14 oz. can artichoke hearts

SPECTACULAR SAUCES AND DRESSINGS

HOT ORANGE DRESSING

EASY - DO AHEAD

✦ ✦ ✦

INGREDIENTS:
¾ cup orange juice
¼ cup brown sugar
¼ cup vinegar
½ tsp. onion powder

DIRECTIONS:
Combine all ingredients in a small saucepan and heat over medium-high heat; bring to a boil, stirring frequently. Great dressing over spinach salad or as sauce for baked chicken.

Serves: 6

Nutrition per Serving

Calories	49
Carbohydrate	13 grams
Cholesterol	0 milligrams
Dietary Fiber	< 1 gram
Protein	< 1 gram
Sodium	3 milligrams

Exchanges
¾ fruit

SHOPPING LIST:
6 oz. orange juice, brown sugar, 2 oz. vinegar, onion powder

MANGO SALAD DRESSING

EASY - DO AHEAD

INGREDIENTS:
2 cups mango, cut in chunks
½ cup lime juice
⅓ cup orange juice
⅓ cup cider vinegar
1 tsp. ground ginger

DIRECTIONS:
Combine all ingredients in a food processor or blender and process until smooth. Refrigerate several hours or overnight before serving. Dressing will keep in refrigerator 5 to 7 days.

Serves: 16

Nutrition per Serving		Exchanges
Calories	37	⅔ fruit
Carbohydrate	10 grams	
Cholesterol	0 milligrams	
Dietary Fiber	1 gram	
Protein	< 1 gram	
Sodium	1 milligram	

SHOPPING LIST:
1¾ lb. fresh mango, 4 oz. lime juice, 3 oz. orange juice, 3 oz. cider vinegar, ground ginger

PARMESAN CHEESE SALAD DRESSING

EASY - DO AHEAD

INGREDIENTS:

¾ cup fat-free mayonnaise
½ cup fat-free Parmesan cheese
½ cup skim milk
1½ tbsp. white wine vinegar
½ tsp. Worcestershire sauce

DIRECTIONS:

Combine all ingredients in a bowl or blender and mix until blended smooth. Refrigerate several hours before serving. Great over mixed greens and assorted vegetables.

Serves: 8

Nutrition per Serving		Exchanges
Calories	36	½ milk
Carbohydrate	6 grams	
Cholesterol	< 1 milligram	
Dietary Fiber	0 grams	
Protein	3 grams	
Sodium	213 milligrams	

SHOPPING LIST:

6 oz. fat-free mayonnaise, 2 oz. fat-free Parmesan cheese, 4 oz. skim milk, wine vinegar, Worcestershire sauce

POPPY SEED DRESSING

EASY - DO AHEAD

INGREDIENTS:

½ cup fat-free mayonnaise
2 tbsp. fat-free sour cream
2 tbsp. skim milk
⅓ cup sugar
2 tbsp. white wine vinegar
1 tbsp. poppy seeds

DIRECTIONS:

Combine all ingredients in small bowl or blender and mix until smooth and creamy. If dressing is too thick, add more skim milk, 1 tablespoon at a time.

Serves: 6

Nutrition per Serving		Exchanges
Calories	66	1 fruit
Carbohydrate	14 grams	
Cholesterol	0 milligrams	
Dietary Fiber	0 grams	
Protein	1 gram	
Sodium	146 milligrams	

SHOPPING LIST:

4 oz. fat-free mayonnaise, 1 oz. fat-free sour cream, 1 oz. skim milk, sugar, 1 oz. white wine vinegar, poppy seeds

RASPBERRY VINAIGRETTE DRESSING

EASY - DO AHEAD

✦ ✦ ✦

INGREDIENTS:

½ cup raspberry vinegar
½ cup water
¼ cup sugar
2 tsp. powdered fruit pectin
½ cup frozen unsweetened raspberries

DIRECTIONS:

Combine all ingredients in a food processor or blender and process until smooth. Great dressing over fruit salad!

Serves: 6

Nutrition per Serving		Exchanges
Calories	68	1 fruit
Carbohydrate	17 grams	
Cholesterol	0 milligrams	
Dietary Fiber	< 1 gram	
Protein	0 grams	
Sodium	11 milligrams	

SHOPPING LIST:

4 oz. raspberry vinegar, sugar, powdered fruit pectin, 6 oz. frozen unsweetened raspberries

RED PEPPER VINAIGRETTE

EASY - DO AHEAD

INGREDIENTS:
½ cup water
¼ cup red wine vinegar
2 tsp. dried basil
1 tsp. garlic powder
15 oz. roasted red peppers, drained

DIRECTIONS:
Combine all ingredients in a food processor or blender and process until smooth. Store in refrigerator.

Serves: 8

Nutrition per Serving		Exchanges
Calories	15	free
Carbohydrate	4 grams	
Cholesterol	0 milligrams	
Dietary Fiber	1 gram	
Protein	1 gram	
Sodium	624 milligrams	

SHOPPING LIST:
2 oz. red wine vinegar, dried basil, garlic powder, 15 oz. jar roasted red peppers

RUSSIAN DRESSING

EASY - DO AHEAD

INGREDIENTS:

1 cup fat-free mayonnaise
3 tbsp. chili sauce
1 tbsp. grated onions
1 tbsp. chopped chives
1 tsp. dried parsley

DIRECTIONS:

Combine all ingredients in a small bowl and mix until well blended. Refrigerate several hours before serving.

Serves: 6

Nutrition per Serving		Exchanges
Calories	35	½ fruit
Carbohydrate	7 grams	
Cholesterol	0 milligrams	
Dietary Fiber	< 1 gram	
Protein	< 1 gram	
Sodium	381 milligrams	

SHOPPING LIST:

8 oz. fat-free mayonnaise, 1½ oz. chili sauce, grated onions (packaged), chives, dried parsley

SIMPLE SLAW DRESSING

EASY - DO AHEAD

INGREDIENTS:

½ cup fat-free sour cream
½ tsp. sugar
2 tsp. lemon juice
1½ tbsp. mustard
salt and pepper to taste

DIRECTIONS:

Combine all ingredients in a small bowl and mix until blended smooth. Refrigerate several hours before serving. Toss dressing with shredded cabbage, carrots, peppers, and onions for simple slaw.

Serves: 6

Nutrition per Serving		Exchanges
Calories	19	free
Carbohydrate	1 gram	
Cholesterol	0 milligrams	
Dietary Fiber	0 grams	
Protein	1 gram	
Sodium	62 milligrams	

SHOPPING LIST:

4 oz. fat-free sour cream, sugar, lemon juice, mustard, salt, pepper

SWEET AND SPICY
BALSAMIC DRESSING

EASY - DO AHEAD

INGREDIENTS:

¼ cup water
1 cup balsamic vinegar
⅛ cup Dijon mustard
¼ cup lemon juice
2 tsp. minced garlic
1½ tsp. sugar
1 tsp. dried parsley
¼ tsp. pepper

DIRECTIONS:

Combine all ingredients in a food processor or blender and process until smooth. Refrigerate several hours before serving. Great on salads or as marinade for chicken or fish.

Serves: 6

Nutrition per Serving		Exchanges
Calories	54	¾ fruit
Carbohydrate	12 grams	
Cholesterol	0 milligrams	
Dietary Fiber	0 grams	
Protein	< 1 gram	
Sodium	133 milligrams	

SHOPPING LIST:

8 oz. balsamic vinegar, 1 oz. Dijon mustard, 2 oz. lemon juice, minced garlic, sugar, dried parsley, pepper

EXOTIC MANGO SALSA

EASY - DO AHEAD

INGREDIENTS:

2 cups mango, peeled, seeded and chopped
¼ cup sliced green onions
¼ cup chopped yellow bell pepper
1 tsp. dried basil
2 tsp. chopped jalapeño peppers
2 tbsp. lime juice

DIRECTIONS:

Combine all ingredients in a medium bowl and toss until well mixed. Refrigerate several hours before serving. Great over baked or grilled fish or chicken.

Serves: 4

Nutrition per Serving		Exchanges
Calories	75	1⅓ fruit
Carbohydrate	20 grams	
Cholesterol	0 milligrams	
Dietary Fiber	3 grams	
Protein	1 gram	
Sodium	13 milligrams	

SHOPPING LIST:

1 mango, 1 to 2 green onions, small yellow bell pepper, dried basil, canned chopped jalapeño peppers, 1 oz. lime juice

PINEAPPLE SALSA

EASY - DO AHEAD

INGREDIENTS:
8 oz. pineapple chunks in juice, drained
¼ cup chopped red bell pepper
1 whole sliced green onion
2 tsp. chopped green chilies
2 tbsp. lime juice
1 tsp. dried basil

DIRECTIONS:
Combine all ingredients in a medium bowl and mix well. Refrigerate several hours before serving. Great on grilled chicken or fish.

Serves: 4

Nutrition per Serving		Exchanges
Calories	24	½ fruit
Carbohydrate	6 grams	
Cholesterol	0 milligrams	
Dietary Fiber	1 gram	
Protein	< 1 gram	
Sodium	17 milligrams	

SHOPPING LIST:
8 oz. pineapple chunks in juice, 1 small red bell pepper, 1 green onion, 4 oz. chopped green chilies, 1 oz. lime juice, dried basil

FANTASTIC
FISH,
TURKEY,
AND
CHICKEN

✦ ✦ ✦

BAKED COD

EASY - DO AHEAD

INGREDIENTS:
1½ lbs. cod fillets
1½ cups fat-free sour cream
1 tsp. horseradish
2 tsp. mustard
1 cup fat-free Parmesan cheese

DIRECTIONS:
Preheat oven to 350 degrees. Lightly spray 9x13-inch baking dish with nonfat cooking spray. Place fish fillets in dish. In a small bowl, combine sour cream, horseradish, and mustard and mix until smooth. Spread mixture over top of fish fillets and sprinkle with Parmesan cheese. Bake in preheated oven 20 to 25 minutes, until fish flakes easily in thickest portion.

Serves: 6

Nutrition per Serving		Exchanges
Calories	175	½ starch
Carbohydrate	10 grams	4¼ meat
Cholesterol	41 milligrams	
Dietary Fiber	0 grams	
Protein	30 grams	
Sodium	260 milligrams	

SHOPPING LIST:
1½ lb. cod fillets, 12 oz. fat-free sour cream, horseradish, mustard, 4 oz. fat-free Parmesan cheese

BREADED BAKED FLOUNDER

EASY - DO AHEAD

INGREDIENTS:
1½ lbs. flounder
4 cups fat-free bread crumbs
1 tsp. onion powder
½ tsp. garlic powder
¼ tsp. pepper
1 tbsp. lemon juice
1½ tbsp. fat-free margarine, melted
¾ cup fat-free Parmesan cheese, divided
1 cup chopped tomatoes

DIRECTIONS:
Preheat oven to 400 degrees. Lightly spray 9x13-inch baking dish with nonfat cooking spray. Place fish in dish in a single layer. In a medium bowl, combine bread crumbs, onion powder, garlic powder, pepper, lemon juice, margarine, and ¼ cup Parmesan cheese; blend well. Spread bread mixture over fish and top with chopped tomatoes. Sprinkle remaining Parmesan cheese on top and bake in preheated oven 15 minutes, until fish flakes easily when tested in thickest part.

Serves: 6

Nutrition per Serving		Exchanges
Calories	185	1⅓ starch
Carbohydrate	22 grams	2½ meat
Cholesterol	40 milligrams	
Dietary Fiber	1 gram	
Protein	21 grams	
Sodium	347 milligrams	

SHOPPING LIST:
1½ lb. flounder, ½ lb. fat-free bread (8 slices) or fat-free bread crumbs, onion powder, garlic powder, pepper, lemon juice, fat-free margarine, 3 oz. fat-free Parmesan cheese, 1 large tomato

BROILED FISH KABOBS

EASY - DO AHEAD

INGREDIENTS:
> 1 lb. cod fillets, cut into 1-inch pieces
> ¾ cup fat-free fish marinade
> 1 medium Vidalia onion
> 1 medium red bell pepper
> 1 medium green bell pepper
> 1 cup cherry tomatoes
> 2½ cups fat-free cooked rice

DIRECTIONS:
> Place cod pieces in baking dish; pour ½ cup fish marinade over cod, cover with plastic wrap, and marinate in refrigerator 30 minutes. Preheat broiler on high heat. Line broiler pan with foil and lightly spray with nonfat cooking spray. Remove fish from marinade; discard marinade. Thread fish, onion, peppers, and tomatoes alternately on metal skewers and place on broiler pan. Baste with remaining ¼ cup marinade. Broil kabobs 6 to 7 minutes, until fish is cooked through and vegetables are tender. Brush with marinade and rotate skewers halfway through cooking time. Serve over rice.

Serves: 6

Nutrition per Serving		Exchanges
Calories	237	2 starch
Carbohydrate	37 grams	1½ vegetable
Cholesterol	33 milligrams	1 meat
Dietary Fiber	1 gram	
Protein	16 grams	
Sodium	427 milligrams	

SHOPPING LIST:
> 1 lb. cod fillets, 6 oz. fat-free fish marinade, 1 medium Vidalia onion, 1 red bell pepper, 1 green bell pepper, ½ pint cherry tomatoes, ¾ to 1 cup fat-free rice

CRAB BURRITOS

AVERAGE - DO AHEAD
✦ ✦ ✦

INGREDIENTS:
4 large fat-free flour tortillas
1 cup fat-free salsa
1½ tsp. chili powder
12 oz. imitation crab flakes
1 cup chopped tomatoes, drained
½ tsp. onion powder
2 cups fat-free shredded Cheddar cheese

DIRECTIONS:
Preheat oven to 350 degrees. Lightly spray 9x13-inch baking dish with nonfat cooking spray. Wrap tortillas in foil and heat in oven 10 minutes, or wrap in paper towels and heat in microwave on high 1 minute. In a medium bowl, combine salsa, chili powder, crab flakes, tomatoes, and onion powder and mix well. Remove tortillas from oven; divide filling evenly among flour tortillas and spread down center. Sprinkle ½ cup cheese on each tortilla and fold up burrito-style. Place tortillas, seam-side down, in baking pan. Cover with foil and bake in preheated oven 15 minutes, until cheese is melted and burritos are heated through. Serve with extra salsa, sour cream, and shredded lettuce, if desired.

Serves: 4

Nutrition per Serving		Exchanges
Calories	355	2½ starch
Carbohydrate	55 grams	3 vegetable
Cholesterol	9 milligrams	2½ meat
Dietary Fiber	4 grams	
Protein	32 grams	
Sodium	1,891 milligrams	

SHOPPING LIST:
10 inch fat-free flour tortillas, 8 oz. fat-free salsa, chili powder, 12 oz. imitation crab flakes, 1 large tomato, onion powder, 8 oz. fat-free shredded Cheddar cheese

CRAB SOUFFLÉ

EASY - DO AHEAD

INGREDIENTS:

8 slices fat-free bread
12 oz. imitation crab flakes
8 slices fat-free American cheese
1 cup egg substitute
2 cups skim milk

DIRECTIONS:

Preheat oven to 350 degrees. Lightly spray 1½-quart casserole with nonfat cooking spray. Place 4 bread slices in casserole; top with 6 oz. crab flakes, 4 slices cheese, 4 slices bread, remaining crab, and remaining cheese. In a large bowl, combine egg substitute and skim milk and beat well. Pour over cheese and bake in preheated oven 1 hour.

Serves: 6

Nutrition per Serving		Exchanges
Calories	271	1½ starch
Carbohydrate	33 grams	1 milk
Cholesterol	13 milligrams	2 meat
Dietary Fiber	1 gram	
Protein	28 grams	
Sodium	1,072 milligrams	

SHOPPING LIST:

½ lb. fat-free bread, 12 oz. imitation crab flakes, 8 oz. fat-free American cheese slices, 8 oz. egg substitute, 1 pint skim milk

FISH BAKED IN LETTUCE WRAPS

EASY - DO AHEAD

INGREDIENTS:

8 large lettuce leaves (romaine or head lettuce)
16 oz. cod
¼ cup dried parsley
2 tsp. onion powder
½ cup chopped onions
1 large carrot, grated
½ cup white wine

DIRECTIONS:

Preheat oven to 400 degrees. Lightly spray 9x13-inch baking dish with nonfat cooking spray. Wash and dry lettuce leaves. Line the bottom and sides of dish with lettuce leaves, extending over the edges of dish. Place half the fish in the bottom of the dish; sprinkle with parsley, onion powder, chopped onions, and carrots. Arrange remaining fish pieces on top. Pour wine over fish, cover with foil, and bake in preheated oven 15 to 20 minutes, until fish flakes easily in thickest portion. This can be prepared ahead and refrigerated until ready to bake. Serve immediately.

Serves: 4

Nutrition per Serving		Exchanges
Calories	140	1 vegetable
Carbohydrate	6 grams	3 meat
Cholesterol	49 milligrams	
Dietary Fiber	1 gram	
Protein	21 grams	
Sodium	78 milligrams	

SHOPPING LIST:

1 head romaine or leaf lettuce, 2 10-oz. cod fillets, dried parsley, onion powder, 1 small onion, 1 large carrot, 4 oz. white wine

PARMESAN FISH FILLETS

EASY - DO AHEAD

INGREDIENTS:
2 lbs. cod fillets
4 large onions, sliced
½ cup fat-free mayonnaise
½ tsp. garlic powder
¼ cup fat-free Parmesan cheese
2 tbsp. Worcestershire sauce
2 tbsp. lemon juice

FANTASTIC FISH, TURKEY, AND CHICKEN

DIRECTIONS:
Preheat oven to 350 degrees. Lightly spray 9x13-inch baking dish with nonfat cooking spray. Cut fish into individual portions. Arrange onions on bottom of baking dish and place fish pieces on top. In a small bowl, combine mayonnaise, garlic powder, Parmesan cheese, Worcestershire sauce, and lemon juice and mix until blended. Spread mixture over fish pieces and bake in preheated oven 35 to 40 minutes, or until fish flakes easily.

Serves: 8

Nutrition per Serving		Exchanges
Calories	146	2 vegetable
Carbohydrate	11 grams	2½ meat
Cholesterol	49 milligrams	
Dietary Fiber	1 gram	
Protein	22 grams	
Sodium	228 milligrams	

SHOPPING LIST:
2 lb. cod (or 6 sole fillets), 4 large onions, 4 oz. fat-free mayonnaise, garlic powder, 1 oz. fat-free Parmesan cheese, 1 oz. Worcestershire sauce, 1 oz. lemon juice

SCALLOP AND VEGGIE STIR-FRY

EASY

INGREDIENTS:
2 cups sliced carrots
2 cups cherry tomatoes
2 cups broccoli florets
2 cups cauliflower florets
2 medium baking potatoes, cooked and cubed
2 cups whole mushrooms
3 cups shredded cabbage
8 oz. fat-free scallops
1 cup low-sodium teriyaki sauce
6 oz. canned sliced water chestnuts (optional)

DIRECTIONS:
Lightly spray wok or large nonstick skillet with nonfat cooking spray. Add ¼ cup water and heat over medium-high heat. Add all ingredients to wok and cook, stirring frequently, until vegetables are tender and scallops are cooked through. Pour in teriyaki sauce and cook until heated through. Great served with rice!

Serves: 4

Nutrition per Serving		Exchanges
Calories	284	1 starch
Carbohydrate	56 grams	1 meat
Cholesterol	10 milligrams	1⅓ fruit
Dietary Fiber	10 grams	4 vegetable
Protein	17 grams	
Sodium	1,535 milligrams	

SHOPPING LIST:
¾ lb. carrots, 1 pint cherry tomatoes, 1 lb. head broccoli, 1 lb. head cauliflower, 2 medium baking potatoes, ⅓ lb. mushrooms, 1 small cabbage (or prepackaged, preshredded cabbage), 8 oz. fat-free scallops, 8 oz. low-sodium teriyaki sauce, 6 oz. can sliced water chestnuts (optional)

SHRIMP CREOLE

AVERAGE

INGREDIENTS:

2 tbsp. fat-free chicken broth
½ cup minced onions
1 clove garlic, crushed
1½ pounds fat-free shrimp
1 cup tomato sauce
2 medium tomatoes, peeled and diced
½ tsp. salt
dash pepper
dash ground red pepper
pinch dried oregano
pinch dried basil
2 cups fat-free rice, cooked

DIRECTIONS:

Lightly spray nonstick skillet with nonfat cooking spray. Add chicken broth and heat over medium-high heat. Sauté onions and garlic in broth until soft and lightly browned. Add shrimp and cook 2 to 3 minutes; stir in tomato sauce, tomatoes, salt, pepper, red pepper, oregano, and basil and mix well. Reduce heat to low; cover and simmer 15 minutes, until shrimp are pink and cooked through. Serve over cooked rice.

Serves: 4

Nutrition per Serving		Exchanges
Calories	281	3 starch
Carbohydrate	49 grams	1 vegetable
Cholesterol	20 milligrams	1 meat
Dietary Fiber	3 grams	
Protein	21 grams	
Sodium	1,766 milligrams	

SHOPPING LIST:

1 oz. fat-free chicken broth, 1 medium onion, 1 clove garlic, 1½ lb. fat-free shrimp, 8 oz. tomato sauce, 2 medium tomatoes, salt, pepper, ground red pepper, oregano, basil, fat-free rice

••••••••••••••••••••••

SHRIMP ENCHILADAS

AVERAGE - DO AHEAD

✦ ✦ ✦

INGREDIENTS:

1 lb. fat-free frozen shrimp, cooked and chopped
1 cup fat-free Monterey Jack cheese, shredded
2 cups fat-free chunky-style salsa
1 cup fat-free cream cheese
10 oz. frozen chopped spinach, thawed and drained
1 tbsp. onion powder
½ tsp. garlic powder
6 large fat-free flour tortillas
½ cup fat-free Cheddar cheese, shredded

DIRECTIONS:

Preheat oven to 350 degrees. Lightly spray 9x13-inch baking dish with nonfat cooking spray. In a large bowl, combine shrimp, Monterey Jack cheese, ½ cup salsa, cream cheese, spinach, onion powder, and garlic powder; mix until blended. Spoon ⅓ to ½ cup mixture down center of each tortilla; roll up burrito-style and place, seam-side down, in prepared dish. Spoon remaining salsa over tortillas and bake in preheated oven 20 minutes, until heated through. Sprinkle Cheddar cheese on top and bake 5 minutes, until cheese is melted. This can be prepared and assembled ahead of time, refrigerated, and baked before serving.

Serves: 6

Nutrition per Serving		Exchanges
Calories	281	2 starch
Carbohydrate	44 grams	2½ vegetable
Cholesterol	9 milligrams	2 meat
Dietary Fiber	3 grams	
Protein	27 grams	
Sodium	1,679 milligrams	

SHOPPING LIST:

1 lb. fat-free frozen shrimp, 4 oz. fat-free shredded Monterey Jack cheese, 16 oz. fat-free chunky-style salsa, 8 oz. fat-free cream cheese, 10 oz. frozen chopped spinach, onion powder, garlic powder, large fat-free flour tortillas, 2 oz. fat-free shredded Cheddar cheese

....

CHICKEN AND BROCCOFLOWER QUICHE

AVERAGE - DO AHEAD - FREEZE

INGREDIENTS:

3 cups fat-free chicken tenders, cooked and cubed
1 tsp. onion powder
10 oz. frozen chopped broccoli, thawed and drained
10 oz. frozen cauliflower florets, thawed and drained

2 cups fat-free ricotta cheese
1 cup fat-free sour cream
¾ cup egg substitute
½ cup flour
1 tsp. baking powder
¾ cup fat-free Parmesan cheese, divided

DIRECTIONS:

Preheat oven to 350 degrees. Lightly spray 9x13-inch baking dish with nonfat cooking spray. In a large bowl, combine chicken, onion powder, broccoli, and cauliflower and toss to mix well. Place ½ chicken-mixture into prepared baking dish. In a food processor or blender, combine ricotta cheese, sour cream, egg substitute, flour, baking powder, and ½ cup Parmesan cheese; process until smooth. Pour mixture over chicken-vegetable mixture; top with remaining chicken mixture and sprinkle with remaining Parmesan cheese. Bake in preheated oven 40 to 45 minutes, until knife inserted in center comes out clean. Let quiche sit at room temperature 10 minutes before slicing.

Serves: 8

Nutrition per Serving		Exchanges
Calories	221	3 vegetable
Carbohydrate	16 grams	4 meat
Cholesterol	63 milligrams	
Dietary Fiber	2 grams	
Protein	36 grams	
Sodium	495 milligrams	

SHOPPING LIST:

1½ lbs. fat-free chicken tenders, onion powder, 10 oz. frozen chopped broccoli, 10 oz. frozen cauliflower florets, 16 oz. fat-free ricotta cheese, 8 oz. fat-free sour cream, 6 oz. egg substitute, flour, baking powder, 3 oz. fat-free Parmesan cheese

FANTASTIC FISH, TURKEY, AND CHICKEN

CHICKEN ENCHILADAS

AVERAGE

✦ ✦ ✦

INGREDIENTS:

1 lb. fat-free chicken tenders, cut in half
1 tsp. garlic powder
1 tsp. onion powder
8 fat-free flour tortillas
2 cups fat-free sour cream
¾ cup chopped green onion

4 oz. chopped green chilies
1 tsp. cumin
1 cup fat-free shredded
Cheddar cheese
1 cup fat-free chunky-style
salsa

DIRECTIONS:

Preheat oven to 350 degrees. Lightly spray 9x13-inch baking
dish with nonfat cooking spray. Lightly spray a large nonstick
skillet with nonfat cooking spray and heat over medium-high
heat. Add the chicken tenders and season with garlic and
onion powder; cook 5 to 6 minutes, until chicken is tender and
cooked through. Divide chicken among tortillas and place
down center. In a medium bowl, combine sour cream, green
onions, green chilies, and cumin and mix until blended. Place
½ cup sour cream mixture over chicken and roll tortillas up
burrito-style; place seam-side down in prepared pan. Sprinkle
cheese over top, cover with foil, and bake in preheated oven
30 to 40 minutes, until cheese is melted and bubbly. Remove
from oven and top with chunky salsa. Serve immediately.

Serves: 8

Nutrition per Serving		Exchanges
Calories	235	1 starch
Carbohydrate	28 grams	2 vegetable
Cholesterol	35 milligrams	2½ meat
Dietary Fiber	2 grams	
Protein	24 grams	
Sodium	945 milligrams	

SHOPPING LIST:

1 lb. fat-free chicken tenders, garlic powder, onion powder, 1
package fat-free flour tortillas, 16 oz. fat-free sour cream, 2 to
3 green onions, 4 oz. chopped green chilies, cumin, 4 oz. fat-
free shredded Cheddar cheese, 8 oz. fat-free chunky-style
salsa

CHICKEN FAJITAS

AVERAGE

INGREDIENTS:

¼ cup lime juice
1 tbsp. red wine vinegar
½ cup honey
½ tsp. garlic powder
2 tsp. fresh coriander, chopped fine
¼ tsp. cumin powder
¼ tsp. onion powder

1 lb. fat-free chicken tenders
1 green bell pepper, sliced thin
1 red bell pepper, sliced thin
1 onion, sliced thin
1 tbsp. fat-free chicken broth
4 large fat-free flour tortillas
½ cup fat-free salsa

DIRECTIONS:

Preheat oven to 425 degrees. Lightly spray 9x13-inch baking dish with nonfat cooking spray. In large bowl, combine lime juice, vinegar, honey, garlic powder, coriander, cumin, and onion powder; mix until blended. Add chicken tenders to marinade; let stand 15 minutes, turning chicken to coat. Place sliced peppers and onions in prepared dish and coat with chicken broth. Bake in preheated oven 10 to 15 minutes, until softened. Remove chicken from marinade and place in dish with vegetables. Bake 15 to 20 minutes, basting and turning frequently, until chicken is no longer pink and is cooked through. Divide chicken and vegetables among tortillas and top with 2 tablespoons salsa. Roll tortillas up and serve immediately.

Serves: 4

Nutrition per Serving		Exchanges
Calories	431	2 starch
Carbohydrate	78 grams	9½ vegetable
Cholesterol	71 milligrams	1 meat
Dietary Fiber	4 grams	
Protein	30 grams	
Sodium	921 milligrams	

SHOPPING LIST:

2 oz. lime juice, red wine vinegar, 4 oz. honey, garlic powder, fresh coriander, cumin powder, onion powder, 1 lb. fat-free chicken tenders, 1 green bell pepper, 1 red bell pepper, 1 onion, fat-free chicken broth, large fat-free flour tortillas, 4 oz. fat-free salsa

FANTASTIC FISH, TURKEY, AND CHICKEN

CHICKEN PARMESAN

EASY - DO AHEAD - FREEZE

INGREDIENTS:

¼ cup egg substitute
1 cup fat-free bread crumbs
¼ cup fat-free Parmesan
  cheese
½ tsp. onion powder
½ tsp. garlic powder

½ tsp. oregano
1 lb. fat-free chicken breasts
1½ cups fat-free pasta sauce
4 oz. fat-free mozzarella
  cheese, sliced

DIRECTIONS:

Preheat oven to 425 degrees. Lightly spray 9x13-inch baking dish with nonfat cooking spray. Pour egg substitute into small bowl. In a separate bowl, combine bread crumbs, 2 tablespoons Parmesan cheese, onion powder, garlic powder, and oregano and mix well. Dip each chicken breast into egg substitute; roll in bread crumbs to coat on all sides. Place chicken breasts in baking dish and bake 30 to 35 minutes, until golden brown and cooked through. Pour pasta sauce over chicken and top with cheese slices. Reduce oven temperature to 375 degrees and cook until sauce is hot and cheese is melted, about 5 to 10 minutes. Great with pasta, garlic bread, and salad!

Serves: 4

Nutrition per Serving		Exchanges
Calories	243	4⅔ meat
Carbohydrate	17 grams	1 starch
Cholesterol	71 milligrams	
Dietary Fiber	< 1 gram	
Protein	38 grams	
Sodium	878 milligrams	

SHOPPING LIST:

2 oz. egg substitute, 2 slices fat-free bread (day-old or fat-free bread crumbs), 1 oz. fat-free Parmesan cheese, onion powder, garlic powder, oregano, 1 lb. fat-free chicken breasts, 12 oz. fat-free pasta sauce, 4 oz. fat-free mozzarella cheese (whole or slices)

CHICKEN POCKETS

EASY - DO AHEAD

INGREDIENTS:

2 medium carrots, sliced thin
2 medium zucchini, sliced thin
1 lb. fat-free chicken breasts
½ tsp. garlic powder
1 tsp. onion powder
½ tsp. dried dill weed
½ tsp. paprika
1 medium lemon, sliced

DIRECTIONS:

Preheat oven to 350 degrees. Cut four 12-inch squares of foil and spray lightly with cooking spray. Divide carrot and zucchini slices among foil squares; place chicken on top of vegetables. Sprinkle both sides with garlic powder, onion powder, dill weed, and paprika. Top with lemon slices. Fold foil around chicken and place on baking sheet. Bake in preheated oven 20 to 30 minutes, until chicken is cooked through and vegetables are tender.

Serves: 4

Nutrition per Serving		Exchanges
Calories	130	1½ vegetable
Carbohydrate	7 grams	3 meat
Cholesterol	71 milligrams	
Dietary Fiber	2 grams	
Protein	24 grams	
Sodium	288 milligrams	

SHOPPING LIST:

2 medium carrots, 2 medium zucchini, 1 lb. fat-free chicken breasts, garlic powder, onion powder, dried dill weed, paprika, 1 medium lemon

CREAMY CHICKEN ENCHILADAS

AVERAGE - DO AHEAD - FREEZE

✦ ✦ ✦

INGREDIENTS:

2 lbs. fat-free chicken breasts
½ cup fat-free shredded Cheddar cheese
8 fat-free flour tortillas
14½ oz. can low-fat cream of chicken soup
4 oz. chopped green chilies
1 cup fat-free sour cream

DIRECTIONS:

Preheat oven to 350 degrees. Lightly spray 9x13-inch baking dish with nonfat cooking spray. Place chicken breasts in large soup pot or Dutch oven and cover with water. Bring water to a boil over high heat; reduce to medium-high and cook 25 to 30 minutes, until chicken is tender and cooked through. Remove chicken from pot and cool slightly. Shred chicken or cut into small chunks, and place in a medium bowl. Toss with Cheddar cheese. In a small bowl, combine soup, chilies, and sour cream and blend well. Divide chicken mixture evenly among tortillas and roll up. Place seam-side down in prepared pan. Pour soup mixture over tortillas and sprinkle with extra Cheddar cheese, if desired. Bake in preheated oven 25 to 30 minutes, until cheese is melted and enchiladas are heated through. Enchiladas can be prepared ahead of time and frozen without soup mixture. Top with sauce just before baking.

Serves: 8

Nutrition per Serving		Exchanges
Calories	271	1⅔ starch
Carbohydrate	27 grams	4½ meat
Cholesterol	59 milligrams	
Dietary Fiber	2 grams	
Protein	35 grams	
Sodium	997 milligrams	

SHOPPING LIST:

2 lb. fat-free chicken breasts, 2 oz. fat-free shredded Cheddar cheese, large flour tortillas, 14½ oz. can low-fat cream of chicken soup, 4 oz. can chopped green chilies, 8 oz. fat-free sour cream

CREOLE CHICKEN

AVERAGE - DO AHEAD - FREEZE

INGREDIENTS:
1 cup Pioneer baking mix
1 tsp. paprika
½ tsp. Creole seasoning
2 tbsp. Buttermilk Blend Mix
½ cup water
1 pound fat-free chicken breasts
¼ cup butter-flavored granules

DIRECTIONS:
Preheat oven to 350 degrees. Lightly spray 9x13-inch baking dish with nonfat cooking spray. In a medium bowl, combine baking mix, paprika, and Creole seasoning. In another medium bowl, mix Buttermilk Blend with water and mix until smooth. Dip chicken into buttermilk; roll in crumb mixture and coat on all sides. Place chicken in prepared pan. Drizzle liquid butter over chicken and bake in pre-heated oven 45 to 50 minutes, until no longer pink and cooked through.

Serves: 4

Nutrition per Serving		Exchanges
Calories	280	3 meat
Carbohydrate	44 grams	1⅔ starch
Cholesterol	56 milligrams	2½ vegetable
Dietary Fiber	> 1 gram	
Protein	30 grams	
Sodium	785 milligrams	

SHOPPING LIST:
Pioneer baking mix, paprika, Creole seasoning, Buttermilk Blend Mix, 1 lb. fat-free chicken breasts, butter-flavored granules

GARLIC CHICKEN

EASY - DO AHEAD - FREEZE

INGREDIENTS:
- 1½ tbsp. minced garlic
- 2¼ tbsp. fresh rosemary leaves, chopped
- 1½ tsp. oregano
- ¾ tsp. onion powder
- ½ tsp. pepper
- ¼ cup fat-free chicken broth
- 1½ lbs. fat-free chicken breasts

DIRECTIONS:

Prepare a hot grill and lightly spray with nonfat cooking spray. Combine garlic, rosemary, oregano, onion powder, pepper, and chicken broth in a small bowl and mix well. Place chicken breasts in baking dish; pour broth mixture over chicken and turn several times to coat on all sides. Preheat broiler on high heat. Broil chicken breasts 4 to 6 inches from heat; cook 7-10 minutes per side, until browned and cooked through.

Serves: 4

Nutrition per Serving		Exchanges
Calories	160	4½ meat
Carbohydrate	2 grams	
Cholesterol	106 milligrams	
Dietary Fiber	0 grams	
Protein	35 grams	
Sodium	467 milligrams	

SHOPPING LIST:

minced garlic, fresh rosemary leaves (or 2¼ tsp. dried), oregano, onion powder, pepper, 2 oz. fat-free chicken broth, 1½ lb. fat-free chicken breasts

HONEY CHICKEN

EASY - DO AHEAD

INGREDIENTS:
¾ cup dry sherry
1 tbsp. cinnamon
½ cup honey
2 tbsp. lime juice
1 tsp. minced garlic
pepper to taste
2 pounds fat-free chicken breasts

DIRECTIONS:
Preheat oven to 350 degrees. In a small bowl, combine sherry, cinnamon, honey, lime juice, garlic, and pepper; blend well. Lightly spray shallow glass baking dish with nonfat cooking spray. Arrange chicken in single layer in dish. Pour marinade over chicken, turning pieces to coat. Refrigerate overnight. Drain marinade and reserve. Bake chicken in preheated oven 35 to 45 minutes, basting several times with marinade. Heat broiler on high. Broil chicken 4 inches from heat until crispy and golden brown, about 5 minutes.

Serves: 8

Nutrition per Serving		Exchanges
Calories	200	1⅓ fruit
Carbohydrate	19 grams	3⅓ meat
Cholesterol	71 milligrams	
Dietary Fiber	< 1 gram	
Protein	23 grams	
Sodium	275 milligrams	

SHOPPING LIST:
6 oz. dry sherry, cinnamon, 4 oz. honey, lime juice, minced garlic, pepper, 2 lb. fat-free chicken breasts

FANTASTIC FISH, TURKEY, AND CHICKEN

LEMON-PINEAPPLE BAKED CHICKEN

AVERAGE - DO AHEAD - FREEZE

◆ ◆ ◆

INGREDIENTS:
2 lbs. fat-free chicken breasts
1 tsp. onion powder
½ tsp. pepper
20 oz. pineapple rings in juice, cut in half
1½ tsp. minced garlic
1 tbsp. cornstarch
1 tsp. Worcestershire sauce
2 tsp. Dijon mustard
1 lemon, sliced

DIRECTIONS:
Preheat broiler on high heat. Lightly spray 9x13-inch baking dish with nonfat cooking spray. Place chicken breasts in baking dish and sprinkle with onion powder and pepper. Broil under high heat until lightly browned, about 10 minutes. Remove from oven; set oven temperature to 350 degrees. Drain pineapple juice into small bowl. Add garlic, cornstarch, Worcestershire, and mustard and mix until blended. Pour sauce over chicken breasts and bake in preheated oven 20 minutes. Remove chicken from oven; arrange pineapple and lemon slices around chicken and baste with sauce. Bake an additional 5 to 7 minutes, until heated through.

Serves: 6

Nutrition per Serving		Exchanges
Calories	202	1 fruit
Carbohydrate	17 grams	4 meat
Cholesterol	95 milligrams	
Dietary Fiber	1 gram	
Protein	31 grams	
Sodium	417 milligrams	

SHOPPING LIST:
2 lb. fat-free chicken breasts, onion powder, pepper, 20 oz. pineapple rings in juice, minced garlic, cornstarch, Worcestershire sauce, Dijon mustard, 1 lemon

ORANGE CHICKEN

EASY - DO AHEAD

INGREDIENTS:
1½ lbs. fat-free chicken breasts
1 tsp. onion powder
¾ tsp. garlic powder
2 cups orange juice
¼ tsp. pepper
½ cup sliced green onion
1 cup sliced red bell pepper
1 cup sliced yellow bell pepper
16 oz. can chopped tomatoes, drained

DIRECTIONS:
Preheat oven to 375 degrees. Lightly spray 9x13-inch baking dish with nonfat cooking spray. Place chicken breasts in prepared dish; sprinkle both sides with onion and garlic powder. Bake in preheated oven 20 minutes. In a small saucepan, combine orange juice, pepper, and green onions; heat over medium-high heat 10 minutes. Stir in sliced peppers and cook 5 minutes, until peppers are softened. Stir in drained tomatoes and cook 2 to 3 minutes, until heated through. Remove chicken from oven; top with orange sauce and bake 10 to 15 minutes, until chicken is cooked through. Great with rice!

Serves: 4

Nutrition per Serving		Exchanges
Calories	272	5 meat
Carbohydrate	24 grams	2 vegetable
Cholesterol	84 milligrams	1 fruit
Dietary Fiber	3 grams	
Protein	42 grams	
Sodium	533 milligrams	

SHOPPING LIST:
1½ lb. fat-free chicken breasts, onion powder, garlic powder, 16 oz. orange juice, pepper, 4 green onions, 1 medium red bell pepper, 1 medium yellow bell pepper, 16 oz. can chopped tomatoes

ORIENTAL CHICKEN TENDERS

EASY - DO AHEAD

✦ ✦ ✦

INGREDIENTS:
1½ lbs. fat-free chicken tenders
1½ tsp. garlic powder
1½ tsp. onion powder
¾ cup low-sodium soy sauce
¾ cup brown sugar

DIRECTIONS:
Preheat oven to 350 degrees. Lightly spray 9x13-inch baking dish or roasting dish with nonfat cooking spray. Arrange chicken tenders in dish in a single layer. Sprinkle chicken with garlic and onion powder. In a small bowl, combine soy sauce and brown sugar and mix until blended smooth. Pour mixture over chicken; turn chicken so it is well coated on both sides. Cover with plastic wrap and marinate in refrigerator 20 to 30 minutes. Remove plastic and bake in preheated oven 15 minutes; remove from oven and turn chicken tenders with fork or tongs. Bake 15 to 20 minutes, until browned and cooked through.

Serves: 4

Nutrition per Serving		Exchanges
Calories	355	2⅔ fruit
Carbohydrate	46 grams	6 meat
Cholesterol	84 milligrams	
Dietary Fiber	0 grams	
Protein	43 grams	
Sodium	2,147 milligrams	

SHOPPING LIST:
1½ lb. fat-free chicken tenders, garlic powder, onion powder, 6 oz. low-sodium soy sauce, brown sugar

BEEF BARLEY

EASY - DO AHEAD

INGREDIENTS:

1 pound fat-free beef crumbles
2½ cups sliced mushrooms
1 cup chopped onion
¾ cup sliced carrots
1 tsp. minced garlic
14½ oz. fat-free vegetable broth
½ cup quick cooking pearled barley
¼ tsp. pepper
8 oz. frozen sugar snap peas, thawed
1 tbsp. dried parsley

DIRECTIONS:

Lightly spray a large nonstick skillet with nonfat cooking spray and heat over medium heat. Add beef crumbles, mushrooms, onion, carrot, and garlic to skillet and cook 10 minutes, until beef is cooked through and vegetables are tender. Add vegetable broth, barley, and pepper to skillet; bring to a boil over medium-high heat. Immediately reduce heat to medium-low, cover, and simmer 10 to 15 minutes. Add snap peas and cook until barley is tender, about 5 minutes. Sprinkle with parsley and serve.

Serves: 4

Nutrition per Serving		Exchanges
Calories	277	1 starch
Carbohydrate	40 grams	5 vegetable
Cholesterol	0 milligrams	2 meat
Dietary Fiber	10 grams	
Protein	27 grams	
Sodium	788 milligrams	

SHOPPING LIST:

1 lb. fat-free beef crumbles (Morningstar Farms), 8 oz. mushrooms, 1 medium onion, 1 carrot, minced garlic, 14½ oz. fat-free vegetable broth, quick-cooking pearl barley, pepper, 8 oz. frozen sugar snap peas, dried parsley

MEXICAN MEAT LOAF

EASY - DO AHEAD - FREEZE

✦ ✦ ✦

INGREDIENTS:
1½ lbs. fat-free ground turkey, chicken, or fat-free beef crumbles
½ cup fresh fat-free bread crumbs
1 tbsp. onion flakes
8 oz. tomato sauce
4 oz. chopped green chilies
¼ cup egg substitute
1 envelope taco seasoning mix
1 cup fat-free shredded Cheddar cheese

DIRECTIONS:
Preheat oven to 350 degrees. Lightly spray 9x5-inch loaf pan with nonfat cooking spray. In medium bowl, combine turkey, bread crumbs, onion flakes, tomato sauce, green chilies, egg substitute, and taco seasoning and mix until ingredients are blended. Divide turkey mixture in half and place in prepared loaf pan; top with Cheddar cheese. Press remaining turkey mixture on top and spread smooth. Bake in preheated oven 45 minutes to 1 hour, until lightly browned and cooked through. Serve with sour cream and salsa, if desired.

Serves: 6

Nutrition per Serving		Exchanges
Calories	178	4 meat
Carbohydrate	10 grams	⅔ starch
Cholesterol	51 milligrams	
Dietary Fiber	1 gram	
Protein	31 grams	
Sodium	1,149 milligrams	

SHOPPING LIST:
1½ lb. fat-free ground turkey, 1 slice fat-free bread or fat-free bread crumbs, onion flakes, 8 oz. tomato sauce, 4 oz. diced green chilies, 2 oz. egg substitute, 1 envelope taco seasoning mix, 4 oz. fat-free shredded Cheddar cheese

SLOPPY JOES

EASY - DO AHEAD - FREEZE

INGREDIENTS:
1 lb. fat-free beef crumbles
2 tbsp. onion powder
½ cup ketchup
1 tsp. mustard
1 tsp. garlic powder
¼ tsp. pepper

DIRECTIONS:
Lightly spray a large nonstick skillet with nonfat cooking spray and heat over medium-high heat. Add beef and cook until no longer pink and cooked through; drain well. Add remaining ingredients and heat over medium-high heat until mixture comes to a boil; reduce temperature to low, cover and simmer 20 to 30 minutes. Serve over fat-free bread, stuffed in pita pockets, or rolled in fat-free flour tortillas.

Serves: 4

Nutrition per Serving		Exchanges
Calories	146	3 meat
Carbohydrate	11 grams	2 vegetable
Cholesterol	0 milligrams	
Dietary Fiber	0 grams	
Protein	22 grams	
Sodium	570 milligrams	

SHOPPING LIST:
1 lb. fat-free beef crumbles (Morningstar Farms), onion powder, 4 oz. ketchup, mustard, garlic powder, pepper

SOUTHWEST TURKEY STEW

AVERAGE - DO AHEAD

INGREDIENTS:

1 lb. fat-free ground turkey
1¼ cups fat-free chunky-style salsa
½ tsp. garlic powder
1 tbsp. onion powder
1 cup corn kernels, drained
1 cup fat-free black beans, rinsed and drained

1 cup canned tomatoes, crushed
2 cups fat-free chicken broth
4 oz. can chopped green chilies, drained
dash cayenne pepper
¼ tsp. oregano

DIRECTIONS:

Preheat oven to 400 degrees. Lightly spray 10-inch baking dish with nonfat cooking spray. In medium bowl, combine turkey, ¼ cup salsa, garlic powder, and onion powder and mix until blended. Roll mixture into 1-inch balls; place in prepared pan. Bake in preheated oven 20 to 25 minutes, until lightly browned and cooked through. In a large saucepan or medium soup pot over high heat, combine corn, beans, tomatoes, chicken broth, chilies, cayenne pepper, and oregano; bring mixture to boil. Reduce heat to medium-low; cook an additional 15 to 20 minutes, until heated through. Add turkey meatballs and cook over low heat 5 to 10 minutes, until heated through.

Serves: 4

Nutrition per Serving		Exchanges
Calories	245	1 vegetable
Carbohydrate	35 grams	2 starch
Cholesterol	41 milligrams	2 meat
Dietary Fiber	5 grams	
Protein	23 grams	
Sodium	2,646 milligrams	

SHOPPING LIST:

1 lb. fat-free ground turkey, 10 oz. fat-free chunky-style salsa, garlic powder, onion powder, 8 oz. corn kernels, 8 oz. fat-free black beans, 8 oz. crushed tomatoes, 14½ oz. can fat-free chicken broth (or 2 chicken bouillon cubes + water), 4 oz. can chopped green chilies, cayenne pepper, oregano

TURKEY BURGERS

EASY - DO AHEAD

INGREDIENTS:
1 lb. fat-free ground turkey
⅓ cup fat-free cracker crumbs
1½ tsp. onion powder
2 tbsp. low-sodium ketchup
1 tbsp. low-sodium teriyaki sauce
pepper to taste

DIRECTIONS:
Combine all ingredients in a medium bowl and mix until blended. Form mixture into patties. Refrigerate 1 to 2 hours before cooking. Preheat broiler on high heat and cook burgers 4 inches from heat until cooked through, about 5 minutes per side.

Serves: 6

Nutrition per Serving		Exchanges
Calories	81	⅓ starch
Carbohydrate	6 grams	1½ meat
Cholesterol	27 milligrams	
Dietary Fiber	< 1 gram	
Protein	11 grams	
Sodium	515 milligrams	

SHOPPING LIST:
1 lb. fat-free ground turkey, 3 oz. fat-free cracker crumbs, onion powder, 1 oz. low-sodium ketchup, low-sodium teriyaki sauce, pepper

TURKEY MEAT LOAF

EASY - DO AHEAD - FREEZE

✦ ✦ ✦

INGREDIENTS:

¾ lb. fat-free ground turkey
¾ cup Cornflakes crumbs
¼ cup chopped onion
½ cup tomato sauce
1½ tsp. Worcestershire sauce
1 large egg white
pepper to taste

DIRECTIONS:

Preheat oven to 350 degrees. Lightly spray 8x4-inch loaf pan or baking sheet with nonfat cooking spray. In a large bowl, combine all ingredients and mix well. Form meat mixture into loaf shape or place in loaf pan. Bake in preheated oven 40 minutes, until firm to the touch.

Serves: 4

Nutrition per Serving		Exchanges
Calories	155	1⅓ starch
Carbohydrate	19 grams	1½ meat
Cholesterol	30 milligrams	
Dietary Fiber	1 gram	
Protein	19 grams	
Sodium	1,339 milligrams	

SHOPPING LIST:

¾ lb. fat-free ground turkey, Cornflakes crumbs, ½ small onion, 4 oz. tomato sauce, Worcestershire sauce, 1 egg, pepper

TURKEY ROLLS FLORENTINE

AVERAGE - DO AHEAD

INGREDIENTS:

2 lbs. fat-free turkey cutlets
10 oz. frozen chopped spinach, thawed and
   drained
3 tbsp. fat-free cream cheese
2½ oz. canned mushrooms, chopped
¾ cup chopped onion
2 tbsp. fat-free margarine, melted
¼ tsp. pepper

DIRECTIONS:

Preheat oven to 400 degrees. Lightly spray 10x15x1-inch jel-lyroll pan with nonfat cooking spray. Dry turkey cutlets with a paper towel. In a medium bowl, combine spinach, cream cheese, mushrooms, onions, and pepper and mix well. Divide mixture and spread over top of each turkey cutlet; roll up cutlets and place in single layer, seam-side down, on baking sheet. Brush with melted margarine, cover with plastic wrap and refrigerate 1 hour (or freeze 10 to 15 minutes). Bake turkey cutlets 20 to 30 minutes, until turkey is cooked through.

Serves: 4

Nutrition per Serving

		Exchanges
Calories	250	1½ vegetable
Carbohydrate	8 grams	6½ meat
Cholesterol	101 milligrams	
Dietary Fiber	2 grams	
Protein	52 grams	
Sodium	736 milligrams	

SHOPPING LIST:

2 lb. fat-free turkey cutlets, 10 oz. frozen chopped spinach, 3 oz. fat-free cream cheese, 2½ oz. canned mushrooms, 1 medium onion, pepper, fat-free margarine

GREAT GRILLS AND BARBECUES

✦ ✦ ✦

BARBECUE BASICS

TYPES OF FUEL FOR THE BARBECUE

1. Lump charcoal - This burns hot and slow. It comes in irregular pieces and must be broken up before use. Charcoal should be 2 inches deep and expand 2 inches larger around than the food on the grill. The best charcoal grilling is about 4-6 inches from the coals. Allow 25-35 minutes for the coals to heat for a hot fire, 45 minutes for a medium fire, and an existing fire for low temperature cooking.

2. Standard briquets - These are easier and safer to use than lump charcoal but the chemical base should be burned off before cooking (about 15-20 minutes).

3. Instant-lighting briquets - These are quick and easy to use, but slightly higher in cost.

4. Wood chips and chunks - These tend to give a smoky flavor to foods but must soak in water 30 minutes before they are placed over the charcoal.

5. Propane gas - This is the easiest, least expensive, and quickest type of fuel to use when barbecuing. Gas grills are efficient because they have their own temperature controls to assure correct heating.

Testing for Barbecue Temperature:

Hold your hand 5 inches from the heat and count the number of seconds you can hold your hand in that position before it becomes too hot:
Hot Fire — 2-3 seconds
Medium Hot — 3-4 seconds
Medium — 4-6 seconds
Low — 7-9 seconds

HINTS FOR GREAT GRILLING

1. Spray the grill rack with nonfat cooking spray to prevent the food from sticking.

2. Meats cook the best when they are grilled from room temperature; meat directly from the refrigerator may not cook as evenly.

3. Use tongs instead of a knife or fork for turning meats, to preserve the juices.

4. If you are using bamboo or wooden skewers, always soak them in water for 30 minutes to prevent them from burning.

5. Do not use gasoline to light charcoal or add starter fluid to an existing fire.

6. Use long-handled tools and fireproof mitts for safe grilling.

7. Marinades add flavor and tenderize foods; always marinate foods in the refrigerator to prevent the growth of bacteria.

8. Chicken tenders and turkey tenderloins on a skewer - Fold the tenders into thirds and pierce the skewer through the meat; try not to press the folds too close together, in order to ensure even cooking.

9. Fish cooks great in a wire basket, as it will not break and stick to the grill; lightly spray the wire panels with nonfat cooking spray, place the fish between the panels and lay the basket on the grill. Turn the basket to cook evenly on both sides.

GREAT GRILLS & BARBECUES

CARIBBEAN CHICKEN TENDERS

EASY - DO AHEAD

INGREDIENTS:

¾ cup water
⅓ cup lemon juice
1 tbsp. brown sugar
1 tbsp. onion powder
1 tbsp. vegetable broth
¾ tsp. allspice

¾ tsp. cinnamon
¾ tsp. pepper
½ tsp. thyme
¼ tsp. cayenne pepper
2 lbs. fat-free chicken
  breasts

DIRECTIONS:

Combine water, lemon juice, brown sugar, onion powder, vegetable broth, allspice, cinnamon, pepper, thyme, and cayenne in food processor or blender; process until smooth. Reserve ½ cup marinade and refrigerate. Place chicken breasts in shallow baking dish; pour remaining marinade over chicken, cover with plastic wrap and refrigerate overnight. Prepare a hot grill; lightly spray with nonfat cooking spray. Remove chicken from marinade and discard marinade. Grill chicken 6 to 8 minutes per side, turning several times and brushing with reserved marinade, until chicken is cooked through and no longer pink.

Serves: 4

<table>
<tr><td colspan="2">Nutrition per Serving</td><td>Exchanges</td></tr>
<tr><td>Calories</td><td>250</td><td>7 meat</td></tr>
<tr><td>Carbohydrate</td><td>7 grams</td><td>⅓ fruit</td></tr>
<tr><td>Cholesterol</td><td>111 milligrams</td><td></td></tr>
<tr><td>Dietary Fiber</td><td>< 1 grams</td><td></td></tr>
<tr><td>Protein</td><td>53 grams</td><td></td></tr>
<tr><td>Sodium</td><td>448 milligrams</td><td></td></tr>
</table>

SHOPPING LIST:

3 oz. lemon juice, brown sugar, onion powder, vegetable broth, allspice, cinnamon, pepper, thyme, cayenne pepper, 2 lb. fat-free chicken breasts

CHICKEN ON A STICK

EASY - DO AHEAD

INGREDIENTS:

1 lb. fat-free chicken tenders, cubed
2 cups fat-free bread crumbs
1 tsp. garlic powder
1 tsp. onion powder
¼ tsp. oregano

½ cup lemon juice
½ cup fat-free Parmesan
cheese
½ cup fat-free Italian salad
dressing

DIRECTIONS:

Place chicken cubes in a medium bowl. In a small bowl, combine bread crumbs with garlic powder, onion powder, and oregano and mix well. Add 1 cup crumb mixture, lemon juice, and Parmesan cheese to chicken. Pour in enough Italian dressing to coat chicken; mix thoroughly. Cover and refrigerate overnight. Next day: press crumb mixture into chicken. Thread chicken onto skewers and pack tightly. Roll skewers in remaining bread crumbs. Prepare a medium hot fire and lightly spray grill with nonfat cooking spray; place skewers on grill 10 to 15 minutes, until bread crumbs are golden brown and chicken is cooked through. Rotate skewers halfway through cooking to prevent bread crumbs from burning. Slide chicken off skewers and serve. Great with fat-free honey mustard, B-B-Q sauce, or fat-free pasta sauce.

Serves: 4

Nutrition per Serving		Exchanges
Calories	323	1 starch
Carbohydrates	48 grams	4 meat
Cholesterol	70 milligrams	2 fruit
Dietary Fiber	1 gram	
Protein	35 grams	
Sodium	884 milligrams	

SHOPPING LIST:

1 lb. fat-free chicken tenders, fat-free bread crumbs (or 4 slices bread, crushed), garlic powder, onion powder, oregano, lemon juice, 4 oz. fat-free Parmesan cheese, 4 oz. fat-free Italian salad dressing

GREAT GRILLS & BARBECUES

CHICKEN AND PINEAPPLE KABOBS

EASY - DO AHEAD

INGREDIENTS:
1 lb. fat-free chicken tenders, cut in 1-inch pieces
8 oz. pineapple chunks in juice, drained
1 cup maraschino cherries
1 cup low-sodium teriyaki sauce

DIRECTIONS:
Prepare a medium-hot fire and lightly spray with nonfat cooking spray. Thread chicken pieces, pineapple chunks, and cherries alternately on metal skewers and place on large platter or dish. Brush teriyaki sauce liberally over skewered pieces. Grill 10 to 12 minutes, basting frequently, until chicken is cooked through. This can be prepared ahead of time; marinate skewers in refrigerator several hours or overnight.

Serves: 4

Nutrition per Serving		Exchanges
Calories	222	4 meat
Carbohydrate	27 grams	1½ fruit
Cholesterol	71 milligrams	
Dietary Fiber	1 gram	
Protein	28 grams	
Sodium	1,500 milligrams	

SHOPPING LIST:
1 lb. fat-free chicken tenders, 8 oz. pineapple chunks in juice, 8 oz. maraschino cherries, 8 oz. low-sodium teriyaki sauce (Teriyaki Allegro Marinade is very low in calories and sodium)

CHICKEN-POTATO AND PINEAPPLE KABOBS

EASY - DO AHEAD

INGREDIENTS:

1 large sweet potato, peeled and cut in chunks
1 lb. fat-free chicken tenders, cut in 1-inch pieces
8 oz. pineapple chunks in juice, drained
1 cup maraschino cherries
1 cup low-sodium teriyaki sauce

DIRECTIONS:

Prepare a medium-hot grill and lightly spray with nonfat cooking spray. Place potato chunks in a medium saucepan and cover with water. Bring to a boil over high heat and boil 5 to 6 minutes, until tender. Thread chicken pieces, potato chunks, pineapple chunks, and cherries alternately on metal skewers and place on large platter or dish. Brush teriyaki sauce liberally over skewered pieces. Grill 10 to 15 minutes, basting frequently, until chicken is cooked through. This can be prepared ahead of time; marinate skewers in refrigerator several hours or overnight.

Serves: 4

Nutrition per Serving		Exchanges
Calories	363	3½ fruit
Carbohydrate	53 grams	4 meat
Cholesterol	56 milligrams	
Dietary Fiber	2 grams	
Protein	29 grams	
Sodium	1,621 milligrams	

SHOPPING LIST:

1 large sweet potato, 1 lb. fat-free chicken tenders, 8 oz. pineapple chunks in juice, 8 oz. maraschino cherries, 8 oz. low-sodium teriyaki sauce

CREAMY GARLIC CHICKEN BREASTS

EASY - DO AHEAD - FREEZE

INGREDIENTS:

¾ cup fat-free sour cream
3 tsp. minced garlic
pepper to taste
1½ lbs. fat-free chicken breasts

DIRECTIONS:

In a small bowl, combine sour cream, garlic, and pepper and mix until blended. Place chicken breasts in a shallow baking dish; spread sour cream mixture over all sides of chicken to coat well. Cover with plastic wrap and refrigerate 2 to 3 hours or overnight. Prepare a hot grill and lightly spray with nonfat cooking spray. Place chicken on grill and cook 7 to 10 minutes per side, until browned and cooked through. (Discard any marinade from chicken—do not reuse!) Chicken can be prepared in the same manner and broiled under high heat about 6-inches from heat.

Serves: 6

Nutrition per Serving		Exchanges
Calories	122	3½ meat
Carbohydrate	< 1 gram	
Cholesterol	71 milligrams	
Dietary Fiber	0 grams	
Protein	25 grams	
Sodium	293 milligrams	

SHOPPING LIST:

6 oz. fat-free sour cream, minced garlic, pepper, 1½ lbs. fat-free chicken breasts

GREAT GRILLS & BARBECUES

FRUIT-GLAZED CHICKEN BREASTS

EASY - DO AHEAD - FREEZE

INGREDIENTS:
1½ lbs. fat-free chicken breasts
1 tsp. onion powder
1 tsp. garlic powder
¾ cup fat-free Italian salad dressing
⅓ cup apricot preserves

DIRECTIONS:
Place chicken breasts in shallow baking dish and season with onion and garlic powder. Pour dressing over chicken, cover with plastic wrap, and marinate in refrigerator at least 2 hours or overnight. Remove ⅓ cup marinade from baking dish and pour into microwave-safe dish; cover with plastic wrap and heat on high 45 seconds to 1 minute, until mixture comes to a boil. (Sauce can also be heated in small saucepan over medium-high heat and brought to a boil.) Stir preserves into sauce until melted. Prepare a hot grill and lightly spray with fat-free cooking spray. Place chicken on grill; baste with apricot sauce and cook 7 to 10 minutes per side, basting frequently, until chicken is cooked through.

Serves: 4

GREAT GRILLS & BARBECUES

Nutrition per Serving		Exchanges
Calories	259	1⅔ fruit
Carbohydrate	26 grams	5 meat
Cholesterol	106 milligrams	
Dietary Fiber	< 1 gram	
Protein	35 grams	
Sodium	593 milligrams	

SHOPPING LIST:
1½ lbs. fat-free chicken breasts, onion powder, garlic power, 6 oz. fat-free Italian salad dressing, apricot preserves

GINGER CHICKEN TENDERS

EASY - DO AHEAD

INGREDIENTS:
1½ lbs. fat-free chicken tenders
¾ tsp. onion powder
1 tsp. garlic powder, divided
½ cup apple juice
1½ tsp. ground ginger
3 tbsp. low-sodium soy sauce
2 tsp. brown sugar

GREAT GRILLS & BARBECUES

DIRECTIONS:
Thread chicken tenders onto metal skewers and place in shallow baking dish; sprinkle both sides with onion powder and ½ teaspoon garlic powder. In a small bowl, combine apple juice, ½ teaspoon garlic powder, ginger, soy sauce, and brown sugar; stir until ingredients are blended and sugar is dissolved. Pour marinade over chicken tenders and coat well on all sides. Cover and refrigerate overnight. Prepare a medium-hot grill and lightly spray with nonfat cooking spray. Remove chicken from marinade and grill 10 to 15 minutes, basting and turning frequently, until chicken is no longer pink and cooked through. Discard any remaining marinade.

Serves: 6

Nutrition per Serving		Exchanges
Calories	135	⅓ fruit
Carbohydrate	6 grams	3½ meat
Cholesterol	56 milligrams	
Dietary Fiber	0 grams	
Protein	27 grams	
Sodium	524 milligrams	

SHOPPING LIST:
1½ lb. fat-free chicken tenders, onion powder, garlic powder, 4 oz. apple juice, ground ginger, low-sodium soy sauce, brown sugar

GRILLED CAJUN CHICKEN SALAD

EASY - DO AHEAD

INGREDIENTS:
1 lb. fat-free chicken tenders
1 tsp. Cajun seasoning
6 cups mixed salad greens
1 cup sliced mushrooms
1 medium red bell pepper, thinly sliced
1 cup cherry tomatoes
1 cup fat-free croutons
¼ cup fat-free Parmesan cheese
¾ cup Bernstein's fat-free cheese & garlic Italian dressing

DIRECTIONS:
Place chicken tenders in shallow baking dish; season on both sides with Cajun seasoning. Prepare a medium-hot grill and lightly spray with nonfat cooking spray. Grill chicken 8 to 10 minutes, until cooked through and no longer pink. Slice chicken tenders and set aside. In large bowl, toss salad greens, mushrooms, red pepper, tomatoes, and croutons. Sprinkle with Parmesan cheese. Arrange chicken over top of salad and drizzle with dressing. Toss lightly; serve immediately. Salad and chicken can be prepared ahead of time; toss with dressing just before serving.

Serves: 4

Nutrition per Serving		Exchanges
Calories	262	2⅓ meat
Carbohydrate	35 grams	1 starch
Cholesterol	71 milligrams	4 vegetable
Dietary Fiber	2 grams	
Protein	29 grams	
Sodium	1,081 milligrams	

SHOPPING LIST:
1 lb. fat-free chicken tenders, Cajun seasoning, mixed salad greens (romaine, red leaf, etc.), ¼ lb. mushrooms, 1 medium red bell pepper, ½ pint cherry tomatoes, 6 oz. package fat-free croutons, 2 oz. fat-free Parmesan cheese, 6 oz. Bernstein's fat-free cheese & garlic Italian dressing

GREAT GRILLS
& BARBECUES

GRILLED CHICKEN BURRITOS

EASY

INGREDIENTS:

1½ lbs. fat-free chicken tenders, cubed
1½ tsp. ground cumin
1½ tsp. chili power
1 tsp. onion powder
½ tsp. garlic powder
6 whole fat-free flour tortillas
1½ cups fat-free chunky-style salsa
½ cup corn kernels, drained
¾ cup fat-free sour cream

DIRECTIONS:

Place chicken cubes in large plastic bag. Sprinkle cumin, chili powder, onion powder, and garlic powder into bag; seal tightly and shake to coat all chicken pieces. Prepare a medium-hot grill and spray lightly with nonfat cooking spray. Thread chicken pieces onto metal skewers. Grill chicken on covered grill 7 to 10 minutes, until chicken is no longer pink and cooked through. Remove skewers from grill. Warm tortillas in microwave, foil-wrapped in oven, or brushed lightly on both sides with water and grilled 10 seconds per side. In a small bowl, combine salsa with corn and mix well. Divide chicken evenly among tortillas; top with salsa and sour cream. Roll tortillas up burrito-style and serve immediately.

Serves: 6

Nutrition per Serving		Exchanges
Calories	257	2 starch
Carbohydrate	30 grams	3 meat
Cholesterol	71 milligrams	
Dietary Fiber	3 grams	
Protein	30 grams	
Sodium	883 milligrams	

SHOPPING LIST:

1½ lb. fat-free chicken tenders, ground cumin, chili powder, onion powder, garlic powder, 1 package large fat-free flour tortillas, 12 oz. fat-free chunky-style salsa, 4 oz. canned corn, 6 oz. fat-free sour cream

GRILLED CHICKEN DIJON

EASY - DO AHEAD

INGREDIENTS:
1 lb. fat-free chicken breasts
⅛ tsp. cayenne pepper
¼ cup fat-free Dijon mustard
¼ cup lemon juice
2 tsp. dried parsley
1 tsp. onion powder
1 cup fat-free bread crumbs

DIRECTIONS:
Rinse chicken with cold water and dry well. Place chicken breasts in shallow baking dish and season both sides with cayenne pepper. In a small bowl, combine mustard, lemon juice, parsley, and onion powder and mix well. Pour over chicken and coat well. Cover with plastic wrap and refrigerate at least 2 hours or overnight. Prepare a hot fire. Lightly spray grill with nonfat cooking spray. Place bread crumbs in medium bowl. Coat both sides of chicken breast with crumbs and place on prepared grill. Grill 7 to 10 minutes per side, until outside is lightly browned and chicken is cooked through.

Serves: 4

Nutrition per Serving		Exchanges
Calories	154	⅔ starch
Carbohydrate	10 grams	3 meat
Cholesterol	71 milligrams	
Dietary Fiber	< 1 gram	
Protein	26 grams	
Sodium	692 milligrams	

SHOPPING LIST:
1 lb. fat-free chicken breasts, cayenne pepper, 2 oz. fat-free Dijon mustard, 2 oz. lemon juice, dried parsley, onion powder, fat-free bread crumbs (or 2 slices fat-free bread)

GRILLED LEMON CHICKEN

EASY - DO AHEAD - FREEZE

INGREDIENTS:
14½ oz. can fat-free chicken broth
3 tbsp. lemon juice
½ tsp. onion powder
⅛ tsp. pepper
1 tsp. Italian seasoning
1 lb. fat-free chicken breasts

DIRECTIONS:
Prepare a medium-hot grill and lightly spray with nonfat cooking spray. In a small bowl, combine chicken broth, lemon juice, onion powder, pepper, and Italian seasoning and blend well. Reserve ½ cup broth mixture and set aside; toss chicken with remaining marinade and coat well. Grill chicken 7 to 10 minutes per side, basting frequently with reserved lemon sauce. Chicken can be cooked under high broiler 6 inches from heat for 30 minutes; turn and baste with lemon sauce.

Serves: 4

Nutrition per Serving		Exchanges
Calories	107	3 meat
Carbohydrate	1 gram	
Cholesterol	71 milligrams	
Dietary Fiber	0 grams	
Protein	23 grams	
Sodium	499 milligrams	

SHOPPING LIST:
14½ oz. can fat-free chicken broth, 1½ oz. lemon juice, onion powder, pepper, Italian seasoning, 1 lb. fat-free chicken breasts

ORANGE HONEY-MUSTARD CHICKEN

EASY - DO AHEAD - FREEZE

INGREDIENTS:
1 lb. fat-free chicken breasts
1 tsp. onion powder
1 tsp. garlic powder
pepper to taste
½ tsp. minced garlic
¼ cup fat-free sour cream
1 tsp. Dijon mustard
½ cup orange juice
1 tsp. honey

DIRECTIONS:
Rinse chicken breasts with cold water and dry well. Place chicken breasts in shallow glass baking dish; season both sides with onion powder, garlic powder, and pepper. In small bowl, combine minced garlic, sour cream, mustard, orange juice, and honey and blend well. Pour marinade over chicken and turn to coat well. Cover with plastic wrap and marinate in refrigerator 2 hours or overnight. Prepare a hot fire and lightly spray grill with nonfat cooking spray. Remove chicken from marinade; save marinade. Grill 7 to 10 minutes per side, until chicken is lightly browned and cooked through. Brush chicken breasts with marinade several times while cooking.

Serves: 4

Nutrition per Serving		Exchanges
Calories	137	⅓ fruit
Carbohydrate	6 grams	3½ meat
Cholesterol	71 milligrams	
Dietary Fiber	< 1 gram	
Protein	25 grams	
Sodium	316 milligrams	

SHOPPING LIST:
1 lb. fat-free chicken breasts, onion powder, garlic powder, pepper, minced garlic, 2 oz. fat-free sour cream, Dijon mustard, 4 oz. orange juice, honey

ORANGE-GLAZED CHICKEN

AVERAGE - DO AHEAD

INGREDIENTS:
1 lb. fat-free chicken tenders, cubed
½ cup orange juice
1 tsp. onion powder
2 tbsp. honey
1 tbsp. Dijon mustard
1 tsp. low-sodium soy sauce
1 tsp. fat-free chicken broth
pepper to taste

DIRECTIONS:
Thread an equal number of chicken pieces onto metal skewers and place on baking sheet. In a small bowl, combine orange juice, onion powder, honey, Dijon mustard, soy sauce, chicken broth, and pepper and mix until blended. Pour mixture over chicken and turn pieces to coat well. Cover with plastic wrap and refrigerate at least 2 hours. Prepare a hot grill and lightly spray with nonfat cooking spray. Pour marinade from chicken into a small saucepan and heat over medium-high heat until the mixture thickens. Place chicken skewers on grill and cook 6 to 7 minutes, until chicken is no longer pink and is cooked through. Turn skewers several times while cooking. Remove chicken pieces from skewers and place on serving plate; drizzle with thickened marinade and serve.

Serves: 4

Nutrition per Serving		Exchanges
Calories	155	¾ fruit
Carbohydrate	13 grams	3⅓ meat
Cholesterol	71 milligrams	
Dietary Fiber	< 1 gram	
Protein	24 grams	
Sodium	419 milligrams	

SHOPPING LIST:
1 lb. fat-free chicken tenders, 4 oz. orange juice, onion powder, honey, Dijon mustard, low-sodium soy sauce, fat-free chicken broth, pepper

SIMPLE ITALIAN CHICKEN

EASY - DO AHEAD - FREEZE

INGREDIENTS:
1 lb. fat-free chicken breasts
1 tsp. onion powder
1 cup fat-free Italian salad dressing
¼ cup dry white wine
1 tsp. minced garlic

DIRECTIONS:
Rinse chicken with cold water and dry well. Place chicken breasts in shallow baking dish; season both sides with onion powder. In a small bowl, combine Italian salad dressing, wine, and minced garlic and mix until blended. Pour mixture over chicken; cover with plastic wrap and marinate in refrigerator at least 2 hours or overnight. Prepare a hot fire and lightly spray grill with nonfat cooking spray. Remove chicken breasts from marinade and grill 7 to 10 minutes per side, until cooked through. Discard any remaining marinade.

Serves: 4

Nutrition per Serving		Exchanges
Calories	154	3 meat
Carbohydrate	9 grams	⅔ starch
Cholesterol	71 milligrams	
Dietary Fiber	0 grams	
Protein	23 grams	
Sodium	514 milligrams	

SHOPPING LIST:
1 lb. fat-free chicken breasts, onion powder, 8 oz. fat-free Italian salad dressing, 2 oz. dry white wine, minced garlic

SOFT CHICKEN TACOS

EASY

INGREDIENTS:

1 lb. fat-free chicken tenders, cut in half
1 tbsp. taco seasoning mix
4 fat-free flour tortillas
¼ cup fat-free shredded Cheddar cheese
½ cup fat-free chunky-style salsa

DIRECTIONS:

Prepare a hot grill and lightly spray with nonfat cooking spray. Place chicken pieces in a medium bowl and toss with taco seasoning until coated. Thread chicken onto metal skewers and grill 10 to 15 minutes, until chicken is tender and cooked through. Lightly spray large (about 18-inches) foil with nonfat cooking spray. Fill each tortilla with ¼ chicken pieces, 1 tablespoon cheese, 2 tablespoons salsa; roll up burrito-style and place on foil sheet. Cook on grill 2 to 3 minutes, just until cheese is melted and tacos are heated through.

Serves: 4

Nutrition per Serving		Exchanges
Calories	231	1½ vegetable
Carbohydrate	23 grams	1 starch
Cholesterol	71 milligrams	3½ meat
Dietary Fiber	2 grams	
Protein	29 grams	
Sodium	804 milligrams	

SHOPPING LIST:

1 lb. fat-free chicken tenders, taco seasoning mix, fat-free flour tortillas, 1 oz. fat-free shredded Cheddar cheese, 4 oz. fat-free chunky-style salsa

SOUTHWEST GRILLED CHICKEN

EASY - DO AHEAD

INGREDIENTS:
- 1 tbsp. fat-free chicken broth
- 1 tbsp. lime juice
- ½ tsp. chili power
- ¼ tsp. pepper
- 1 tsp. minced garlic
- 1½ lbs. fat-free chicken breasts
- 1½ cups fat-free chunky-style salsa

DIRECTIONS:

In a small bowl, combine chicken broth, lime juice, chili powder, pepper, and garlic; mix until all ingredients are blended. Place chicken in a shallow baking dish; pour marinade over chicken, cover, and refrigerate overnight. Prepare a medium-hot grill and lightly spray with nonfat cooking spray. Remove chicken from marinade and grill 8 to 10 minutes per side, until chicken is no longer pink and cooked through. Place chicken on plate and top with salsa.

Serves: 4

GREAT GRILLS
& BARBECUES

Nutrition per Serving		Exchanges
Calories	184	1 vegetable
Carbohydrate	4 grams	5 meat
Cholesterol	84 milligrams	
Dietary Fiber	< 1 gram	
Protein	40 grams	
Sodium	724 milligrams	

SHOPPING LIST:

fat-free chicken broth, lime juice, chili powder, pepper, minced garlic, 1½ lb. fat-free chicken breasts, 12 oz. fat-free chunky-style salsa

SPICY APRICOT CHICKEN

AVERAGE - DO AHEAD

INGREDIENTS:
1 lb. fat-free chicken breasts
½ tsp. garlic powder
½ tsp. onion powder
1½ cups apricot preserves
1 tbsp. frozen orange juice concentrate
1 tsp. cinnamon
½ tsp. nutmeg
½ tsp. ginger

DIRECTIONS:
Lightly spray shallow baking dish with nonfat cooking spray. Place chicken breasts in baking dish and sprinkle both sides with garlic and onion powder. In a medium bowl, combine apricot preserves, orange juice concentrate, cinnamon, nutmeg, and ginger; mix until ingredients are blended. Pour over chicken; turn chicken until well coated. Cover with plastic wrap and refrigerate at least 2 hours. Prepare a medium-hot grill and lightly spray with nonfat cooking spray. Remove chicken from marinade and place on grill; brush with marinade. Grill chicken 8 to 10 minutes per side, brushing frequently with marinade, until no longer pink and cooked through. Pour remaining marinade into small saucepan; heat to boiling over high heat and boil 1 minute. Serve with chicken, if desired.

Serves: 4

Nutrition per Serving		Exchanges
Calories	353	3¾ meat
Carbohydrate	61 grams	4 fruit
Cholesterol	56 milligrams	
Dietary Fiber	1 gram	
Protein	26 grams	
Sodium	232 milligrams	

SHOPPING LIST:
1 lb. fat-free chicken breasts, garlic powder, onion powder, 12 oz. apricot preserves, frozen orange juice concentrate, cinnamon, nutmeg, ginger

CURRIED TURKEY BURGERS

EASY - DO AHEAD - FREEZE

INGREDIENTS:
1 lb. fat-free ground turkey
1 tsp. onion powder
¼ tsp. garlic powder
¼ cup fat-free bread crumbs
3 tsp. curry powder

DIRECTIONS:
Prepare a hot grill and lightly spray with nonfat cooking spray. In a large bowl, combine all ingredients and mix well. Shape mixture into 4 patties, about ½-inch thick. Place patties on hot grill and cook 4 to 5 minutes per side, until no longer pink and cooked through.

Serves: 4

Nutrition per Serving		Exchanges
Calories	116	⅓ starch
Carbohydrate	3 grams	3 meat
Cholesterol	51 milligrams	
Dietary Fiber	1 gram	
Protein	24 grams	
Sodium	255 milligrams	

SHOPPING LIST:
1 lb. fat-free ground turkey, onion powder, garlic powder, fat-free bread crumbs, curry powder

GRILLED TURKEY SANDWICH

EASY - DO AHEAD

INGREDIENTS:
½ cup fat-free mayonnaise
¼ cup spicy mustard
2 tbsp. horseradish
12 slices fat-free bread
1 lb. fat-free deli turkey, sliced thin
1 large tomato, sliced
½ medium red onion, sliced in rings
6 oz. fat-free Swiss cheese, sliced

DIRECTIONS:
Prepare a medium-hot grill and lightly spray with nonfat cooking spray. In a small bowl, combine mayonnaise, mustard, and horseradish and blend well. Spread mixture on one side of each bread slice. Layer turkey, tomato, red onion, and Swiss cheese on one slice of bread and top with second bread slice. Place sandwiches on hot grill and cook 5 to 7 minutes, until bread is toasted and cheese is melted. Serve immediately

Serves: 6

Nutrition per Serving		Exchanges
Calories	331	2⅔ starch
Carbohydrate	44 grams	1 vegetable
Cholesterol	27 milligrams	2 meat
Dietary Fiber	2 grams	
Protein	23 grams	
Sodium	1,888 milligrams	

SHOPPING LIST:
4 oz. fat-free mayonnaise, 2 oz. mustard, 1 oz. horseradish, 1 lb. fat-free bread, 1 lb. fat-free deli-style turkey (sliced thin), 1 large tomato, 1 red onion, 6 oz. fat-free Swiss cheese (sliced)

GREAT GRILLS & BARBECUES

SPICY TURKEY KABOBS

EASY - DO AHEAD

INGREDIENTS:
  ½ cup fat-free mayonnaise
  1¼ tsp. hot pepper sauce
  1½ lbs. fat-free turkey tenders, cut in chunks
  1 medium red bell pepper, cut in chunks
  1 medium yellow pepper, cut in chunks
  2 medium onions, cut in quarters

DIRECTIONS:
  Prepare a hot grill and lightly spray with nonfat cooking spray. In a medium bowl, combine nonfat mayonnaise with hot pepper sauce and blend well. Stir in turkey; let turkey marinate in sauce at room temperature 15 to 20 minutes. Alternately thread turkey, peppers, and onions on metal skewers and cook, turning frequently, 15 minutes, until turkey is cooked through and vegetables are tender. Baste turkey and vegetables with mayonnaise mixture several times while cooking. Serve with fat-free Ranch dressing, if desired.

Serves: 6

Nutrition per Serving		Exchanges
Calories	125	1 vegetable
Carbohydrate	5 grams	3 meat
Cholesterol	51 milligrams	
Dietary Fiber	1 gram	
Protein	24 grams	
Sodium	385 milligrams	

SHOPPING LIST:
  4 oz. fat-free mayonnaise, hot pepper sauce, 1½ lbs. fat-free turkey tenders, 1 medium red bell pepper, 1 medium yellow bell pepper, 2 medium onions

TURKEY CHEESEBURGERS

EASY- DO AHEAD

INGREDIENTS:
1½ lbs. fat-free ground turkey
1 tsp. Worcestershire sauce
1 tsp. onion powder
4 small portabello mushrooms
4 slices fat-free Swiss cheese
1 tbsp. deli-style mustard
4 fat-free sandwich rolls

DIRECTIONS:

Prepare a medium-hot grill and lightly spray with nonfat cooking spray. In a large bowl, combine ground turkey, Worcestershire sauce, and onion powder and mix well. Shape mixture into 4 patties. Place burgers on grill and cook 6 to 7 minutes per side until cooked through. Lightly spray square foil sheet (large enough for mushrooms) with nonfat cooking spray. Place mushrooms on sheet and grill next to burgers until tender. When burgers are cooked through, top each with one slice of cheese and cook until cheese is melted. To serve: Spread 1 teaspoon mustard on bottom half of each bun; top with burger, mushrooms, and remaining bun. Serve immediately. Turkey burgers can be prepared ahead of time, refrigerated, and cooked just before serving.

Serves: 4

Nutrition per Serving		Exchanges
Calories	329	2 starch
Carbohydrate	28 grams	5 meat
Cholesterol	76 milligrams	
Dietary Fiber	1 gram	
Protein	45 grams	
Sodium	874 milligrams	

SHOPPING LIST:

1½ lbs. fat-free ground turkey, Worcestershire sauce, onion powder, 4 small-medium portabello mushrooms, 4 oz. fat-free sliced Swiss cheese, deli-style mustard, 4 fat-free sandwich rolls or 8 slices fat-free bread

TURKEY VEGGIE BURGERS

EASY - DO AHEAD

INGREDIENTS:
1½ lbs. fat-free ground turkey
1 small zucchini, grated
1 tbsp. onion flakes
1 large carrot, peeled and grated
1 tbsp. Worcestershire sauce
1 tbsp. Dijon mustard
1 tbsp. low-sodium ketchup
pepper to taste

DIRECTIONS:
Prepare a hot grill and lightly spray with nonfat cooking spray. In a large bowl, combine all ingredients and mix until blended. Shape into 6 large patties and place on hot grill. Cook 6 to 8 minutes per side, until no longer pink and cooked through. Serve on fat-free bread with lettuce, tomato, and onions, if desired.

Serves: 6

Nutrition per Serving		Exchanges
Calories	120	1 vegetable
Carbohydrate	4 grams	3 meat
Cholesterol	51 milligrams	
Dietary Fiber	1 gram	
Protein	25 grams	
Sodium	349 milligrams	

SHOPPING LIST:
1½ lbs. fat-free ground turkey, 1 small zucchini, onion flakes, 1 large carrot (or ¾ cup preshredded carrot), Worcestershire sauce, Dijon mustard, low-sodium ketchup, pepper

GREAT GRILLS & BARBECUES

GRILLED COD PACKETS

EASY - DO AHEAD

INGREDIENTS:

2 lbs. cod fillets
salt and pepper to taste
1 tsp. dried parsley
¼ cup dry vermouth
1 tbsp. lemon juice

DIRECTIONS:

Prepare a medium fire and spray grill lightly with nonfat cooking spray. Lightly spray large rectangle of heavy-duty foil with nonfat cooking spray. Sprinkle fillets on both sides with salt, pepper, and parsley; roll up jellyroll fashion and place, seam-side down, on prepared foil. In a small bowl, combine vermouth and lemon juice and mix until blended. Pour mixture over fish fillets. Cover fish with another rectangle of heavy-duty foil and seal edges to form tight packet. Place packet on grill and cook, turning occasionally, 20 to 25 minutes, until fish flakes easily and is opaque throughout.

Serves: 6

Nutrition per Serving		Exchanges
Calories	125	3½ meat
Carbohydrate	< 1 gram	
Cholesterol	60 milligrams	
Dietary Fiber	< 1 gram	
Protein	25 grams	
Sodium	86 milligrams	

SHOPPING LIST:

2 lbs. cod fillets, salt, pepper, dried parsley, 2 oz. dry vermouth, lemon juice

GRILLED SHRIMP ON A STICK

EASY - DO AHEAD

✦ ✦ ✦

INGREDIENTS:
1 cup low-sodium ketchup
1 tbsp. horseradish
1 tbsp. lemon juice
1 tsp. onion powder
1 tbsp. dried parsley
1 lb. fat-free frozen shrimp (large)

DIRECTIONS:
In a small bowl, combine ketchup, horseradish, lemon juice, onion powder, and parsley and mix well. Cover and refrigerate several hours or overnight before serving. Prepare a hot fire and lightly spray grill with nonfat cooking spray. Thread shrimp on metal skewers and lightly spray with nonfat cooking spray. Grill until shrimp turn pink and are cooked through, about 5 to 6 minutes. Serve with cocktail sauce.

Serves: 4

GREAT GRILLS & BARBECUES

Nutrition per Serving		Exchanges
Calories	138	1⅓ starch
Carbohydrate	22 grams	1 meat
Cholesterol	13 milligrams	
Dietary Fiber	0 grams	
Protein	12 grams	
Sodium	1,033 milligrams	

SHOPPING LIST:
8 oz. low-sodium ketchup, horseradish, lemon juice, onion powder, dried parsley, 1 lb. fat-free frozen shrimp (large)

ORIENTAL GRILLED COD

EASY - DO AHEAD

INGREDIENTS:
¼ cup Swanson's Oriental broth
1 tsp. garlic powder
1 tsp. crushed rosemary
¾ tsp. dry mustard
2½ tsp. low-sodium soy sauce
¼ cup red wine vinegar
1 lb. cod fillets

DIRECTIONS:
In a small bowl, combine broth, garlic powder, rosemary, mustard, soy sauce, and vinegar; mix until all ingredients are blended. Place fish in shallow baking dish; pour broth mixture over fish and turn until coated on all sides. Cover with plastic wrap and refrigerate 1 to 2 hours, turning once. Lightly spray grill with nonfat cooking spray; prepare a medium-hot grill. Remove fish from marinade; reserve marinade for basting. Cook fish 4 to 6 minutes per side, brushing frequently with marinade, until fish flakes easily with fork. Discard any remaining marinade.

Serves: 4

Nutrition per Serving		Exchanges
Calories	101	3 meat
Carbohydrate	2 grams	
Cholesterol	49 milligrams	
Dietary Fiber	0 grams	
Protein	21 grams	
Sodium	252 milligrams	

SHOPPING LIST:
2 oz. Oriental broth, garlic powder, rosemary, dry mustard, low-sodium soy sauce, 2 oz. red wine vinegar, 1 lb. cod fillets

SCALLOPS KABOBS

EASY - DO AHEAD

INGREDIENTS:
1 lb. fat-free frozen scallops
13½ oz. pineapple chunks in juice, drained
½ cup small mushrooms
1 medium red bell pepper, cut in chunks
1 cup cherry tomatoes
½ cup K.C. Masterpiece honey-teriyaki barbecue sauce

DIRECTIONS:
Place scallops in bowl and cover with cold water to thaw; rinse well. In a medium bowl, combine scallops, pineapple, mushrooms, peppers, and tomatoes; pour barbecue sauce over mixture and marinate 30 minutes at room temperature. Alternately thread metal skewers with scallops, pineapple, mushrooms, peppers, and tomatoes until skewers are filled. Prepare medium-hot grill and lightly spray with nonfat cooking spray. Place skewers on grill and cook 12 to 15 minutes, turning halfway through cooking time. Scallops should be opaque when done. Great served with rice.

Serves: 6

GREAT GRILLS & BARBECUES

Nutrition per Serving

Calories	120
Carbohydrate	21 grams
Cholesterol	9 milligrams
Dietary Fiber	1 gram
Protein	9 grams
Sodium	534 milligrams

Exchanges
1 meat
1 vegetable
1 fruit

SHOPPING LIST:
1 lb. fat-free frozen scallops (large size), 13½ oz. pineapple chunks in juice, 4 oz. mushrooms, 1 medium red bell pepper, ½ pint cherry tomatoes, 4 oz. K.C. Masterpiece honey-teriyaki barbecue sauce

BARBECUE STIR-FRY

EASY

INGREDIENTS:
2 cups broccoli florets
2 cups cauliflower florets
2 medium baked potatoes, cooked and cubed
2 cups sliced carrots
2 cups cherry tomatoes
2 cups sliced mushrooms
½ lb. fat-free cooked shrimp
2 cups barbecue sauce

DIRECTIONS:
Prepare a low-heat grill. Combine all ingredients in a grill basket or barbecue wok and brush with barbecue sauce. Cook, stirring and basting frequently, until vegetables are tender and cooked through. Top with additional barbecue sauce before serving, if desired.

Serves: 6

Nutrition per Serving		Exchanges
Calories	252	2⅓ fruit
Carbohydrate	56 grams	1 starch
Cholesterol	4 milligrams	4 vegetable
Dietary Fiber	6 grams	¼ meat
Protein	8 grams	
Sodium	1,123 milligrams	

SHOPPING LIST:
1 lb. head broccoli, 1 lb. head cauliflower, 2 baking potatoes, ¾ lb. carrots, 1 pint cherry tomatoes, ⅓ lb. mushrooms, ½ lb. fat-free cooked shrimp, 16 oz. barbecue sauce

HOT DOG KABOBS

EASY - DO AHEAD

INGREDIENTS:
1 lb. fat-free hot dogs, cut in 1-inch pieces
1 medium onion, cut in 1-inch pieces
1 medium red bell pepper, cut in 1-inch pieces
1 pint cherry tomatoes
8 oz. pineapple chunks in juice

DIRECTIONS:
Prepare a hot fire and lightly spray grill with nonfat cooking spray. Thread hot dog pieces, onions, red peppers, tomatoes, and pineapple chunks alternately on metal skewers. Grill 8 to 10 minutes, until hot dogs are browned and vegetables are tender.

Serves: 4

GREAT GRILLS & BARBECUES

Nutrition per Serving		Exchanges
Calories	172	1 fruit
Carbohydrate	24 grams	2 vegetable
Cholesterol	38 milligrams	2 meat
Dietary Fiber	2 grams	
Protein	16 grams	
Sodium	1,310 milligrams	

SHOPPING LIST:
1 lb. fat-free hot dogs, 1 medium onion, 1 medium red bell pepper, 1 pint cherry tomatoes, 8 oz. pineapple chunks in juice

BEAN AND RICE BURRITOS

EASY - DO AHEAD

INGREDIENTS:
4 large fat-free flour tortillas
16 oz. fat-free refried beans
1½ cups fat-free cooked rice
1½ cups fat-free shredded Cheddar cheese
14½ oz. can Mexican tomatoes and jalapeños

DIRECTIONS:
Prepare a medium-hot grill and lightly spray with nonfat cooking spray. Cut four 18-inch sheets of heavy-duty foil and set aside. Wrap tortillas in paper towel and heat in microwave on high, about 1 to 2 minutes, just until slightly warmed. Place one tortilla on each foil sheet. Spread ¼ cup beans down center of each tortilla; top with rice, cheese, and tomato/jalapeños. Roll tortillas up burrito-style and place, seam-side down, on foil. Loosely fold foil around tortilla and place packet on grill. Cook 15 to 20 minutes, until cheese is melted and tortilla is heated through. Turn packets halfway through cooking.

Serves: 4

Nutrition per Serving		Exchanges
Calories	430	4⅓ starch
Carbohydrate	77 grams	2 vegetable
Cholesterol	0 milligrams	1½ meat
Dietary Fiber	7 grams	
Protein	27 grams	
Sodium	1,824 milligrams	

SHOPPING LIST:
large fat-free flour tortillas, 16 oz. fat-free refried beans, ½ cup fat-free rice, 6 oz. fat-free shredded Cheddar cheese, 14½ oz. can Mexican-style tomatoes and jalapeños

CAJUN FRIES

EASY - DO AHEAD

INGREDIENTS:
4 large baking potatoes, cut into thin strips
4 tsp. Cajun seasoning

DIRECTIONS:
Prepare a medium-hot grill and lightly spray with nonfat cooking spray. Preheat oven to 425 degrees. Lightly spray baking sheets(s) with nonfat cooking spray. Place potato strips in a single layer on baking sheet(s) and spray lightly with nonfat cooking spray. Sprinkle evenly with Cajun seasoning; turn potatoes and season other side. Bake potatoes in oven 20 minutes; remove from oven and place on grill. Cover grill and cook 15 to 20 minutes, until potatoes are browned and crispy.

Serves: 8

Nutrition per Serving		Exchanges
Calories	86	1 starch
Carbohydrate	20 grams	
Cholesterol	0 milligrams	
Dietary Fiber	2 grams	
Protein	2 grams	
Sodium	110 milligrams	

SHOPPING LIST:
4 large baking potatoes, Cajun seasoning (i.e. Schilling Cajun Seasoning—Great for Chicken)

GRILLED POTATOES

EASY

INGREDIENTS:
2 large baking potatoes
2 large sweet potatoes

DIRECTIONS:
Prepare a medium fire. Wrap each potato in heavy-duty foil and pierce several times with fork through foil. Grill 45 to 60 minutes, until potatoes are tender and soft. Potatoes can be baked on the side while grilling other foods.

Serves: 4

Nutrition per Serving		Exchanges
Calories	131	1¾ starch
Carbohydrate	31 grams	
Cholesterol	0 milligrams	
Dietary Fiber	4 grams	
Protein	3 grams	
Sodium	10 milligrams	

SHOPPING LIST:
2 large baking potatoes, 2 large sweet potatoes

GRILLED RATATOUILLE

EASY - DO AHEAD

INGREDIENTS:
¾ pound eggplant, cut into ¼-inch slices
1 medium Vidalia onion, quartered and separated
1 pint cherry tomatoes
¾ lb. mushrooms
1 large red bell pepper, cut in 1-inch pieces
1 medium yellow squash, sliced ¼-inch thick
1 medium zucchini, sliced ¼-inch thick
½ cup fat-free French salad dressing

DIRECTIONS:
Prepare a medium-hot grill and lightly spray with nonfat cooking spray. Alternately thread eggplant, onion, tomatoes, mushrooms, red pepper, squash, and zucchini on 6 metal skewers; place on large platter. Pour salad dressing over vegetables and turn to coat well; marinate at room temperature 15 to 30 minutes. Place skewers on grill and cook 20 minutes, until tender and cooked through. Remove from skewers and serve with chicken, fish, rice, or potatoes.

Serves: 6

Nutrition per Serving		Exchanges
Calories	90	3 vegetable
Carbohydrate	20 grams	⅓ fruit
Cholesterol	0 milligrams	
Dietary Fiber	3 grams	
Protein	3 grams	
Sodium	222 milligrams	

SHOPPING LIST:
¾ lb. eggplant, 1 medium Vidalia onion, 1 pint cherry tomatoes, ¾ lb. mushrooms, 1 large red bell pepper, 1 medium yellow squash, 1 medium zucchini, 4 oz. fat-free French salad dressing (Western Valley or Kraft Catalina)

GRILLED SUMMER SQUASH

EASY - DO AHEAD

INGREDIENTS:

1 medium zucchini, cut in half
1 medium yellow squash, cut in half
¼ cup Swanson's Oriental broth
1 tbsp. lime juice
⅛ tsp. dried mint leaves
½ tsp. ginger
⅛ tsp. crushed basil
⅛ tsp. pepper
1½ tsp. low-sodium soy sauce

DIRECTIONS:

Place zucchini and squash in a shallow baking dish. In a small bowl, combine broth, lime juice, mint, ginger, basil, pepper, and soy sauce; mix until blended. Pour mixture over vegetables, cover, and refrigerate 1 to 2 hours. Prepare a medium-hot grill; remove vegetables from marinade and cook 5 to 7 minutes per side, brushing frequently with marinade, until golden brown and cooked through. Slice cooked vegetables; toss with remaining marinade and serve.

Serves: 4

Nutrition per Serving		Exchanges
Calories	18	free
Carbohydrate	4 grams	
Cholesterol	0 milligrams	
Dietary Fiber	1 gram	
Protein	1 gram	
Sodium	125 milligrams	

SHOPPING LIST:

1 zucchini, 1 yellow squash, 2 oz. Oriental broth, lime juice, dried mint, ground ginger, dried basil, pepper, low-sodium soy sauce

GREAT GRILLS
& BARBECUES

HONEY-MUSTARD GRILLED ONIONS AND PEPPERS

EASY - DO AHEAD

INGREDIENTS:

1 large Vidalia onion, cut into rings
1 small red bell pepper, cut into rings
1 small yellow bell pepper, cut into rings
¼ cup Wish-Bone fat-free Honey Dijon dressing

DIRECTIONS:

Prepare a medium-hot grill and lightly spray with nonfat cooking spray. Cut a large (about 18-inches) square of heavy-duty foil. Arrange onions and pepper on foil and drizzle with Honey-Dijon dressing. Wrap foil over top and seal packet. Place packet, seam up, on hot grill and cook 20 minutes, until vegetables are tender-crisp; turn packet several times during cooking.

Serves: 4

Nutrition per Serving		Exchanges
Calories	43	2 vegetable
Carbohydrate	10 grams	
Cholesterol	0 milligrams	
Dietary Fiber	2 grams	
Protein	1 gram	
Sodium	63 milligrams	

SHOPPING LIST:

1 large Vidalia onion, 1 small red bell pepper, 1 yellow bell pepper, 2 oz. Wish-Bone fat-free Honey-Dijon dressing

ITALIAN VEGGIE KABOBS

EASY - DO AHEAD

INGREDIENTS:

1 medium yellow squash, cut in 1-inch pieces
1 medium zucchini, cut in 1-inch pieces
1 medium onion, cut into strips
2 cups cherry tomatoes
½ pound mushrooms
1 cup fat-free Italian salad dressing

DIRECTIONS:

In a large bowl, combine vegetables and toss with Italian dressing. Cover with plastic wrap and marinate at least 2 hours or overnight in the refrigerator. Prepare a hot fire and lightly spray with nonfat cooking spray. Thread vegetables alternately on metal skewers and place on prepared grill. Brush frequently with reserved marinade and grill 8 to 10 minutes, until all vegetables are tender-crisp. Slide vegetables off skewers and serve over rice, if desired.

Serves: 4

Nutrition per Serving

Calories	121
Carbohydrate	25 grams
Cholesterol	0 milligrams
Dietary Fiber	4 grams
Protein	4 grams
Sodium	440 milligrams

Exchanges

4 vegetable
⅓ fruit

SHOPPING LIST:

1 yellow squash, 1 zucchini, 1 onion, 1 pint cherry tomatoes, ½ lb. mushrooms, 8 oz. fat-free Italian salad dressing

BAR-B-Q SAUCE

EASY - DO AHEAD

INGREDIENTS:
    1 cup low-sodium ketchup
    3 tbsp. honey
    1 tbsp. minced garlic
    2 drops hot pepper sauce

DIRECTIONS:
    Combine all ingredients in a small bowl and mix until blended smooth. Store in refrigerator up to one week. Great on chicken, "burgers," and potatoes.

Yields: 1 cup

Nutrition per Serving (2 tbsp.)		Exchanges
Calories	41	⅔ fruit
Carbohydrate	11 grams	
Cholesterol	0 milligrams	
Dietary Fiber	< 1 gram	
Protein	< 1 gram	
Sodium	180 milligrams	

SHOPPING LIST:
    8 oz. low-sodium ketchup, 1½ oz. honey, minced garlic, hot pepper sauce

HONEY-MUSTARD BAR-B-Q SAUCE

EASY - DO AHEAD

INGREDIENTS:

1 cup mustard
½ cup barbecue sauce
¼ cup honey
2 tsp. onion powder

DIRECTIONS:

Combine all ingredients in a food processor or blender and process until smooth and blended. Use as sauce or glaze for chicken, turkey, or fish.

Yields: 1 cup

Nutrition per Serving (1 tbsp.)		Exchanges
Calories	24	⅓ fruit
Carbohydrate	4 grams	
Cholesterol	0 milligrams	
Dietary Fiber	< 1 gram	
Protein	< 1 gram	
Sodium	149 milligrams	

SHOPPING LIST:

8 oz. mustard, 4 oz. barbecue sauce, 2 oz. honey, onion powder

PINEAPPLE GINGER MARINADE

EASY - DO AHEAD

INGREDIENTS:
1 cup pineapple juice
2½ tsp. minced garlic
5 tbsp. brown sugar
4½ tbsp. cider vinegar
1½ tsp. ground ginger
1 drop hot pepper sauce

DIRECTIONS:
Place all ingredients in a food processor or blender and blend until smooth. Store in tightly sealed jar in refrigerator 2 to 3 days. Great marinade for chicken or turkey.

Yields: 1 cup

Nutrition per Serving (2 tbsp.)		Exchanges
Calories	51	1 fruit
Carbohydrate	14 grams	
Cholesterol	0 milligrams	
Dietary Fiber	0 grams	
Protein	< 1 gram	
Sodium	3 milligrams	

SHOPPING LIST:
8 oz. pineapple juice, minced garlic, brown sugar, 3 oz. cider vinegar, ground ginger, hot pepper sauce

BARBECUED BANANA SPLITS

EASY

INGREDIENTS:
6 large bananas
2 tsp. lemon juice
2½ cups miniature marshmallows
3 cups fat-free frozen vanilla yogurt
¾ cup fat-free Cool Whip
¾ cup maraschino cherries

DIRECTIONS:

Prepare a hot grill and lightly spray with nonfat cooking spray. Cut six rectangular sheets (about 12-inches) foil and lightly spray with nonfat cooking spray. Peel banana on one side and remove peel; place peel-side down on foil and cut in center (do not cut all the way through). Sprinkle lemon juice down center of banana and top each banana with ½ cup marshmallows. Fold foil loosely over bananas and place on grill. Cook 5 to 6 minutes, until marshmallows are melted. Remove bananas carefully from packets and place each on a separate plate. Top each banana with ½ cup vanilla yogurt, 2 tablespoons fat-free Cool Whip, and cherry. Serve immediately.

Serves: 6

Nutrition per Serving		Exchanges	
Calories	341	4¾ fruit	
Carbohydrate	80 grams	¾ milk	
Cholesterol	0 milligrams		
Dietary Fiber	3 grams		
Protein	6 grams		
Sodium	80 milligrams		

SHOPPING LIST:
6 large bananas, lemon juice, 1 lb. package miniature marshmallows, 48 oz. fat-free frozen vanilla yogurt, 6 oz. fat-free Cool Whip, maraschino cherries

GREAT GRILLS
& BARBECUES

PERFECT
PASTA
AND
RICE

✦ ✦ ✦

PICKING AND PREPARING PERFECT PASTA

Pasta is highly popular because of its versatility, as well as its nutritious content. Plain pasta is relatively low in calories, cholesterol, and fat—watch out for butter or cream sauces that can add several hundred calories and unwanted fat. One cup of plain pasta (2 oz. uncooked) has about 175 calories and .5-1 gram of fat. You can create hundreds of dishes with a variety of vegetables, fat-free cheeses, fat-free pasta sauces, chicken, seafood, and more. Here are some suggestions for selecting and preparing the perfect pasta.

- Use about 4-5 quarts of water in a large pot per pound of pasta.

- Bring the water to a boil and add pasta, stirring with a spoon or wooden fork to prevent sticking.

- Pasta should be cooked "al denté"—it should be slightly undercooked for the best texture and flavor.

- Place hot pasta in a warm serving bowl, toss with sauce and serve immediately.

- Dried pasta takes longer to cook than fresh pasta.

- Immediately drain cooked pasta and only rinse if it is being used in a salad or baked casserole.

- Slightly undercook the pasta when it is being used in baked casseroles.

- Hearty meat and vegetable sauces are great with rotelle or penne pasta.

- Simple tomato or light cheese sauces are perfect for spaghetti, vermicelli, capellini, or angel hair pasta.

- Fettucine or linguini are perfect choices for cream or seafood sauces.

- Jumbo shells or cannelloni are designed to be stuffed with cheese or vegetable fillings.

- Elbow macaroni, ditalini, orzo, or rotini are great additions to soups or baked pasta dishes.

CHEESY-RICE AND PEPPERS

AVERAGE - DO AHEAD

INGREDIENTS:

1 cup fat-free chicken broth
1 cup chopped red bell pepper
1 cup chopped yellow bell pepper
1 cup chopped green bell pepper
1 tbsp. onion powder

2 tsp. minced garlic
2 cups fat-free cooked rice
2 cups cooked wild rice
2 cups fat-free ricotta cheese
1 cup egg substitute
¾ cup fat-free Parmesan cheese

DIRECTIONS:

Preheat oven to 375 degrees. Lightly spray 3-quart casserole with nonfat cooking spray. Pour ¼ cup chicken broth into large saucepan and heat over medium-high heat. Add peppers, onion powder, and garlic to saucepan; cook until vegetables are tender and broth has evaporated. Add ¼ cup broth to saucepan; mix with vegetables. Stir in rice; mix lightly. Spread mixture into prepared casserole. In medium bowl, combine remaining broth, ricotta cheese, egg substitute, and ½ cup Parmesan cheese. Spread cheese mixture over rice and sprinkle with remaining Parmesan cheese. Bake in preheated oven 40 to 45 minutes, until golden brown and cooked through.

Serves: 6

Nutrition per Serving		Exchanges
Calories	236	2 starch
Carbohydrate	37 grams	1 vegetable
Cholesterol	13 milligrams	2 meat
Dietary Fiber	2 grams	
Protein	23 grams	
Sodium	458 milligrams	

SHOPPING LIST:

8 oz. fat-free chicken broth, 1 red bell pepper, 1 yellow bell pepper, 1 green bell pepper, onion powder, minced garlic, fat-free rice, wild rice, 15 oz. fat-free ricotta cheese, 8 oz. egg substitute, 3 oz. fat-free Parmesan cheese

CHICKEN RISOTTO WITH VEGETABLES

AVERAGE - DO AHEAD

INGREDIENTS:

1 cup sliced zucchini
1 cup sliced yellow squash
1½ cups sliced mushrooms
¾ cup chopped onions
2 tsp. minced garlic
½ tsp. poultry seasoning
1¾ cups uncooked orzo

36 oz. fat-free chicken broth
1½ cups fat-free chicken
tenders, cooked and diced
1 cup frozen peas, thawed
and drained
¾ cup fat-free Parmesan
cheese

DIRECTIONS:

Lightly spray a large saucepan with nonfat cooking spray and heat over medium-high heat. Add zucchini and squash to saucepan and cook 3 to 4 minutes, until vegetables are tender. Remove from pan and set aside. Lightly respray saucepan and heat over medium heat. Add mushrooms, onions, garlic, and poultry seasoning; cook 3 to 4 minutes, until vegetables are tender. Stir in orzo; cook until lightly browned. Heat chicken broth in another saucepan or microwave until hot; gradually add to saucepan with orzo, stirring constantly, and cook 15 minutes, until liquid is absorbed and orzo is tender. Stir in diced chicken, peas, and squash mixture; cook 4 to 5 minutes, until heated through. Sprinkle with Parmesan cheese; mix lightly.

Serves: 6

PERFECT PASTA AND RICE

Nutrition per Serving		Exchanges
Calories	222	1 meat
Carbohydrates	36 grams	1⅔ starch
Cholesterol	24 milligrams	2 vegetable
Dietary Fiber	2 grams	
Protein	18 grams	
Sodium	509 milligrams	

SHOPPING LIST:

1 small zucchini, 1 small yellow squash, ¼ to ⅓ lb. mushrooms, 1 large onion, minced garlic, poultry seasoning, orzo, 3–14½ oz. cans fat-free chicken broth, ½ lb. fat-free chicken tenders, 6 oz. frozen peas, 3 oz. fat-free Parmesan cheese

CHILI AND CHEESE RICE CASSEROLE

EASY - DO AHEAD

INGREDIENTS:

1 tbsp. vegetable broth
1 cup chopped onion
½ cup chopped celery
3 cups fat-free rice, cooked
15 oz. canned corn kernels, drained
4 oz. chopped green chilies
½ tsp. onion powder
2 cups fat-free shredded Cheddar cheese
1½ cups skim milk
¾ tsp. chili powder
pepper to taste

DIRECTIONS:

Preheat oven to 350 degrees. Lightly spray 2-quart casserole with nonfat cooking spray. Combine all ingredients in prepared casserole and mix well. Bake in preheated oven 45 minutes.

Serves: 6

Nutrition per Serving		Exchanges
Calories	238	2 starch
Carbohydrate	42 grams	2 vegetable
Cholesterol	1 milligram	1 meat
Dietary Fiber	3 grams	
Protein	17 grams	
Sodium	645 milligrams	

SHOPPING LIST:

vegetable broth, 1 medium onion, 1 to 2 stalks celery, 1 cup fat-free rice (raw), 15 oz. canned corn kernels, 4 oz. can diced green chilies, onion powder, 8 oz. fat-free shredded Cheddar cheese, 12 oz. skim milk, chili powder, pepper

"FRIED" RICE

AVERAGE - DO AHEAD

INGREDIENTS:
½ cup egg substitute
1 cup fat-free uncooked rice
14½ oz. can fat-free chicken broth
1 tsp. minced garlic
¼ tsp. onion powder
¾ cup frozen peas
¾ cup carrot slices

DIRECTIONS:
Lightly spray large nonstick skillet with nonfat cooking spray and heat over medium heat. Add egg substitute and cook, stirring frequently, until set; remove from skillet, cut into small pieces, and set aside. Respray skillet with nonfat cooking spray and heat over medium heat. Add rice and cook, stirring constantly, until lightly browned. Stir in chicken broth, garlic, and onion powder; increase heat to high and bring to a boil. Immediately reduce heat to low, cover and simmer 15 minutes. Add peas and carrots to rice and cook until most of the liquid is absorbed. Stir in egg pieces and heat 5 minutes. Serve immediately or place rice in casserole and reheat before serving (it may be necessary to add a little broth to rice if reheating).

Serves: 4

PERFECT PASTA AND RICE

Nutrition per Serving		Exchanges
Calories	169	2 starch
Carbohydrate	34 grams	½ vegetable
Cholesterol	0 milligrams	
Dietary Fiber	3 grams	
Protein	7 grams	
Sodium	355 milligrams	

SHOPPING LIST:
4 oz. egg substitute, fat-free rice, 14½ oz. can fat-free chicken broth, minced garlic, onion powder, 6 oz. frozen peas, 6 oz. frozen sliced carrots

GREEN CHILE CHEESE RICE

EASY - DO AHEAD

INGREDIENTS:
1 cup fat-free rice (raw)
2 cups fat-free sour cream
7 oz. can chopped green chilies
2 cups fat-free shredded Cheddar cheese
½ cup fat-free Parmesan cheese

DIRECTIONS:
Preheat oven to 350 degrees. Lightly spray 1½- to 2-quart baking dish with nonfat cooking spray. Cook rice according to package directions. In a small bowl, combine sour cream and green chilies. Layer ½ rice, ½ sour cream mixture, and 1 cup Cheddar cheese in casserole. Repeat layers and top with Parmesan cheese. Bake in preheated oven 35 to 40 minutes, until cheese is lightly browned and mixture is bubbly.

Serves: 6

Nutrition per Serving		Exchanges
Calories	223	1⅔ starch
Carbohydrate	25 grams	2½ meat
Cholesterol	0 milligrams	
Dietary Fiber	1 gram	
Protein	21 grams	
Sodium	877 milligrams	

SHOPPING LIST:
fat-free rice, 16 oz. fat-free sour cream, 7 oz. can diced green chilies (mild), 8 oz. fat-free shredded Cheddar cheese, 2 oz. fat-free Parmesan cheese

HERBED RICE

EASY - DO AHEAD

INGREDIENTS:
1 cup fat-free rice, uncooked
14½ oz. can fat-free chicken broth
1 cup sliced zucchini
1 cup corn kernels
½ tsp. pepper
1 tsp. onion powder
1 cup diced tomatoes with roasted garlic
1 tsp. dried basil

DIRECTIONS:
In a medium saucepan, combine rice, chicken broth, zucchini, corn, pepper, and onion powder and heat over high heat to boiling. Reduce heat to low, cover, and simmer 15 to 20 minutes, until liquid is absorbed. Stir in tomatoes and basil; cook 10 to 15 minutes, until heated through.

Serves: 4

PERFECT PASTA AND RICE

Nutrition per Serving		Exchanges
Calories	202	1 starch
Carbohydrate	48 grams	3 vegetable
Cholesterol	0 milligrams	1 fruit
Dietary Fiber	2 grams	
Protein	5 grams	
Sodium	470 milligrams	

SHOPPING LIST:
fat-free rice, 14½ oz. can fat-free chicken broth, 2 zucchini, 8 oz. corn kernels, pepper, onion powder, 14 oz. can diced tomatoes with roasted garlic, dried basil

ITALIAN BEEF AND RICE

AVERAGE

INGREDIENTS:
1 lb. fat-free beef crumbles
1 tbsp. onion powder
1 tsp. minced garlic
½ cup chopped green bell pepper
10¾ oz. fat-free beef broth
14½ oz. diced tomatoes with roasted garlic
1¾ cups fat-free instant rice, uncooked

DIRECTIONS:
Lightly spray large nonstick skillet with nonfat cooking spray and heat over medium-high heat. Add beef crumbles, onion powder, minced garlic, and bell pepper to skillet and cook until vegetables are tender and beef is cooked through; drain well and return to skillet. Add broth and tomatoes to beef mixture and bring to a boil over high heat. Remove skillet from heat; immediately stir in rice, cover, and let stand 15 minutes, until rice is tender. Serve immediately.

Serves: 6

Nutrition per Serving		Exchanges
Calories	196	2 starch
Carbohydrate	30 grams	1⅓ meat
Cholesterol	0 milligrams	
Dietary Fiber	4 grams	
Protein	16 grams	
Sodium	786 milligrams	

SHOPPING LIST:
1 lb. fat-free beef crumbles (Morningstar Farms), onion powder, minced garlic powder, 1 small green pepper, 10¾ oz. fat-free beef broth, 14½ oz. diced tomatoes with roasted garlic, fat-free instant rice

LEMON RICE

EASY - DO AHEAD

INGREDIENTS:
2 cups fat-free chicken broth
⅓ cup chopped green onions
1 tsp. grated lemon peel
1 cup fat-free rice (raw)
1 tbsp. lemon juice
⅛ tsp. ground pepper

DIRECTIONS:
Lightly spray medium nonstick saucepan with nonfat cooking spray. Add 2 teaspoons chicken broth and heat over medium-high heat. Add green onions and lemon peel and cook 2 minutes. Add rice, remaining chicken broth, lemon juice, and pepper. Bring mixture to a boil over high heat; reduce heat to low, cover, and simmer 20 minutes.

Serves: 4

Nutrition per Serving		Exchanges
Calories	85	1 starch
Carbohydrate	18 grams	
Cholesterol	0 milligrams	
Dietary Fiber	1 gram	
Protein	2 grams	
Sodium	228 milligrams	

SHOPPING LIST:
15 oz. can fat-free chicken broth, 1 to 2 green onions, grated lemon peel, fat-free rice, lemon juice, pepper

PERFECT PASTA AND RICE

ORIENTAL RICE PILAF

EASY - DO AHEAD

INGREDIENTS:

¾ cup fat-free rice (raw)
14½ oz. can Swanson's Oriental broth
¼ c. chopped red and green bell peppers
¾ cup frozen broccoli, carrots, and water chestnuts

DIRECTIONS:

Lightly spray medium saucepan with nonfat cooking spray and heat over medium heat. Add rice to saucepan and cook, stirring constantly, 1 minute. Pour broth into saucepan; increase heat to high and bring broth to a boil. Immediately reduce heat to low, cover, and simmer until most of the liquid is absorbed (this will depend on whether Minute Rice or regular rice is used). Stir in peppers and frozen vegetables. Cover saucepan and cook 15 minutes, until vegetables are tender and heated through.

Serves: 4

Nutrition per Serving		Exchanges
Calories	122	1 starch
Carbohydrate	28 grams	2 vegetable
Cholesterol	0 milligrams	
Dietary Fiber	1 gram	
Protein	3 grams	
Sodium	230 milligrams	

SHOPPING LIST:

fat-free rice, 14½ oz. can Swanson's Oriental broth, 1 small red bell pepper, 1 small green pepper, 10 to 16 oz. frozen vegetable mix (broccoli, carrots, water chestnuts)

RED BEANS AND RICE

AVERAGE - DO AHEAD

INGREDIENTS:
1 medium sweet potato, peeled and cubed
1 cup chopped onion
½ cup chopped yellow bell pepper
1½ tsp. minced garlic
2 15-oz. cans fat-free red kidney beans, drained
2 cups fat-free chicken broth
¼ tsp. pepper
3 cups fat-free cooked rice

DIRECTIONS:
Lightly spray medium saucepan with nonfat cooking spray and heat over medium heat. Add potato, onion, bell pepper, and garlic to saucepan and cook until potatoes and onion are tender. Add beans, chicken broth, and pepper to pan; bring to a boil over medium heat. Stir in rice, cover, and simmer over low heat 30 to 35 minutes.

Serves: 6

Nutrition per Serving		Exchanges
Calories	250	3 starch
Carbohydrate	49 grams	1 vegetable
Cholesterol	0 milligrams	
Dietary Fiber	10 grams	
Protein	12 grams	
Sodium	650 milligrams	

SHOPPING LIST:
1 medium sweet potato, 1 medium onion, 1 small yellow bell pepper, minced garlic, 2 15-oz. cans fat-free red kidney beans, 16 oz. fat-free chicken broth, pepper, 1 cup fat-free rice

RICE AND VEGETABLES PROVENCAL

EASY - DO AHEAD

INGREDIENTS:

¼ cup water
¼ cup fat-free chicken broth
1 tsp. minced garlic
1 tbsp. tomato paste
1 small zucchini, cubed
1 small yellow squash, cubed
1 large tomato, chopped

1 medium green pepper, chopped
½ cup chopped red onion
1 cup sliced mushrooms
1 tbsp. dried parsley
1 tbsp. dried basil
¼ tsp. pepper
2 cups fat-free cooked rice

DIRECTIONS:

Combine water and chicken broth in large saucepan or Dutch oven; add garlic and tomato paste and heat over medium-high heat 5 to 7 minutes. Add zucchini, yellow squash, tomato, green pepper, onion, and mushrooms to pan. Cover and simmer over low heat, about 10 to 15 minutes. Stir in parsley, basil, and pepper and mix until blended. Serve over cooked rice. Vegetables can be prepared ahead of time and reheated just before serving.

Serves: 4

Nutrition per Serving		Exchanges
Calories	134	1 starch
Carbohydrate	29 grams	2 vegetable
Cholesterol	0 milligrams	
Dietary Fiber	4 grams	
Protein	4 grams	
Sodium	155 milligrams	

SHOPPING LIST:

2 oz. fat-free chicken broth, minced garlic, tomato paste, 1 small zucchini, 1 small yellow squash, 1 large tomato, 1 medium green bell pepper, 1 small red onion, ¼ lb. mushrooms, dried parsley, dried basil, pepper, ¾ cup fat-free rice

SPANISH RICE

EASY - DO AHEAD

INGREDIENTS:

2 tbsp. fat-free chicken broth
1 cup fat-free rice (raw)
¾ cup chopped onion
½ cup sliced green pepper
2 tsp. chili powder
1 cup crushed tomatoes
2 cups water

DIRECTIONS:

Lightly spray a large nonstick skillet with nonfat cooking spray. Add chicken broth and heat over medium-high heat. Stir in rice and cook until rice is lightly browned. Add onions, green pepper, chili powder, tomatoes and water. Cover and simmer over low heat 20 to 25 minutes, until all liquid has been absorbed.

Serves: 4

Nutrition per Serving		Exchanges
Calories	154	2 starch
Carbohydrate	33 grams	
Cholesterol	0 milligrams	
Dietary Fiber	< 1 gram	
Protein	4 grams	
Sodium	155 milligrams	

SHOPPING LIST:

1 oz. fat-free chicken broth (canned, bouillon cube, or granules), fat-free rice, 1 medium onion, 1 green pepper, chili powder, 1 large fresh tomato or 15 oz. can crushed tomatoes

WILD RICE AND BARLEY

AVERAGE - DO AHEAD

INGREDIENTS:
2 cups fat-free beef broth
1 tbsp. onion powder
½ tsp. thyme
6 oz. wild rice
¼ cup pearled barley, uncooked
1 tbsp. dried parsley

DIRECTIONS:
Lightly spray large nonstick skillet with nonfat cooking spray and heat over medium heat. Add 1 tablespoon beef broth, onion powder, and thyme to skillet and cook 1 minute. Add rice and barley to skillet and cook 1 minute, stirring constantly. Add remaining broth and bring to a boil over high heat. Reduce heat to low, cover, and simmer 45 to 60 minutes, until rice is tender. Stir in parsley.

Serves: 8

Nutrition per Serving		Exchanges
Calories	102	1⅓ starch
Carbohydrate	22 grams	
Cholesterol	0 milligrams	
Dietary Fiber	1 gram	
Protein	4 grams	
Sodium	116 milligrams	

SHOPPING LIST:
16 oz. fat-free beef broth, onion powder, thyme, 6 oz. wild rice, pearled barley, dried parsley

PERFECT PASTA AND RICE

BULGUR WITH MUSHROOMS

AVERAGE

INGREDIENTS:
2 cups + 2 tbsp. fat-free chicken broth
2 tbsp. onion powder
¾ cup sliced mushrooms
2 tbsp. chopped green pepper
1 cup uncooked bulgur
¼ tsp. pepper

DIRECTIONS:
Lightly spray large nonstick skillet with nonfat cooking spray. Pour 2 tablespoons chicken broth into skillet and heat over medium-high heat. Add onion powder, mushrooms, and green pepper to skillet; cook, stirring constantly, until tender. Add remaining chicken broth, bulgur, and pepper. Reduce heat to low, cover and simmer 15 to 20 minutes, until liquid is absorbed and bulgur is cooked through.

Serves: 4

PERFECT PASTA AND RICE

Nutrition per Serving		Exchanges
Calories	138	1½ starch
Carbohydrate	30 grams	1 vegetable
Cholesterol	0 milligrams	
Dietary Fiber	8 grams	
Protein	5 grams	
Sodium	258 milligrams	

SHOPPING LIST:
16 oz. fat-free chicken broth, onion powder, ¼ lb. mushrooms, green bell pepper, bulgur (cracked wheat), pepper

CINCINNATI CHILI

EASY - DO AHEAD - FREEZE

INGREDIENTS:

1 lb. fat-free beef crumbles (Morningstar Farms)
1½ tbsp. onion powder
1½ tbsp. minced garlic
1½ cups low-sodium tomato sauce
¾ cup water
2 tsp. cider vinegar
2 tbsp. chili powder
1½ tsp. cinnamon
1¼ tbsp. unsweetened cocoa powder
¼ tsp. nutmeg
¾ cup canned red kidney beans, drained
1½ cups cooked spaghetti
¾ cup fat-free shredded Cheddar cheese (optional)

DIRECTIONS:

Lightly spray large saucepan with nonfat cooking spray; heat over medium heat. Add beef crumbles, onion powder, and minced garlic; cook until browned. Add tomato sauce, water, vinegar, chili powder, cinnamon, cocoa, and nutmeg; heat over medium-high heat to boiling. Reduce heat to low, cover; simmer 15 to 20 minutes, until sauce thickens. Stir in beans; mix lightly. Spoon cooked spaghetti into bowls; top with chili. Sprinkle with Cheddar cheese, if desired.

Serves: 6

Nutrition per Serving		Exchanges
Calories	223	2 starch
Carbohydrate	30 grams	2⅓ meat
Cholesterol	0 mg	
Dietary Fiber	7 grams	
Protein	23 grams	
Sodium	646 milligrams	

SHOPPING LIST:

1 lb. fat-free beef crumbles (Morningstar Farms), onion powder, minced garlic, 12 oz. low-sodium tomato sauce, cider vinegar, chili powder, cinnamon, unsweetened cocoa powder, nutmeg, 6 oz. can red kidney beans, 3 oz. spaghetti, 3 oz. fat-free shredded Cheddar cheese (optional)

COUSCOUS WITH SUN-DRIED TOMATOES

EASY - DO AHEAD

INGREDIENTS:

¾ cup sun-dried tomatoes, sliced thin
½ cup onion flakes
¾ tsp. garlic powder
6 cups fat-free chicken broth
2½ cups instant couscous

DIRECTIONS:

Combine tomatoes, onion flakes, garlic powder, and chicken broth; bring to a boil over high heat. Stir in couscous; reduce temperature to low, cover, and simmer 5 to 8 minutes, until all liquid is absorbed.

Serves: 6

Nutrition per Serving		Exchanges
Calories	332	4 vegetable
Carbohydrate	66 grams	3 starch
Cholesterol	0 milligrams	
Dietary Fiber	12 grams	
Protein	11 grams	
Sodium	915 milligrams	

SHOPPING LIST:

1 package sun-dried tomatoes (not oil-packed), onion flakes, garlic powder, 3 15½-oz. cans fat-free chicken broth, instant couscous

GREEN ONION COUSCOUS

EASY - DO AHEAD

INGREDIENTS:

1 cup couscous
2 tbsp. fat-free chicken broth
3 cups chopped tomatoes
3 whole green onions, sliced
¼ tsp. garlic powder
1½ tsp. ground cumin
pepper to taste

DIRECTIONS:

Cook couscous according to package directions; stir occasionally with a fork to separate. Stir in 1½ tablespoons chicken broth and mix well; cool at room temperature 10 to 15 minutes. In a separate bowl, combine tomatoes, green onions, garlic powder, cumin, pepper, and remaining chicken broth and mix well. Stir mixture into couscous; refrigerate at least 1 hour before serving.

Serves: 6

Nutrition per Serving		Exchanges
Calories	141	1 starch
Carbohydrate	29 grams	2½ vegetable
Cholesterol	0 milligrams	
Dietary Fiber	6 grams	
Protein	5 grams	
Sodium	215 milligrams	

SHOPPING LIST:

1 box couscous, 1 oz. fat-free chicken broth (or chicken bouillon cube + water), 3 large tomatoes, 3 green onions, garlic powder, ground cumin, pepper

PERFECT PASTA AND RICE

KASHA WITH VEGETABLES

EASY - DO AHEAD - FREEZE

INGREDIENTS:

1 tbsp. vegetable broth
1 cup chopped onion
½ cup chopped celery
1 cup chopped green pep-
  per
½ tsp. minced garlic
¾ tsp. oregano

1 tsp. chili powder
¾ cup kasha
2½ cups crushed tomatoes,
  liquid reserved
pepper to taste
1 cup fat-free shredded
  Monterey Jack cheese

DIRECTIONS:

Lightly spray large nonstick skillet with nonfat cooking spray. Add vegetable broth to skillet and heat over medium-high heat. Stir in onion, celery, green pepper, and garlic and cook 5 to 7 minutes, until vegetables are soft. Add oregano, chili powder, kasha, tomatoes with liquid, and pepper. Bring to a boil over high heat; reduce heat to low, cover, and simmer 10 to 15 minutes, until kasha is cooked through. Sprinkle cheese over kasha, cover skillet, and let stand until cheese is melted. This can be prepared ahead and refrigerated and frozen after kasha is finished cooking. Sprinkle cheese on top after reheating and let stand until cheese is melted.

Serves: 6

Nutrition per Serving

Calories	172
Carbohydrate	24 grams
Cholesterol	0 milligrams
Dietary Fiber	3 grams
Protein	16 grams
Sodium	449 milligrams

Exchanges

1 vegetable
1⅓ starch
1 meat

SHOPPING LIST:

fat-free vegetable broth, 1 large onion, 1 medium stalk celery, 1 green pepper, minced garlic, oregano, chili powder, kasha or buckwheat groats, 2 16-oz. cans crushed tomatoes, pepper, 4 oz. fat-free shredded Monterey Jack cheese

LENTIL PILAF

AVERAGE - DO AHEAD

INGREDIENTS:

¼ cup diced green bell pepper
¼ cup diced red bell pepper
½ cup diced carrots
½ cup diced zucchini
¼ cup diced yellow squash
1 tbsp. onion powder
¾ cup dried lentils
1½ cups fat-free vegetable broth
1 tsp. minced garlic

DIRECTIONS:

Lightly spray a large nonstick skillet with nonfat cooking spray and heat over medium-high heat. Add peppers, carrots, zucchini, and squash to skillet; sprinkle with onion powder and cook 5 to 7 minutes, stirring constantly, until vegetables soften. Add lentils, vegetable broth, and garlic to skillet; increase heat to high and bring mixture to a boil. Immediately reduce heat to low, cover and simmer 10 to 15 minutes. Great with barbecued scallops or shrimp.

Serves: 6

Nutrition per Serving		Exchanges
Calories	102	1 starch
Carbohydrate	18 grams	½ vegetable
Cholesterol	0 milligrams	½ meat
Dietary Fiber	4 grams	
Protein	7 grams	
Sodium	156 milligrams	

SHOPPING LIST:

1 small green bell pepper, 1 small red bell pepper, 1 to 2 carrots, 1 small zucchini, 1 small yellow squash, onion powder, dried lentils, 14½ oz. fat-free vegetable broth, minced garlic

VEGETABLE PAELLA

EASY - DO AHEAD

INGREDIENTS:

½ cup diced red bell pepper
½ cup diced green bell pepper
1 cup chopped onion
1 tsp. minced garlic
1½ cups fat-free rice (raw)
3 cups fat-free chicken broth
2 10-oz. packages frozen chopped spinach, thawed and drained
15 oz. can low sodium tomatoes, chopped
¾ tsp. paprika
15 oz. can fat-free black beans, drained
½ cup peas

DIRECTIONS:

Lightly spray large saucepan with nonfat cooking spray and heat over medium-high heat. Add bell pepper, onion, and garlic and cook until vegetables are soft and tender. Add rice, chicken broth, spinach, tomatoes, and paprika and increase heat to high. Bring mixture to a boil; reduce heat to low, cover, and simmer, 13 to 15 minutes, until liquid is almost absorbed. Stir in black beans and peas and heat through.

Serves: 6

Nutrition per Serving

Calories	273
Carbohydrate	56 grams
Cholesterol	0 milligrams
Dietary Fiber	6 grams
Protein	11 grams
Sodium	430 milligrams

Exchanges

3 starch
2 vegetable

SHOPPING LIST:

1 small red bell pepper, 1 small green pepper, 1 large onion, minced garlic, 1½ cups fat-free rice, 2 15½-oz. cans fat-free chicken broth (chicken bouillon cubes or granules), 2 10-oz. packages frozen chopped spinach, 15 oz. can low sodium chopped tomatoes, paprika, 15 oz. can fat-free black beans, frozen peas

ANGEL HAIR PASTA WITH SMOKED TURKEY

AVERAGE

INGREDIENTS:

9 oz. angel hair pasta
1 cup +1 tbsp. fat-free chicken broth
1 tbsp. onion powder
1 tbsp. minced garlic
1 cup frozen Chinese pea pods

¼ pound fat-free smoked deli turkey, thinly sliced
¾ cup canned sliced water chestnuts
1 cup red bell pepper, thinly sliced
⅛ tsp. pepper

DIRECTIONS:

Prepare pasta according to package directions; drain well and set aside in a large bowl. Lightly spray a large nonstick skillet with nonfat cooking spray; pour 1 tablespoon chicken broth into skillet and heat over medium-high heat about 1 minute. Add garlic, bell pepper, water chestnuts, and pea pods to broth; reduce heat to medium, cover; cook over medium-low heat 5 minutes. Add turkey, onion powder, and pepper to vegetables, cover, and cook over medium-low heat 5 minutes. Pour 1 cup chicken broth into microwave-safe dish or saucepan and heat to almost boiling. Pour hot broth over pasta, add chicken-vegetable mixture and toss until well mixed. Serve immediately.

Serves: 6

Nutrition per Serving		Exchanges
Calories	205	2 starch
Carbohydrate	39 grams	2 vegetable
Cholesterol	7 milligrams	
Dietary Fiber	< 1 gram	
Protein	9 grams	
Sodium	366 milligrams	

SHOPPING LIST:

9 oz. angel hair pasta, 14½ oz. can fat-free chicken broth, onion powder, minced garlic, 10 oz. frozen Chinese pea pods, ¼ lb. fat-free cooked smoked deli turkey breast, 6 oz. can sliced water chestnuts, 1 medium red bell pepper, pepper

CHICKEN AND BROCCOLI FETTUCCINE ALFREDO

AVERAGE

INGREDIENTS:

12 oz. fettuccine
1 lb. fat-free chicken tenders
1¼ cups chopped onion
2½ cups sliced mushrooms
13½ oz. can fat-free chicken broth

1 cup fat-free cream cheese, softened
2 10-oz. packages frozen broccoli florets
1 tsp. white pepper

DIRECTIONS:

Prepare fettuccine according to package directions; drain and keep warm. Lightly spray a large nonstick skillet with nonfat cooking spray and heat over medium-high heat. Add chicken tenders and cook until chicken is no longer pink and is cooked through; remove chicken from skillet and set aside. Lightly respray skillet; sauté onions until soft and transparent, about 5 minutes. Add mushrooms and continue cooking until mushrooms are tender. Stir in chicken broth and cream cheese; heat over medium-high heat until mixture almost comes to a boil and thickens. Add chicken, broccoli, and pepper to skillet; cook over medium heat until heated through. Toss with fettuccine; serve immediately.

Serves: 8

PERFECT PASTA AND RICE

Nutrition per Serving

Calories	162
Carbohydrate	19 grams
Cholesterol	50 milligrams
Dietary Fiber	1 gram
Protein	20 grams
Sodium	445 milligrams

Exchanges

1 starch
1 vegetable
2 meat

SHOPPING LIST:

12 oz. fettuccine, 1 lb. fat-free chicken tenders, 2 small onions, ½ lb. mushrooms, 13½ oz. can fat-free chicken broth, 8 oz. fat-free cream cheese, 2 10-oz. packages frozen broccoli florets, white pepper

CHICKEN AND PASTA WITH ORANGE DRESSING

EASY - DO AHEAD

INGREDIENTS:
12 oz. spaghetti
½ cup orange juice frozen concentrate, thawed
¾ cup fat-free mayonnaise
¼ tsp. dry mustard
3 cups fat-free chicken tenders, cooked
1½ cups diced celery

DIRECTIONS:
Cook spaghetti according to package directions; drain and rinse. In a small bowl, combine orange juice concentrate, mayonnaise, and mustard and mix until blended. In a large bowl, combine spaghetti, chicken, and celery; toss with dressing and chill several hours before serving.

Serves: 8

Nutrition per Serving		Exchanges
Calories	291	3 vegetable
Carbohydrate	44 grams	2 starch
Cholesterol	41 milligrams	2 meat
Dietary Fiber	1 gram	
Protein	25 grams	
Sodium	346 milligrams	

SHOPPING LIST:
12 oz. spaghetti, 4 oz. frozen orange juice concentrate, 6 oz. fat-free mayonnaise, dry mustard, 2 lbs. fat-free chicken tenders, 4 stalks celery

CHICKEN PEPPER PASTA

AVERAGE

INGREDIENTS:

1½ lbs fat-free chicken
   breasts
1 tsp. garlic powder
1½ tsp. onion powder
½ tsp. pepper
4 oz. angel hair pasta
1½ cups sliced yellow bell
   pepper

1 cup sliced green bell pepper
1½ cups sliced red bell pepper
3 cups sliced Vidalia onion
3 tsp. minced garlic
1 tsp. dried basil
½ cup fat-free Parmesan
   cheese

DIRECTIONS:
Preheat oven to 375 degrees. Lightly spray a 9x13-inch baking dish with nonfat cooking spray. Place chicken breasts in dish; sprinkle both sides with garlic powder, onion powder, and pepper. Bake in preheated oven 20 to 25 minutes, until no longer pink and cooked through. Cut chicken breasts into thin slices and keep warm. Cook pasta according to package directions; drain and keep warm. Lightly spray a large nonstick skillet with nonfat cooking spray and heat over medium-high heat. Add peppers, onions, garlic, and basil to skillet and cook 1 to 2 minutes, stirring frequently. Reduce heat to medium, cover skillet and continue cooking until vegetables are soft, about 25 minutes. Add sliced chicken to skillet and mix lightly; cook 5 minutes, until heated through. Spoon pasta onto plates; top with chicken-vegetable mixture and sprinkle with Parmesan cheese.

Serves: 6

Nutrition per Serving

Calories	186
Carbohydrate	22 grams
Cholesterol	53 milligrams
Dietary Fiber	2 grams
Protein	23 grams
Sodium	255 milligrams

Exchanges
1 starch
1½ vegetable
2 meat

SHOPPING LIST:
1½ lbs. fat-free chicken breasts, garlic powder, onion powder, pepper, 4 oz. angel hair pasta, 2 yellow bell peppers, 1 green bell pepper, 2 red bell peppers, 3 Vidalia onions (or other sweet variety), minced garlic, dried basil, 2 oz. fat-free Parmesan cheese

CREAMY VEGETABLE PASTA

AVERAGE

INGREDIENTS:

12 oz. pasta shells
2 cups fat-free cottage cheese
¼ cup + 2 tbsp. fat-free
  Parmesan cheese
¼ tsp. hot chili flakes
2 tbsp. fat-free chicken broth
1 medium onion, chopped

½ tsp. minced garlic
1 cup broccoli florets
1 cup cauliflower florets
1 small red bell pepper,
  sliced
1 large carrot, shredded
¼ lb. sliced mushrooms

DIRECTIONS:

Cook pasta according to package directions and drain well. Combine cottage cheese, ¼ cup Parmesan cheese, and hot chili flakes in a food processor or blender and process until smooth and creamy. Lightly spray large nonstick skillet with nonfat cooking spray. Add chicken broth to skillet and heat over medium-high heat. Add onion and garlic and cook just until tender, about 2 to 3 minutes. Add broccoli, cauliflower, red pepper, and carrots; cook 5 to 7 minutes over medium heat, until vegetables are tender-crisp. Add mushrooms and cook just until softened. Stir in cottage cheese mixture and cook over low heat until heated through. In a large bowl or serving platter, combine pasta with vegetables and toss lightly. Sprinkle with remaining Parmesan cheese and serve immediately.

Serves: 8

Nutrition per Serving		Exchanges
Calories	227	2 starch
Carbohydrate	40 grams	2 vegetable
Cholesterol	5 milligrams	½ meat
Dietary Fiber	1 gram	
Protein	15 grams	
Sodium	231 milligrams	

SHOPPING LIST:

12 oz. pasta shells, 16 oz. fat-free cottage cheese, 1½ oz. fat-free Parmesan cheese, hot chili flakes, 1 oz. fat-free chicken broth, 1 medium onion, minced garlic, ½ lb. broccoli, 1 lb. cauliflower, 1 large carrot, ¼ lb. mushrooms, 1 small red bell pepper

LINGUINE WITH CLAM SAUCE

EASY - DO AHEAD

INGREDIENTS:
6 oz. linguine
1 cup fat-free pasta sauce
14½ oz. can diced tomatoes with roasted garlic, drained
¾ tsp. onion powder
½ tsp. Italian seasoning
15 oz. canned clams, drained
1 tbs. lemon juice

DIRECTIONS:
Prepare linguine according to package directions; drain well and keep warm. In a small saucepan over medium-high heat, combine pasta sauce, diced tomatoes, onion powder, and Italian seasoning; bring to a boil, reduce heat and simmer 10 minutes. Add clams and lemon juice to pasta sauce; increase heat to medium and cook 10 minutes, until heated through. Combine clam sauce with linguine; toss lightly and serve.

Serves: 4

Nutrition per Serving		Exchanges
Calories	234	1 meat
Carbohydrate	42 grams	2 vegetable
Cholesterol	19 milligrams	2 starch
Dietary Fiber	< 1 gram	
Protein	14 grams	
Sodium	1,285 milligrams	

SHOPPING LIST:
6 oz. linguine, 8 oz. fat-free pasta sauce, 14½ oz. diced tomatoes with roasted garlic, onion powder, Italian seasoning, 2 7½-oz. cans fat-free clams, lemon juice

MACARONI AND CHEESE

AVERAGE - DO AHEAD

INGREDIENTS:

2 tbsp. reconstituted Butter
Buds
¼ cup chopped onions
½ cup chopped green bell
pepper
2 tbsp. flour
2 cups skim milk

¾ tsp. dry mustard
¾ tsp. hot pepper sauce
2 cups fat-free shredded
Cheddar cheese
2 cups cooked macaroni
1 cup chopped tomatoes

DIRECTIONS:

Preheat oven to 350 degrees. Lightly spray baking dish with
nonfat cooking spray. Lightly spray nonstick skillet with
nonfat cooking spray. Add reconstituted Butter Buds to skillet and heat over medium-high heat. Add onions and bell
pepper; cook until tender, about 5 minutes. Blend in flour;
gradually add milk, mustard, and hot pepper sauce and
cook over medium heat, stirring constantly, until mixture
thickens. Add cheese and mix until cheese is melted. Remove sauce from heat and stir in macaroni and tomatoes
until mixed well. Place mixture into prepared baking dish
and bake in preheated oven 20 to 25 minutes.

Serves: 8

Nutrition per Serving		Exchanges
Calories	132	1 starch
Carbohydrate	18 grams	½ vegetable
Cholesterol	1 milligram	1 meat
Dietary Fiber	1 gram	
Protein	12 grams	
Sodium	371 milligrams	

SHOPPING LIST:

Butter Buds flavored granules, 1 small onion, 1 small green
pepper, flour, 1 pint skim milk, dry mustard, hot pepper
sauce, 8 oz. fat-free shredded Cheddar cheese, 8 oz. macaroni, 1 large tomato

NOODLE KUGEL

EASY - DO AHEAD - FREEZE

INGREDIENTS:
  8 oz. yolk-free noodles
  1½ cups egg substitute
  1 cup fat-free sour cream
  1 cup fat-free cottage cheese
  ½ cup sugar
  ½ cup skim milk
  ¼ cup golden raisins
  ½ cup Cornflakes crumbs
  ½ cup brown sugar
  2 tbsp. fat-free margarine, melted

DIRECTIONS:
  Preheat oven to 350 degrees. Lightly spray 8x12-inch baking dish with nonfat cooking spray. Cook noodles according to package directions. Drain well and set aside. In a large bowl, combine egg substitute, sour cream, cottage cheese, sugar, and milk. Add raisins and noodles and mix well. Pour into baking dish. In a small bowl, combine Cornflakes crumbs and brown sugar, stir in margarine and mix lightly. Sprinkle Cornflakes mixture over casserole. Bake in preheated oven 1 hour. Let casserole stand 5 minutes before cutting.

Serves: 12

Nutrition per Serving		Exchanges
Calories	192	2⅓ starch
Carbohydrate	37 grams	
Cholesterol	1 milligram	
Dietary Fiber	1 gram	
Protein	8 grams	
Sodium	142 milligrams	

SHOPPING LIST:
  8 oz. yolk-free noodles, 12 oz. egg substitute, 8 oz. fat-free sour cream, 8 oz. fat-free cottage cheese, sugar, 4 oz. skim milk, 2 oz. golden raisins, Cornflakes crumbs, brown sugar, fat-free margarine

PASTA RISOTTO

EASY - DO AHEAD

INGREDIENTS:

3 cups fat-free chicken broth
1 cup orzo
1 cup asparagus, cut into 1-inch pieces
1 cup broccoli florets
½ cup fat-free Parmesan cheese

DIRECTIONS:

Pour chicken broth into 2- or 3-quart saucepan and bring to a boil over high heat. Add orzo; reduce heat to medium and gently boil 6 to 8 minutes. Add asparagus pieces and broccoli and cook, stirring frequently, until liquid is absorbed and pasta is tender, about 5 to 7 minutes. Stir in ¼ cup cheese. Spoon pasta mixture into serving bowl and sprinkle with remaining cheese.

Serves: 4

Nutrition per Serving		Exchanges
Calories	164	1 starch
Carbohydrate	29 grams	3½ vegetable
Cholesterol	0 milligrams	
Dietary Fiber	2 grams	
Protein	11 grams	
Sodium	773 milligrams	

SHOPPING LIST:

2 15½-oz. cans fat-free chicken broth (bouillon cubes or granules), 4 oz. orzo, ⅓ to ¼ lb. asparagus, 1 small head broccoli (or 10 oz. frozen broccoli florets), 2 oz. fat-free Parmesan cheese

PESTO PASTA

EASY - DO AHEAD

INGREDIENTS:

9 oz. pasta, cooked and drained
1 cup fresh basil leaves, rinsed and dried
2 tsp. minced garlic
½ tsp. onion powder
1½ cups chopped zucchini
⅓ cup fat-free chicken broth
⅓ cup fat-free Parmesan cheese

DIRECTIONS:

Cook pasta according to package directions and drain well.
Combine basil, garlic, and onion powder in food processor
or blender and process until chopped. Add zucchini,
chicken broth, and cheese and process until smooth. Pour
pesto sauce into small saucepan and heat over medium heat
just until heated through. Serve over hot pasta.

Serves: 6

PERFECT
PASTA
AND RICE

Nutrition per Serving		Exchanges
Calories	180	2 starch
Carbohydrate	35 grams	1 vegetable
Cholesterol	0 milligram	
Dietary Fiber	1 gram	
Protein	8 grams	
Sodium	98 milligrams	

SHOPPING LIST:

9 oz. pasta, fresh basil leaves (1 cup), minced garlic, onion
powder, 2 to 3 zucchini, 3 oz. fat-free chicken broth, 1½ oz.
fat-free Parmesan cheese

PIZZA BAKE

AVERAGE - DO AHEAD - FREEZE

INGREDIENTS:

1 lb. fat-free beef crumbles (Morningstar Farms)	1 tsp. Italian seasoning
1 tbsp. onion powder	¼ tsp. pepper
¼ cup chopped mushrooms	4 oz. uncooked pasta
28 oz. can diced tomatoes with roasted garlic	1 cup fat-free shredded pizza cheese
¾ cup tomato sauce	¼ cup fat-free Parmesan cheese

DIRECTIONS:

Preheat oven to 350 degrees. Lightly spray 10-inch baking dish with nonfat cooking spray. Lightly spray large saucepan with nonfat cooking spray and heat over medium heat, about 1 minute. Add beef crumbles and onion powder to pan and cook until browned. Stir in mushrooms, tomatoes, tomato sauce, Italian seasoning, and pepper; increase heat to medium-high and bring mixture to a boil. Immediately reduce heat and simmer over low heat 10 to 15 minutes.

Prepare pasta according to package directions and drain well. Stir pasta into sauce and mix well. Pour mixture into prepared baking dish; top with pizza and Parmesan cheeses. Bake in preheated oven 30 to 35 minutes, until cheese is lightly browned.

Serves: 6

Nutrition per Serving		**Exchanges**
Calories	226	1½ starch
Carbohydrate	29 grams	2⅔ meat
Cholesterol	0 milligrams	1 vegetable
Dietary Fiber	4 grams	
Protein	25 grams	
Sodium	1,226 milligrams	

SHOPPING LIST:

1 lb. fat-free beef crumbles (Morningstar Farms), onion powder, 4 oz. mushrooms, 28 oz. can diced tomatoes with roasted garlic, 6 oz. tomato sauce, Italian seasoning, pepper, 4 oz. pasta (rigatoni, rotini, etc.), 2 oz. fat-free shredded pizza cheese, 1 oz. fat-free Parmesan cheese

SOUTHWESTERN-STYLE FETTUCCINE

AVERAGE

INGREDIENTS:

10 oz. fettuccine
15 oz. can low-calorie
   creamed corn
⅔ cup skim milk
2 tsp. fat-free chicken broth
¼ tsp. ground cumin
1 medium red bell pepper,
   thinly sliced

1 tbsp. onion powder
15 oz. canned corn kernels,
   drained
1 cup fat-free Monterey Jack
   cheese, shredded
15 oz. can Mexican toma-
   toes and jalapeños,
   drained

DIRECTIONS:

Cook fettuccine according to package directions; drain well
and return to pan to keep warm. Combine creamed corn and
milk in a food processor or blender and process until
smooth. Lightly spray a large nonstick skillet with nonfat
cooking spray. Pour chicken broth into skillet and heat over
medium-high heat. Add cumin, red pepper, and onion powder to hot broth and cook about 5 minutes, until peppers
soften. Gradually add corn-milk mixture, corn kernels, and
shredded cheese to skillet and cook until cheese is melted
and sauce thickens. Heat tomatoes in small saucepan or microwave until heated through. Pour corn sauce over pasta
and toss with tomatoes. Serve immediately.

Serves: 6

Nutrition per Serving		Exchanges
Calories	334	3 starch
Carbohydrate	63 grams	3 vegetable
Cholesterol	0 milligrams	½ meat
Dietary Fiber	4 grams	
Protein	18 grams	
Sodium	663 milligrams	

SHOPPING LIST:

10 oz. fettuccine, 15 oz. can low-calorie creamed corn, 5 to 6
oz. skim milk, fat-free chicken broth, ground cumin, 1
medium red bell pepper, onion powder, 15 oz. can corn kernels, 4 oz. fat-free Monterey Jack cheese, 15 oz. can tomatoes
with green chilies or Mexican tomatoes with jalapeños

PERFECT
PASTA
AND RICE

SPAGHETTI PIE

AVERAGE - DO AHEAD

INGREDIENTS:

12 oz. spaghetti
½ cup fat-free Parmesan
  cheese
½ cup fat-free ricotta cheese
¼ tsp. oregano
¼ tsp. basil
¼ tsp. thyme
¼ tsp. garlic powder
¼ tsp. cayenne pepper
½ cup egg substitute

¼ cup frozen chopped
  spinach, thawed and
  drained
2 cups chopped tomatoes
4 oz. fat-free Swiss cheese,
  sliced
2 cups fat-free pasta sauce

DIRECTIONS:

Preheat oven to 350 degrees. Lightly spray 9-inch springform pan with nonfat cooking spray. Cook spaghetti according to package directions; rinse with cold water; drain. In large bowl, combine spaghetti, Parmesan, ricotta, oregano, basil, thyme, garlic powder, cayenne pepper, and egg substitute; toss until well mixed and spaghetti is coated. Press half the spaghetti mixture in bottom of prepared pan. Top with spinach, half the tomatoes, and half the cheese slices. Press remaining spaghetti on top; layer with remaining tomatoes and cheese. Bake in preheated oven 30 to 35 minutes; let stand at room temperature 10 to 15 minutes, until set. In medium saucepan or microwave-safe bowl, heat pasta sauce until hot. Remove spaghetti pie from pan; cut in wedges; serve with pasta sauce.

Serves: 4

Nutrition per Serving		Exchanges
Calories	244	½ meat
Carbohydrate	42 grams	2 starch
Cholesterol	2 milligrams	2½ vegetable
Dietary Fiber	1 gram	
Protein	14 grams	
Sodium	483 milligrams	

SHOPPING LIST:

12 oz. spaghetti, 2 oz. fat-free Parmesan cheese, 4 oz. fat-free ricotta cheese, oregano, basil, thyme, garlic powder, cayenne pepper, 4 oz. egg substitute, frozen chopped spinach, 2 large tomatoes or 28 oz. can chopped tomatoes, 4 oz. fat-free sliced Swiss cheese, 16 oz. fat-free pasta sauce

SPAGHETTI WITH MEATBALLS

AVERAGE - DO AHEAD

✦ ✦ ✦

INGREDIENTS:
¾ lb. fat-free beef crumbles (Morningstar Farms)
2 tsp. onion flakes
¼ cup fat-free Parmesan cheese
½ tsp. Italian seasoning
⅛ tsp. garlic powder
6 oz. cooked angel hair pasta
2½ cups fat-free pasta sauce with vegetables

DIRECTIONS:
Preheat broiler on high heat. Lightly spray baking sheet or broiler pan with nonfat cooking spray. In a medium bowl, combine beef crumbles, onions, Parmesan cheese, Italian seasoning, and garlic powder; mix well. Shape meat mixture into 15 to 20 balls and place on prepared baking sheet. Broil meatballs 10 to 12 minutes, until browned on all sides (turn frequently during cooking). Cook pasta according to package directions; drain well and keep warm. Pour pasta sauce into medium saucepan and heat over medium-high heat until heated through, about 5 minutes. Add meatballs to sauce; reduce heat to medium and cook 5 to 10 minutes. Place pasta on large platter and top with meatball-pasta sauce. Sprinkle with extra Parmesan cheese, if desired, and serve.

Serves: 4

Nutrition per Serving		Exchanges
Calories	319	3⅓ starch
Carbohydrate	51 grams	2 meat
Cholesterol	0 milligrams	
Dietary Fiber	3 grams	
Protein	24 grams	
Sodium	885 milligrams	

SHOPPING LIST:
¾ lb. fat-free beef crumbles (Morningstar Farms), minced onion flakes, 1 oz. fat-free Parmesan cheese, Italian seasoning, garlic powder, 6 oz. angel hair pasta, 26 oz. jar fat-free pasta sauce with vegetables

· ·

SPAGHETTI WITH PEPPERS AND MUSHROOMS

AVERAGE - DO AHEAD

INGREDIENTS:

12 oz. angel hair pasta
4 cups sliced mushrooms
1 cup chopped green bell pepper
1 cup chopped red bell pepper
2 cups sliced onions

1 tbsp. minced garlic
1 lb. fat-free beef crumbles (Morningstar Farms)
28 oz. can crushed tomatoes
½ cup water
2 tbsp. dried parsley
1 tsp. dried basil

DIRECTIONS:

Prepare pasta according to package directions; drain well and keep warm. Lightly spray large nonstick skillet with nonfat cooking spray and heat over medium-high heat. Add sliced mushrooms and peppers and cook 5 minutes, until softened; remove from skillet and set aside. Lightly respray skillet and add onions and garlic; cook 5 minutes, stirring frequently. Reduce heat to medium. Add beef crumbles and cook until cooked through. Stir in tomatoes, water, parsley, and basil; increase temperature to high and bring to a boil. Reduce heat to low and simmer 10 to 15 minutes, until sauce has slightly thickened. Serve over cooked spaghetti. Sauce can be prepared ahead of time; refrigerate or freeze until ready to use. Heat in microwave or nonstick skillet until heated through.

Serves: 8

Nutrition per Serving		Exchanges
Calories	261	2 starch
Carbohydrate	39 grams	2 vegetable
Cholesterol	28 milligrams	2 meat
Dietary Fiber	3 grams	
Protein	23 grams	
Sodium	485 milligrams	

SHOPPING LIST:

12 oz. angel hair pasta, ¾ lb. mushrooms, 1 green bell pepper, 1 red bell pepper, 2 onions, minced garlic, 1 lb. Morningstar Farms fat-free beef crumbles, 28 oz. can crushed tomatoes, dried parsley, dried basil

SPAGHETTI WITH WHITE CREAM SAUCE

EASY

✦ ✦ ✦

INGREDIENTS:

10 oz. angel hair pasta, cooked and drained
¾ cup fat-free ricotta cheese
¼ cup fat-free cream cheese
1½ cups fat-free chicken broth
¾ cup fat-free Parmesan cheese

DIRECTIONS:

Cook pasta according to package directions and drain well. Lightly spray large saucepan with nonfat cooking spray; add ricotta cheese and cream cheese to saucepan and cook over medium heat until blended. Gradually add chicken broth to cheese and cook over low heat, stirring constantly, until blended and thick. Add pasta to sauce and toss until well coated. Sprinkle with Parmesan cheese and serve.

Serves: 6

PERFECT PASTA AND RICE

Nutrition per Serving		Exchanges
Calories	237	2⅔ starch
Carbohydrate	42 grams	1 meat
Cholesterol	5 milligrams	
Dietary Fiber	2 grams	
Protein	16 grams	
Sodium	370 milligrams	

SHOPPING LIST:

10 oz. angel hair pasta, 6 oz. fat-free ricotta cheese, 2 oz. fat-free cream cheese, 12 oz. fat-free chicken broth, 3 oz. fat-free Parmesan cheese

SPINACH-CHEESE PASTA

EASY - DO AHEAD

INGREDIENTS:

16 oz. yolk-free noodles
2 tsp. minced garlic
2 10-oz. packages frozen chopped spinach, thawed and drained
½ tsp. onion powder
½ tsp. dried basil
1 cup fat-free ricotta cheese
salt and pepper to taste
¼ cup fat-free Parmesan cheese

DIRECTIONS:

Cook the noodles according to package directions and drain well; keep warm. Lightly spray a large nonstick skillet with nonfat cooking spray and heat over medium-high heat. Add the garlic and spinach and cook about 5 minutes, until softened. Add onion powder, basil, ricotta cheese, salt, and pepper, and cook over low heat, stirring frequently, until mixture is blended and heated through. In a large serving bowl, toss spinach mixture with cooked noodles; sprinkle with Parmesan cheese.

Serves: 8

Nutrition per Serving		Exchanges
Calories	253	2 starch
Carbohydrate	49 grams	3 vegetable
Cholesterol	5 milligrams	½ meat
Dietary Fiber	3 grams	
Protein	14 grams	
Sodium	1,188 milligrams	

SHOPPING LIST:

1 lb. yolk-free noodles, minced garlic, 2 10-oz. packages frozen chopped spinach, onion powder, dried basil, 8 oz. fat-free ricotta cheese, salt and pepper, 1 oz. fat-free Parmesan cheese

VEGETABLE LASAGNA

AVERAGE - DO AHEAD - FREEZE

INGREDIENTS:

1 lb. spinach lasagna noodles
2 cups fat-free ricotta cheese
1 lb. frozen chopped spinach, thawed and drained
2 cups sliced zucchini
1½ cups sliced yellow squash
1 medium red bell pepper, sliced
1 medium green bell pepper, sliced
1 medium yellow bell pepper, sliced
¾ pound eggplant, peeled and sliced
3 cups fat-free pasta sauce
2 cups fat-free Parmesan cheese

DIRECTIONS:

Cook noodles according to package directions. Preheat oven to 300 degrees. Lightly spray 9x13-inch baking dish with nonfat cooking spray. Place ricotta cheese in food processor or blender and process until smooth. In medium bowl, combine spinach, zucchini, squash, peppers, and eggplant; toss lightly. Pour 1 cup pasta sauce into baking dish; top with single layer of lasagna noodles. Sprinkle ½ vegetable mixture on top of noodles; top vegetables with ½ ricotta cheese and ⅓ Parmesan cheese. Repeat layers, ending with pasta, sauce, and Parmesan cheese on top. Cover baking dish with foil and bake in preheated oven 30 minutes. Uncover; cook additional 15 minutes. Remove from oven; let stand at room temperature 15 minutes to set.

Serves: 12

Nutrition per Serving		Exchanges
Calories	260	2 starch
Carbohydrate	46 grams	3 vegetable
Cholesterol	7 milligrams	1 meat
Dietary Fiber	2 grams	
Protein	19 grams	
Sodium	411 milligrams	

SHOPPING LIST:

1 lb. spinach lasagna noodles, 16 oz. fat-free ricotta cheese, 16 oz. frozen chopped spinach, 4 small zucchini, 3 small yellow squash, 1 medium red bell pepper, 1 medium green bell pepper, 1 medium yellow bell pepper, ¾ lb. eggplant, 24 oz. fat-free pasta sauce, 8 oz. fat-free Parmesan cheese

PERFECT PASTA AND RICE

SHRIMP JAMBALAYA

AVERAGE - DO AHEAD

INGREDIENTS:
29 oz. + 2 tbsp. fat-free chicken broth, divided
¾ cup chopped celery
1 cup chopped green pepper
1 tbsp. onion powder
2 cups fat-free uncooked rice
28 oz. can chopped tomatoes, drained
½ tsp. thyme
½ tsp. garlic powder
¼ tsp. pepper
3 drops hot pepper sauce
1 lb. fat-free frozen cooked shrimp, thawed

DIRECTIONS:

Lightly spray a large Dutch oven or soup pot with nonfat cooking spray. Pour 2 tablespoons chicken broth into pot and heat over medium-high heat. Add celery, green pepper, and onion powder to hot broth and cook until vegetables are tender, about 5 minutes. Add 2 cans broth, rice, tomatoes, thyme, garlic powder, pepper, and hot pepper sauce to vegetables; bring to a boil over high heat. Reduce heat to low and simmer 6 to 8 minutes. Add shrimp and cook over medium heat 5 to 10 minutes, until heated through.

Serves: 6

Nutrition per Serving		Exchanges
Calories	220	2 starch
Carbohydrate	42 grams	½ meat
Cholesterol	9 milligrams	2 vegetable
Dietary Fiber	3 grams	
Protein	12 grams	
Sodium	1,031 milligrams	

SHOPPING LIST:
3 14½-oz. cans fat-free chicken broth, 3 stalks celery, 1 small green pepper, onion powder, fat-free rice, 28 oz. can chopped tomatoes, thyme, garlic powder, pepper, hot pepper sauce, 1 lb. fat-free frozen cooked shrimp

PICTURE PERFECT PIZZA

✦ ✦ ✦

MIX-A-PIZZA-CRUST

EASY - DO AHEAD - FREEZE

INGREDIENTS:
1½ cups Pioneer Baking Mix
⅓ cup hot water
1 cup Boboli pizza sauce
1½ cups fat-free shredded mozzarella cheese
¼ cup fat-free Parmesan cheese

DIRECTIONS:
Preheat oven to 450 degrees. Lightly spray cookie sheet or pizza pan with nonfat cooking spray. In a large bowl, combine baking mix and hot water. Lightly sprinkle surface with baking mix; turn dough onto surface and roll in mix. Knead until dough is smooth. Press dough into circle or rectangle on cookie sheet or press into pizza pan. Pour sauce over crust and top with your favorite toppings (vegetables, fat-free beef, chicken, etc.); top with mozzarella and Parmesan cheeses. Bake in preheated oven 10 to 15 minutes, until crust is lightly browned and cheese is melted.

Serves: 8

Nutrition per Serving		Exchanges
Calories	164	½ meat
Carbohydrate	33 grams	2 starch
Cholesterol	0 milligrams	
Dietary Fiber	< 1 gram	
Protein	10 grams	
Sodium	659 milligrams	

SHOPPING LIST: •
Pioneer Baking Mix, 8 oz. Boboli pizza sauce, 8 oz. fat-free shredded mozzarella cheese, 1 oz. fat-free Parmesan cheese

THIN NEW YORK PIZZA CRUST

AVERAGE - DO AHEAD - FREEZE

INGREDIENTS:
⅔ cup warm water (110 to 115 degrees)
1 tsp. sugar
1⅛ tsp. active dry yeast
1¾ cups flour
½ tsp. salt

DIRECTIONS:
Combine water and sugar in a small bowl; stir until sugar is dissolved. Sprinkle yeast into bowl and stir until mixed; let stand 5 minutes. In a large bowl, combine flour and salt; add yeast mixture to flour and mix until soft dough forms. Place dough on lightly-floured surface and knead until smooth and elastic, adding more flour as needed. Lightly spray the large bowl with nonfat cooking spray. Place pizza dough into bowl; cover with towel or plastic wrap and let rise 30 minutes, until doubled in size.

Punch dough down and place on lightly-floured surface. Knead 2 to 3 minutes, until dough is smooth. Lightly spray 12- to 14-inch pizza pan or baking sheet with nonfat cooking spray. Stretch dough and pat into prepared pan. Follow baking instructions for favorite pizza recipe.

Serves: 6

Nutrition per Serving		Exchanges
Calories	139	1⅔ starch
Carbohydrate	29 grams	
Cholesterol	0 milligrams	
Dietary Fiber	1 gram	
Protein	4 grams	
Sodium	178 milligrams	

SHOPPING LIST:
sugar, active dry yeast, flour, salt

PICTURE PERFECT PIZZA

THICK CHICAGO PIZZA CRUST

AVERAGE -DO AHEAD - FREEZE

INGREDIENTS:
¾ cup warm water
1½ tsp. sugar
1⅛ tsp. yeast
2½ cups bread flour
¼ tsp. salt

DIRECTIONS:
In a small bowl, combine water and sugar; stir until sugar is dissolved. Sprinkle yeast into bowl; mix and let stand 5 minutes. In a large bowl, combine flour and salt. Stir in yeast mixture and mix until soft dough forms. Place dough onto lightly-floured surface and knead until dough is smooth. Lightly spray large bowl with nonfat cooking spray; place dough into bowl; cover with towel or plastic wrap and let rise in warm place until doubled in size. Place dough on lightly-floured surface and knead 2 minutes until smooth. Pat and stretch dough into 12- to 14-inch round. Lightly spray pizza pan or baking sheet with nonfat cooking spray. Place pizza dough on prepared pan, cover, and let rise in warm place for 15 to 20 minutes. Preheat oven to 500 degrees. Lightly prick dough several times with fork and bake in preheated oven for 4 to 5 minutes. Remove crust from oven and follow favorite pizza recipe for toppings and baking instructions.

Serves: 6

Nutrition per Serving		Exchanges
Calories	174	2 starch
Carbohydrate	38 grams	⅓ fruit
Cholesterol	0 milligrams	
Dietary Fiber	< 1 gram	
Protein	6 grams	
Sodium	89 milligrams	

SHOPPING LIST:
sugar, yeast, bread flour, salt

WHOLE WHEAT PIZZA CRUST

AVERAGE - DO AHEAD - FREEZE

✦ ✦ ✦

INGREDIENTS:
1¼ cups water (110 to 115 degrees)
1 tbsp. sugar
1 tbsp. honey
2¼ tsp. active dry yeast
2¼ cups flour
1 cup whole wheat flour
¼ tsp. salt

DIRECTIONS:
In a small bowl, combine water, sugar, and honey; mix until honey and sugar are dissolved. Sprinkle yeast into bowl; stir to mix and let stand 5 minutes. In a large bowl, combine flour, whole wheat flour, and salt. Add yeast mixture to bowl and mix until soft dough forms. Place dough onto lightly-floured surface and knead 5 to 10 minutes, adding more flour as needed. Lightly spray a large bowl with non-fat cooking spray. Roll dough into ball and place in bowl; cover with towel or plastic wrap and let rise in warm place until doubled in size. Preheat oven according to pizza recipe directions. Lightly spray a 14-inch pizza pan or baking sheet with nonfat cooking spray. Turn dough onto floured surface; punch dough down and knead lightly. Press dough into prepared pan. Follow topping and baking instructions for favorite pizza recipes.

Serves: 6

PICTURE PERFECT PIZZA

Nutrition per Serving		Exchanges
Calories	195	2 starch
Carbohydrate	42 grams	⅔ fruit
Cholesterol	0 milligrams	
Dietary Fiber	3 grams	
Protein	6 grams	
Sodium	68 milligrams	

SHOPPING LIST:
sugar, honey, ¼ oz. active dry yeast, flour, whole wheat flour, salt

BARBECUE CHICKEN PIZZA

AVERAGE - DO AHEAD - FREEZE

INGREDIENTS:
1 fat-free pizza crust (pages 274–277)
1 cup barbecue sauce
¾ cup sliced red onion
½ pound fat-free chicken tenders, cooked and cubed
½ cup frozen artichoke hearts, thawed and drained
¾ cup sliced red bell pepper
1 cup fat-free shredded pizza cheese

DIRECTIONS:
Prepare favorite fat-free pizza crust. Preheat oven to 450 degrees. Spread barbecue sauce over pizza crust. Arrange onions, chicken, artichokes, and bell pepper over sauce and top with cheese. Bake in preheated oven for 10 to 15 minutes, until crust is lightly browned and cheese is melted.

Serves: 4

Nutrition per Serving		Exchanges
Calories	210	2⅓ starch
Carbohydrate	36 grams	1 meat
Cholesterol	18 milligrams	
Dietary Fiber	1 gram	
Protein	14 grams	
Sodium	812 milligrams	

SHOPPING LIST:
8 oz. barbecue sauce, 1 small red onion, ½ lb. fat-free chicken tenders, frozen artichoke hearts, 1 small red bell pepper, 4 oz. fat-free pizza cheese

BASIC CHEESE AND TOMATO PIZZA

EASY - DO AHEAD - FREEZE

INGREDIENTS:
1 fat-free pizza crust (pages 274–277)
¾ cup Boboli pizza sauce
1 cup fat-free shredded mozzarella cheese
1 cup diced tomatoes with roasted garlic, drained
¼ cup fat-free Parmesan cheese

DIRECTIONS:
Prepare favorite fat-free pizza crust. Preheat oven to 450 degrees. Spread pizza sauce over crust. Sprinkle mozzarella cheese over crust and bake in preheated oven 5 minutes. Remove pizza from oven; top with tomatoes and sprinkle with Parmesan cheese. Bake 5 to 8 minutes, until golden brown. Fresh diced tomatoes can be substituted for canned tomatoes; sprinkle fresh tomatoes lightly with ½ teaspoon garlic powder. This is a great basic pizza—add your favorite toppings and bake accordingly.

Serves: 6

PICTURE PERFECT PIZZA

Nutrition per Serving		Exchanges
Calories	197	2 starch
Carbohydrate	34 grams	1 vegetable
Cholesterol	0 milligrams	½ meat
Dietary Fiber	2 grams	
Protein	12 grams	
Sodium	511 milligrams	

SHOPPING LIST:
6 oz. Boboli pizza sauce, 4 oz. fat-free shredded mozzarella cheese, 14½ oz. can diced tomatoes with roasted garlic (or 1 large fresh tomato + garlic powder), 1 oz. fat-free Parmesan cheese

MEXICAN VEGETABLE PIZZA

EASY - DO AHEAD

INGREDIENTS:
1 fat-free pizza crust (pages 274–277)
1½ cups fat-free shredded pizza cheese
¾ cup Mexican stewed tomatoes, drained
½ cup fat-free chunky-style salsa
½ cup chopped green bell pepper
¼ cup chopped green onion
2 tsp. chopped fresh cilantro

DIRECTIONS:
Prepare favorite fat-free pizza crust. Preheat oven to 450 degrees. Sprinkle ½ cup pizza cheese on crust. Drain stewed tomatoes; spread on top of cheese. Top with salsa, bell pepper, and green onions; sprinkle with remaining cheese and fresh cilantro. Bake 10 to 12 minutes, until cheese is melted and crust is lightly browned.

Serves: 6

Nutrition per Serving		Exchanges
Calories	198	1 starch
Carbohydrate	32 grams	3 vegetable
Cholesterol	0 milligrams	1 meat
Dietary Fiber	2 grams	
Protein	14 grams	
Sodium	582 milligrams	

SHOPPING LIST:
6 oz. fat-free shredded pizza cheese, 14 oz. Mexican-style stewed tomatoes, 4 oz. fat-free chunky-style salsa, 1 small green bell pepper, 2 green onions, fresh cilantro

PEPPER-ONION PIZZA

AVERAGE - DO AHEAD

INGREDIENTS:
1 fat-free pizza crust (pages 274–277)
2 tsp. vegetable broth
1 large Vidalia onion, sliced thin
3 cups sliced mushrooms
1 cup sliced red bell pepper
1 cup fat-free pizza sauce
1 cup fat-free shredded mozzarella cheese
¼ cup fat-free Parmesan cheese

DIRECTIONS:
Prepare favorite fat-free pizza crust. Preheat oven to 425 degrees. Lightly spray large nonstick skillet with nonfat cooking spray. Pour vegetable broth into skillet and heat over medium-high heat. Add onions, mushrooms, and peppers to skillet and cook 8 to 10 minutes, until vegetables are tender. Spread pizza sauce over crust; sprinkle with mozzarella cheese. Place cooked vegetables on top of cheese and sprinkle with Parmesan cheese. Bake in preheated oven 10 to 15 minutes, until crust is golden brown.

Serves: 6

PICTURE
PERFECT
PIZZA

Nutrition per Serving		Exchanges
Calories	231	2 starch
Carbohydrate	42 grams	2½ vegetable
Cholesterol	0 milligrams	½ meat
Dietary Fiber	3 grams	
Protein	14 grams	
Sodium	487 milligrams	

SHOPPING LIST:
fat-free vegetable broth, 1 large Vidalia onion, ½ lb. mushroms, 1 medium red bell pepper, 8 oz. fat-free pizza sauce (or ingredients for homemade sauce), 4 oz. fat-free shredded mozzarella cheese, 1 oz. fat-free Parmesan cheese

PIZZA PRIMAVERA

AVERAGE - DO AHEAD - FREEZE

INGREDIENTS:

1 fat-free pizza crust (pages 274–277)
1 cup Boboli pizza sauce
1½ cups frozen broccoli florets, thawed and drained
½ cup frozen carrot slices, thawed and drained
1 cup frozen asparagus spears, thawed, drained, and chopped
¾ cup sugar snap peas, thawed and drained
¾ cup frozen artichoke hearts, thawed and drained
1½ cups fat-free shredded pizza cheese
¼ cup fat-free Parmesan cheese

DIRECTIONS:

Prepare favorite fat-free pizza crust. Preheat oven to 450 degrees. Spread Boboli pizza sauce over pizza crust; top with broccoli, carrots, asparagus pieces, snap peas, and artichoke hearts. Sprinkle pizza cheese over vegetables and top with Parmesan cheese. Bake in preheated oven for 5 to 10 minutes, until crust is lightly browned and cheese is melted. Let pizza stand 3 to 5 minutes before slicing.

Serves: 6

Nutrition per Serving		Exchanges
Calories	250	2 starch
Carbohydrate	44 grams	3 vegetable
Cholesterol	0 milligrams	½ meat
Dietary Fiber	4 grams	
Protein	18 grams	
Sodium	635 milligrams	

SHOPPING LIST:

8 oz. Boboli pizza sauce, 10 oz. frozen broccoli florets, 6 oz. frozen carrot slices, 10 oz. frozen asparagus spears, 6 oz. frozen sugar snap peas, 10 oz. frozen artichoke hearts, 6 oz. fat-free shredded pizza cheese, 1 oz. fat-free Parmesan cheese

SEAFOOD-PINEAPPLE PIZZA

AVERAGE - DO AHEAD

INGREDIENTS:
1 fat-free pizza crust (pages 274–277)
¾ cup fat-free shredded mozzarella cheese
8 oz. fat-free frozen cooked shrimp, thawed and drained
8 oz. pineapple tidbits in juice, drained
¾ cup chopped red bell pepper
¼ cup sliced mushrooms
¼ cup fat-free Parmesan cheese

DIRECTIONS:
Prepare favorite fat-free pizza crust. Preheat oven to 450 degrees. Lightly spray pizza crust with nonfat cooking spray; immediately sprinkle with mozzarella cheese. Top with cooked shrimp, pineapple, bell pepper, and mushrooms. Sprinkle Parmesan cheese on top. Bake in preheated oven 10 to 15 minutes, until crust is golden brown.

Serves: 6

PICTURE
PERFECT
PIZZA

Nutrition per Serving		Exchanges
Calories	224	½ meat
Carbohydrate	39 grams	2 starch
Cholesterol	4 milligrams	2 vegetable
Dietary Fiber	2 grams	
Protein	14 grams	
Sodium	529 milligrams	

SHOPPING LIST:
3 oz. fat-free shredded mozzarella cheese, ½ lb. fat-free frozen cooked shrimp (small-medium), 8 oz. pineapple tidbits in juice, 1 small red bell pepper, 3 to 4 mushrooms, 1 oz. fat-free Parmesan cheese.

SIMPLE CHEESE PIZZA

EASY - DO AHEAD - FREEZE

INGREDIENTS:

1 whole fat-free pizza crust (Sassafrass mix)
2 cups fat-free shredded mozzarella cheese
2 cups fat-free pasta sauce

DIRECTIONS:

Preheat oven to 450 degrees. Lightly spray 12-inch pizza pan with nonfat cooking spray. Prepare pizza crust according to package directions. Sprinkle crust with half of shredded mozzarella cheese. Pour pasta sauce over cheese and top with remaining mozzarella cheese. Add sliced mushrooms, onions, or green peppers, if desired. Bake in preheated oven 20 minutes, or until crust is golden brown.

Serves: 10

Nutrition per Serving		Exchanges
Calories	136	1⅓ starch
Carbohydrate	21 grams	1 meat
Cholesterol	0 milligrams	
Dietary Fiber	< 1 gram	
Protein	10 grams	
Sodium	408 milligrams	

SHOPPING LIST:

fat-free pizza crust mix (i.e. Sassafrass), 8 oz. fat-free mozzarella cheese, 16 oz. fat-free pasta sauce

VEGETARIAN PIZZA

AVERAGE - DO AHEAD

✦ ✦ ✦

INGREDIENTS:
1 fat-free pizza crust (pages 274–277)
15 oz. can fat-free refried beans
2 tsp. onion powder
1 tsp. chili powder
½ tsp. ground cumin
1 cup fat-free shredded pizza cheese
¾ cup tomatoes with green chilies
½ cup frozen corn kernels, thawed and drained
1 cup fat-free salsa

DIRECTIONS:
Prepare favorite fat-free pizza crust. Preheat oven to 450 degrees. Lightly spray saucepan with nonfat cooking spray. Place refried beans into saucepan; add onion powder, chili powder, and cumin to beans and heat over medium heat 5 to 6 minutes, until heated through. Spread bean mixture over pizza crust. Top with ½ cup cheese, tomatoes, corn, and remaining cheese. Bake in preheated oven 10 to 15 minutes, until crust is lightly browned and cheese is melted. Serve pizza with fat-free salsa.

Serves: 6

Nutrition per Serving		Exchanges
Calories	271	2½ starch
Carbohydrate	48 grams	2 vegetable
Cholesterol	0 milligrams	½ meat
Dietary Fiber	4 grams	
Protein	16 grams	
Sodium	900 milligrams	

SHOPPING LIST:
15 oz. can fat-free refried beans, onion powder, chili powder, ground cumin, 4 oz. fat-free shredded pizza cheese, 14½ oz. can tomatoes with green chilies, 10 oz. frozen corn kernels, 8 oz. fat-free salsa

CHICKEN PIZZA ON VEGGIE CRUST

AVERAGE - DO AHEAD

INGREDIENTS:

6 cups shredded zucchini
½ cup + 2 tbsp. egg substitute
1 tbsp. onion flakes
½ tsp. garlic powder
½ tsp. dried basil
⅓ cup flour
1½ cups fat-free shredded
   mozzarella cheese

¾ cup fat-free Parmesan
   cheese, divided
1 cup fat-free chicken tenders, cooked and diced
½ cup chopped red pepper
½ cup chopped green pep-
   per
2 cups fat-free pasta sauce

DIRECTIONS:

Preheat oven to 350 degrees. Lightly spray 13-inch shallow baking dish with nonfat cooking spray. Wrap zucchini in paper towels and squeeze as much moisture out as possible; dry well. In large bowl, combine zucchini, egg substitute, onion flakes, garlic powder, basil, flour, ½ cup mozzarella cheese and ½ cup Parmesan cheese. Mix ingredients until well blended; press mixture into prepared pan to form crust. Bake in preheated oven 30 minutes, until lightly browned and firm. Sprinkle crust with shredded chicken and peppers. Top with pasta sauce; spread evenly over top. Sprinkle remaining mozzarella and Parmesan cheese on top and bake 25 to 30 minutes, until cooked through and cheese is melted.

Serves: 6

Nutrition per Serving		Exchanges
Calories	243	4 meat
Carbohydrate	21 grams	1 starch
Cholesterol	24 milligrams	1 vegetable
Dietary Fiber	2 grams	
Protein	35 grams	
Sodium	853 milligrams	

SHOPPING LIST:

9 to 10 medium zucchini, 5 oz. egg substitute, onion flakes, garlic powder, dried basil, flour, 6 oz. fat-free shredded mozzarella cheese, 3 oz. fat-free Parmesan cheese, ½ lb. fat-free chicken tenders, 1 small red pepper, 1 small green pepper, 16 oz. fat-free pasta sauce

PICTURE PERFECT PIZZA

FRENCH BREAD PIZZA

EASY - DO AHEAD - FREEZE

INGREDIENTS:
1 cup fat-free shredded mozzarella cheese
2 tbsp. fat-free sour cream
1 tsp. minced garlic
½ tsp. Italian seasoning
1 lb. fat-free French bread loaf
¼ cup tomato paste, divided

DIRECTIONS:
Preheat broiler on high. In a medium bowl, combine mozzarella cheese, sour cream, garlic, and Italian seasoning; mix well. Line a baking sheet with foil and lightly spray with nonfat cooking spray. Cut French bread loaf in half and place bread slices, crust down, on baking sheet. Spread ⅛ cup tomato paste on each bread slice. Divide cheese mixture and drop on top of each slice. Broil in heated oven (about 6 inches from heat) 1½ minutes, until cheese is melted and lightly browned. Let pizza stand at room temperature 5 minutes before slicing. Vegetables or fat-free chicken strips can be added to top of pizza before baking, if desired.

Serves: 8

PICTURE PERFECT PIZZA

Nutrition per Serving		Exchanges
Calories	193	2⅓ starch
Carbohydrate	34 grams	½ meat
Cholesterol	0 milligrams	
Dietary Fiber	2 grams	
Protein	11 grams	
Sodium	456 milligrams	

SHOPPING LIST:
4 oz. fat-free shredded mozzarella cheese, 1 oz. fat-free sour cream, minced garlic, Italian seasoning, 1 lb. loaf fat-free French bread, 2 oz. tomato paste

SHRIMP PIZZA ON RICE

EASY - DO AHEAD

INGREDIENTS:

3 cups fat-free cooked rice
¼ cup + 2 tbsp. egg substitute
2 cups fat-free shredded mozzarella cheese
1 cup fat-free pasta sauce
1½ cups fat-free shrimp, cooked and diced
¼ cup fat-free Parmesan cheese

DIRECTIONS:

Preheat oven to 450 degrees. Lightly spray 12-inch pizza pan or two 9-inch pie plates with nonfat cooking spray. In a medium bowl, combine rice, egg substitute, and 1 cup mozzarella cheese; mix until ingredients are blended. Press mixture into prepared pan(s) and bake in preheated oven 15 to 20 minutes. Spread pasta sauce over rice crust and top with shrimp. Sprinkle with remaining mozzarella and Parmesan cheese. Bake an additional 10 to 15 minutes, until cheese is melted and lightly browned.

Serves: 8

Nutrition per Serving		Exchanges
Calories	203	1⅓ starch
Carbohydrate	20 grams	3 meat
Cholesterol	4 milligrams	
Dietary Fiber	< 1 gram	
Protein	25 grams	
Sodium	714 milligrams	

SHOPPING LIST:

1 cup fat-free rice (raw), 3 oz. egg substitute, 8 oz. fat-free shredded mozzarella cheese, 8 oz. fat-free pasta sauce, 12 oz. fat-free shrimp, 1 oz. fat-free Parmesan cheese

TURKEY PITA PIZZAS

EASY - DO AHEAD

INGREDIENTS:
4 fat-free pita pockets
¼ cup fat-free Italian salad dressing
2 medium tomatoes, sliced
1 large green bell pepper, sliced
½ lb. fat-free deli turkey, thinly sliced
2 cups fat-free shredded mozzarella cheese

DIRECTIONS:
Preheat oven to 350 degrees. Lightly spray baking sheet(s) with nonfat cooking spray. Place pita breads on baking sheet; brush the top of each pita with 1 tablespoon salad dressing. Top with tomato slices, green peppers, and sliced turkey; sprinkle ½ cup mozzarella cheese on each pita. Bake in preheated oven 10 to 15 minutes, until pita is crisp and cheese is melted.

Serves: 4

Nutrition per Serving		Exchanges
Calories	277	1 starch
Carbohydrate	27 grams	2½ vegetable
Cholesterol	25 milligrams	4 meat
Dietary Fiber	2 grams	
Protein	35 grams	
Sodium	806 milligrams	

SHOPPING LIST:
4 fat-free pita pockets, 2 oz. fat-free Italian salad dressing, 2 medium tomatoes, 1 large green bell pepper, ½ lb. fat-free deli turkey, 8 oz. fat-free shredded mozzarella cheese

PICTURE PERFECT PIZZA

FRUIT TORTILLA PIZZA

EASY

INGREDIENTS:
4 small fat-free flour tortillas
1 cup fat-free ricotta cheese
⅓ cup fat-free cottage cheese
2½ tbsp. brown sugar
½ tsp. cinnamon
1 cup mixed berries (raspberries, blueberries, strawberries)

DIRECTIONS:
Preheat oven to 450 degrees. Line baking sheet with foil and lightly spray with nonfat cooking spray. Place tortillas on baking sheet and bake in preheated oven 3 to 5 minutes, just until crisp. In a food processor or blender, combine ricotta cheese, cottage cheese, 1 tablespoon brown sugar, and cinnamon; blend until smooth and creamy. Divide cheese mixture evenly among tortillas; top each tortilla with ¼ cup mixed berries. Sprinkle remaining brown sugar on top of berries and bake 5 minutes, until heated through. Serve immediately.

Serves: 4

Nutrition per Serving		Exchanges
Calories	232	1 milk
Carbohydrate	47 grams	2⅓ fruit
Cholesterol	10 milligrams	½ meat
Dietary Fiber	5 grams	
Protein	14 grams	
Sodium	480 milligrams	

SHOPPING LIST:
4 small fat-free flour tortillas, 8 oz. fat-free ricotta cheese, 3 to 4 oz. fat-free cottage cheese, brown sugar, cinnamon, mixed berries (strawberries, blueberries, raspberries to equal 1 cup)

MEXICAN PIZZA

EASY - DO AHEAD

INGREDIENTS:
4 fat-free flour tortillas
15 oz. can fat-free refried beans
2 cups fat-free shredded mozzarella cheese
3 medium tomatoes, sliced

DIRECTIONS:
Lightly spray large nonstick skillet with nonfat cooking spray. Place tortillas on surface and top each tortilla with ½ cup refried beans, ¼ cup cheese, 1 sliced tomato, and another ¼ cup cheese. Heat skillet over medium heat; add "pizzas," one at a time, and cook 5 to 7 minutes, until cheese is melted and tortilla is lightly browned. Repeat with remaining "pizzas."

Serves: 4

Nutrition per Serving		Exchanges
Calories	294	2 starch
Carbohydrate	40 grams	2 meat
Cholesterol	0 milligrams	2½ vegetable
Dietary Fiber	6 grams	
Protein	28 grams	
Sodium	863 milligrams	

SHOPPING LIST:
4 fat-free flour tortillas, 15 oz. can fat-free refried beans, 8 oz. fat-free shredded mozzarella cheese, 3 medium tomatoes

TURKEY TACO PIZZA

EASY

INGREDIENTS:
4 fat-free flour tortillas
½ lb. fat-free ground turkey
1 tbsp. taco seasoning mix
1 cup fat-free refried beans
1 cup fat-free chunky-style salsa
2 cups fat-free shredded Cheddar cheese

DIRECTIONS:
Preheat oven to 400 degrees. Lightly spray baking sheet(s) with nonfat cooking spray. Place tortillas on baking sheet. Lightly spray medium nonstick skillet with nonfat cooking spray and heat over medium-high heat. Add turkey to skillet and cook until no longer pink; stir in taco seasonings and mix well. Remove turkey from heat. Top each tortilla with ¼ cup refried beans, ¼ cup salsa, ½ cup turkey, and ½ cup cheese. Bake in preheated oven for 10 to 12 minutes, until cheese is melted and tortilla is crisp. Serve immediately.

Serves: 4

Nutrition per Serving		Exchanges
Calories	329	2½ starch
Carbohydrate	42 grams	4 meat
Cholesterol	25 milligrams	
Dietary Fiber	4 grams	
Protein	36 grams	
Sodium	1,545 milligrams	

SHOPPING LIST:
4 fat-free flour tortillas, ½ lb. fat-free ground turkey (or chicken), taco seasoning mix, 8 oz. fat-free refried beans, 8 oz. fat-free chunky-style salsa, 8 oz. fat-free shredded Cheddar cheese

VIGOROUS
VEGETABLES

◆ ◆ ◆

BROCCOLI CASSEROLE

EASY - DO AHEAD

INGREDIENTS:

2 10-oz. packages frozen chopped broccoli, cooked and
   drained
2 cups fat-free sour cream
1 envelope onion soup mix
¾ cup fat-free shredded Cheddar cheese

DIRECTIONS:

Preheat oven to 350 degrees. Lightly spray 1-quart casserole
dish with nonfat cooking spray. Combine broccoli, sour
cream, and onion soup mix in a medium bowl and mix well.
Spread broccoli mixture into prepared dish; sprinkle with
cheese and bake in preheated oven 30 minutes. Serve immediately.

Serves: 6

Nutrition per Serving		Exchanges
Calories	121	2 vegetable
Carbohydrate	10 grams	1½ meat
Cholesterol	< 1 milligram	
Dietary Fiber	4 grams	
Protein	13 grams	
Sodium	798 milligrams	

SHOPPING LIST:

2 10-oz. packages frozen chopped broccoli, 16 oz. fat-free
sour cream, 1 envelope onion soup mix, 6 oz. fat-free shredded Cheddar cheese

VIGOROUS VEGETABLES

CINNAMON-GLAZED CARROTS AND YAMS

EASY

INGREDIENTS:

½ lb. carrots, sliced ¼-inch thick
½ lb. yams, sliced ¼-inch thick
⅓ cup frozen orange juice concentrate, thawed
¾ tsp. cinnamon

DIRECTIONS:

Combine all ingredients in a medium saucepan and heat over medium-high heat; reduce heat to medium, cover, and cook 15 to 20 minutes, until carrots and yams are tender. Uncover saucepan and cook 5 minutes. Serve immediately.

Serves: 6

Nutrition per Serving		Exchanges
Calories	66	1 vegetable
Carbohydrate	16 grams	⅔ fruit
Cholesterol	0 milligrams	
Dietary Fiber	3 grams	
Protein	1 gram	
Sodium	26 milligrams	

SHOPPING LIST:

½ lb. carrots, ½ lb. yams, frozen orange juice concentrate, cinnamon

VIGOROUS VEGETABLES

GINGER CARROTS

EASY

INGREDIENTS:
4 cups sliced carrots
½ cup water
½ cup orange juice
2 tsp. reconstituted butter-flavored granules
1 tsp. ginger
½ tsp. cinnamon
1 tbsp. lemon juice
2 tsp. brown sugar

DIRECTIONS:
Lightly spray large nonstick skillet with nonfat cooking spray and heat over medium-high heat. Add carrots, water, orange juice, liquid butter, ginger, and cinnamon to skillet; cook over medium heat until carrots are tender, about 10 to 15 minutes. Reduce heat to medium-low; stir in lemon juice and sugar. Cook, stirring constantly, until carrots are glazed.

Serves: 6

Nutrition per Serving		Exchanges
Calories	65	1 vegetable
Carbohydrate	15 grams	⅔ fruit
Cholesterol	0 milligrams	
Dietary Fiber	4 grams	
Protein	1 gram	
Sodium	70 milligrams	

VIGOROUS VEGETABLES

SHOPPING LIST:
8 carrots, 4 oz. orange juice, butter-flavored granules, ginger, cinnamon, lemon juice, brown sugar

HONEY-ORANGE GLAZED CARROTS

AVERAGE

INGREDIENTS:

1 lb. fresh baby carrots
1 cup water
½ cup orange juice
2 tsp. cornstarch
2 tbsp. reconstituted butter-flavored granules
2 tbsp. honey

DIRECTIONS:

Place carrots in a small saucepan and cover with water. Bring to a boil over high heat; cover pan, reduce heat to medium and cook 7 to 10 minutes, until tender. Drain carrots well. Combine orange juice and cornstarch in saucepan; mix until cornstarch is dissolved. Add butter-flavored granules and honey to orange mixture; cook over medium-high heat 2 to 3 minutes, stirring constantly, until mixture becomes thick and bubbly. Pour over cooked carrots and serve immediately.

Serves: 6

Nutrition per Serving		Exchanges
Calories	57	1 vegetable
Carbohydrate	13 grams	½ fruit
Cholesterol	0 milligrams	
Dietary Fiber	2 grams	
Protein	< 1 gram	
Sodium	30 milligrams	

SHOPPING LIST:

1 lb. baby carrots, 4 oz. orange juice, cornstarch, butter-flavored granules, honey

VIGOROUS VEGETABLES

CREAMED SPINACH

EASY - DO AHEAD

INGREDIENTS:
2 10-oz. packages frozen chopped spinach, thawed and drained
1 tsp. onion flakes
1 tsp. garlic powder
¼ tsp. pepper
1 cup fat-free sour cream
½ cup fat-free shredded Cheddar cheese

DIRECTIONS:
Preheat oven to 350 degrees. Lightly spray 1-quart baking dish with nonfat cooking spray. Drain spinach well and place in medium bowl. Sprinkle spinach with onion flakes, garlic powder, and pepper; mix well. Stir in sour cream and mix until blended. Spoon spinach mixture into prepared casserole and top with cheese. Bake in preheated oven 25 to 30 minutes, until cheese is lightly browned and casserole is bubbly.

Serves: 6

Nutrition per Serving		Exchanges
Calories	70	1 vegetable
Carbohydrate	6 grams	1 meat
Cholesterol	0 milligrams	
Dietary Fiber	2 grams	
Protein	8 grams	
Sodium	201 milligrams	

SHOPPING LIST:
2 10-oz. packages frozen chopped spinach, onion flakes, garlic powder, pepper, 8 oz. fat-free sour cream, 2 oz. fat-free shredded Cheddar cheese

CURRIED CORN WITH RED PEPPERS

EASY

INGREDIENTS:
2 tbsp. fat-free margarine
2 large red bell peppers, sliced
2 tbsp. chopped jalapeño peppers
1 tbsp. curry powder
¼ tsp. salt
pepper to taste
½ cup fat-free creamer
1½ cups corn kernels

DIRECTIONS:
Place margarine in large saucepan and melt over medium-high heat. Add peppers and cook until tender and soft. Stir in curry powder, salt, pepper, and creamer (mocha mix); blend well. Add corn and heat over high heat until mixture comes to a boil. Reduce heat; cover and simmer 3 to 5 minutes.

Serves: 4

Nutrition per Serving		Exchanges
Calories	123	1 starch
Carbohydrate	29 grams	¾ fruit
Cholesterol	0 milligrams	
Dietary Fiber	3 grams	
Protein	3 grams	
Sodium	293 milligrams	

SHOPPING LIST:
fat-free margarine, 2 large red bell peppers, 4 oz. can chopped jalapeño peppers, curry powder, salt, pepper, 4 oz. fat-free creamer, 15 oz. can corn kernels

VIGOROUS VEGETABLES

SWEET AND SPICY CORN

EASY

INGREDIENTS:
 1½ cups cooked corn kernels
 ½ cup white vinegar
 ¼ cup lime juice
 1 tbsp. onion powder
 3 tbsp. sugar
 ⅛ tsp. dry mustard
 dash of cayenne pepper

DIRECTIONS:
 Prepare frozen or canned corn kernels according to package directions. Lightly spray 1-quart casserole with nonfat cooking spray. Spoon cooked corn into casserole and keep warm. In a small saucepan, combine vinegar, lime juice, onion powder, sugar, mustard, and cayenne pepper. Bring to a boil over high heat; reduce heat to medium and cook, stirring constantly, until sugar is dissolved and mixture is blended. Pour sauce over corn and serve immediately.

Serves: 6

Nutrition per Serving		Exchanges
Calories	64	1 vegetable
Carbohydrate	17 grams	⅔ fruit
Cholesterol	0 milligrams	
Dietary Fiber	1 gram	
Protein	1 gram	
Sodium	6 milligrams	

SHOPPING LIST:
 10 oz. frozen corn kernels or 16 oz. canned corn kernels, 4 oz. white vinegar, 2 oz. lime juice, onion powder, sugar, dry mustard, cayenne pepper

EGGPLANT GRATIN

EASY - DO AHEAD

INGREDIENTS:
1 lb. zucchini, cut into ¼-inch slices
1 lb. yellow squash, cut into ¼-inch slices
1 lb. tomatoes, cut into ½-inch slices
¾ lb. eggplant
1 medium onion, cut into rings
¾ tsp. garlic powder
¼ tsp. pepper
¾ cup fat-free Parmesan cheese

DIRECTIONS:
Preheat oven to 400 degrees. Lightly spray 9x13-inch baking dish with nonfat cooking spray. Alternately layer zucchini, yellow squash, tomatoes, eggplant, and onion in dish. Lightly spray vegetables with nonfat cooking spray. Sprinkle vegetables with garlic powder, pepper, and Parmesan cheese. Bake in preheated oven 35 to 40 minutes, until vegetables are tender and lightly browned.

Serves: 6

Nutrition per Serving		Exchanges
Calories	97	4 vegetable
Carbohydrate	19 grams	
Cholesterol	0 milligrams	
Dietary Fiber	< 1 gram	
Protein	7 grams	
Sodium	103 milligrams	

SHOPPING LIST:
2 medium zucchini, 2 medium yellow squash, 2 large tomatoes, ¾ lb. eggplant, 1 medium onion, garlic powder, pepper, 3 oz. fat-free Parmesan cheese

VIGOROUS VEGETABLES

FRENCH-FRIED PEPPERS

AVERAGE - DO AHEAD

INGREDIENTS:
½ cup egg substitute
1½ cups skim milk
¾ cup fat-free bread crumbs
1 tsp. Italian seasoning
½ cup Parmesan cheese
2 large green bell peppers, sliced into rings
2 large red bell peppers, sliced into rings

DIRECTIONS:
Preheat oven to 425 degrees. Lightly spray baking sheet(s) with nonfat cooking spray. Combine egg substitute and milk in a medium bowl and mix until blended. Combine bread crumbs, seasoning, and cheese in separate bowl and mix until blended. Dip pepper rings in egg mixture; roll in crumb mixture until well coated and place in single layer on baking sheet(s). Sprinkle with remaining crumbs; bake in preheated oven 15 to 20 minutes, until lightly browned and crisp.

Serves: 4

Nutrition per Serving		Exchanges
Calories	127	1 starch
Carbohydrate	20 grams	1 vegetable
Cholesterol	2 milligrams	1 meat
Dietary Fiber	2 grams	
Protein	11 grams	
Sodium	223 milligrams	

SHOPPING LIST:
4 oz. egg substitute, 12 oz. skim milk, fat-free bread crumbs, Italian seasoning, 2 oz. fat-free Parmesan cheese, 2 green bell peppers, 2 red bell peppers

HONEY-BAKED ONIONS

EASY - DO AHEAD

INGREDIENTS:
3 large Vidalia onions
2 tbsp. fat-free chicken broth
⅓ cup honey
¼ cup water
3 tbsp. reconstituted butter-flavored granules
1 tsp. paprika
⅛ tsp. cayenne pepper

DIRECTIONS:
Preheat oven to 350 degrees. Lightly spray shallow baking dish with nonfat cooking spray. Peel and cut onions in half horizontally and place onions, cut-side down, in dish in single layer. Sprinkle onions with chicken broth. Bake in preheated oven 25 to 30 minutes. Remove from oven and turn onions, cut-side up. In a small bowl, combine honey, water, liquid butter granules, paprika, and cayenne and mix well. Pour half the honey mixture over onions and bake, uncovered, 10 to 15 minutes; remove from oven; brush with remaining sauce and bake 15 minutes, until tender and glazed.

Serves: 4

VIGOROUS VEGETABLES

Nutrition per Serving		Exchanges
Calories	93	1 vegetable
Carbohydrate	22 grams	1 fruit
Cholesterol	0 milligrams	
Dietary Fiber	1 gram	
Protein	1 gram	
Sodium	20 milligrams	

SHOPPING LIST:
3 large Vidalia onions, 1 oz. fat-free chicken broth, 3 oz. honey, butter-flavored granules, paprika, cayenne pepper

BREADED PORTABELLO MUSHROOMS

EASY - DO AHEAD

INGREDIENTS:
½ cup egg substitute
⅔ cup fat-free bread crumbs
2 tbsp. fat-free Parmesan cheese
¾ tsp. garlic powder
½ tsp. onion powder
8 oz. portabello mushrooms

DIRECTIONS:
Preheat oven to 400 degrees. Lightly spray foil-lined baking sheet with nonfat cooking spray. Pour egg substitute into small bowl. In a separate bowl, combine bread crumbs with Parmesan cheese, garlic powder, and onion powder; mix well. Dip mushroom slices into egg substitute; roll in seasoned bread crumbs to coat. Place on prepared baking sheet and bake in preheated oven 15 minutes, until golden brown.

Serves: 4

Nutrition per Serving		Exchanges
Calories	57	½ meat
Carbohydrate	8 grams	½ starch
Cholesterol	0 milligrams	
Dietary Fiber	1 gram	
Protein	5 grams	
Sodium	103 milligrams	

VIGOROUS VEGETABLES

SHOPPING LIST:
4 oz. egg substitute, 2 slices bread (dried) or fat-free bread crumbs, ½ oz. fat-free Parmesan cheese, garlic powder, onion powder, 8 oz. portabello mushrooms

STUFFED PORTABELLO MUSHROOMS

DIFFICULT - DO AHEAD

INGREDIENTS:

4 large portabello mushrooms
¼ cup fat-free chicken
broth, divided
1 cup chopped onion
1 medium eggplant, peeled
and sliced
1 cup chopped tomato

¼ tsp. cumin
½ cup fat-free Parmesan
cheese, divided
1 tsp. lemon juice
1 tsp. chopped parsley
1½ tsp. dried basil

DIRECTIONS:

Clean mushrooms and pat dry; remove stems and chop into
small pieces. Lightly spray large nonstick skillet with nonfat
cooking spray; add 2 tablespoons chicken broth and heat
over medium-high heat. Add portabello mushrooms to hot
skillet and cook 5 minutes on each side. Remove from skillet
and set aside. Add 1 to 2 tablespoons chicken broth to skillet
and heat over medium-high heat. Add chopped onion to hot
skillet and cook until tender, about 5 minutes. Add eggplant
and mushroom stems and cook until tender. Add tomato,
cumin, ¼ cup Parmesan cheese, lemon juice, parsley, and
basil and cook over medium heat until heated through,
about 10 to 15 minutes. Preheat oven to 350 degrees. Lightly
spray 9x13-inch baking dish with nonfat cooking spray.
Place mushrooms in dish and fill each mushroom with eggplant mixture; sprinkle with remaining Parmesan cheese.
Bake in preheated oven for 20 to 25 minutes.

Serves: 4

VIGOROUS
VEGETABLES

Nutrition per Serving		Exchanges
Calories	101	4 vegetable
Carbohydrate	19 grams	½ meat
Cholesterol	0 milligrams	
Dietary Fiber	8 grams	
Protein	11 grams	
Sodium	173 milligrams	

SHOPPING LIST:

4 large portabello mushrooms, 2 oz. fat-free chicken broth, 1
medium onion, 1 medium eggplant, 1 large tomato, cumin,
4 oz. fat-free Parmesan cheese, lemon juice, chopped parsley, dried basil

SWEET AND SOUR ASPARAGUS

EASY

INGREDIENTS:

2 tbsp. vegetable broth
1 lb. asparagus, cut and trimmed
½ cup red currant jelly
¼ cup red wine vinegar
2 tbsp. lemon juice
1 tbsp. onion powder

DIRECTIONS:

Lightly spray large nonstick skillet with nonfat cooking spray; add vegetable broth and heat over medium-high heat until hot. Add asparagus and cook, uncovered, until tender, about 3 to 5 minutes; drain and place on serving platter. In a small saucepan, combine jelly, vinegar, lemon juice, and onion powder; mix well. Heat over high heat until jelly is completely melted and mixture is blended. Spoon sauce over asparagus and serve.

Serves: 4

Nutrition per Serving		Exchanges
Calories	83	1½ vegetable
Carbohydrate	20 grams	⅔ fruit
Cholesterol	0 milligrams	
Dietary Fiber	< 1 gram	
Protein	3 grams	
Sodium	64 milligrams	

SHOPPING LIST:

1 oz. vegetable broth, 1 lb. asparagus, 4 oz. red currant jelly, 2 oz. red wine vinegar, 1 oz. lemon juice, onion powder

VIGOROUS VEGETABLES

CURRY VEGETABLES AND FRUIT

EASY

INGREDIENTS:
2 medium zucchini, shredded
3 medium carrots, shredded
1 tbsp. onion powder
¼ tsp. garlic powder
14½ oz. can fat-free chicken broth
3 tsp. curry powder
3 tbsp. cider vinegar
2 tbsp. sugar
¼ cup raisins

DIRECTIONS:
Combine all ingredients in a small saucepan and bring to a boil over high heat; reduce heat to low, cover, and simmer 8 to 10 minutes, until vegetables are tender. Drain and serve immediately.

Serves: 4

Nutrition per Serving		Exchange
Calories	110	1 vegetable
Carbohydrate	28 grams	1⅓ fruit
Cholesterol	0 milligrams	
Dietary Fiber	4 grams	
Protein	2 grams	
Sodium	249 milligrams	

VIGOROUS VEGETABLES

SHOPPING LIST:
2 medium zucchini, 3 medium carrots, onion powder, garlic powder, 14½ oz. can fat-free chicken broth, curry powder, 3 oz. cider vinegar, sugar, 2 oz. raisins

GINGER SAUTÉED VEGETABLES

EASY

INGREDIENTS:

2 tbsp. fat-free chicken broth
½ lb. sugar snap peas, trimmed
1 cup shredded carrots
1 small yellow bell pepper, cut into strips
1 small red bell pepper, cut into strips
1 tsp. ground ginger
⅓ cup orange juice
1⅓ tsp. honey
¾ tsp. orange peel
Pepper to taste

DIRECTIONS:

Lightly spray large nonstick skillet with nonfat cooking spray. Pour chicken broth into skillet and heat over medium-high heat 1 minute. Add sugar snap peas, carrots, and peppers to skillet; sprinkle with ginger. Sauté vegetables 3 to 5 minutes, until tender-crisp. Add orange juice, honey, orange peel, and pepper to vegetables and stir until all vegetables are evenly coated.

Serves: 4

Nutrition per Serving		Exchanges
Calories	78	2 vegetable
Carbohydrate	19 grams	½ fruit
Cholesterol	0 milligrams	
Dietary Fiber	3 grams	
Protein	2 grams	
Sodium	37 milligrams	

SHOPPING LIST:

1 oz. fat-free chicken broth, ½ lb. sugar snap peas, 2 carrots (or prepackaged shredded carrots), 1 small yellow bell pepper, 1 small red bell pepper, ground ginger, 3 oz. orange juice, honey, orange peel, pepper

VIGOROUS VEGETABLES

ONION-PEPPER STIR-FRY

EASY

✦ ✦ ✦

INGREDIENTS:
¼ cup vegetable broth
½ tsp. garlic powder
1 tsp. ginger
1 medium red bell pepper, thinly sliced
1 medium yellow bell pepper, thinly sliced
1 medium green bell pepper, thinly sliced
1 small Vidalia onion, thinly sliced
1 tbsp. hoisin sauce

DIRECTIONS:
Lightly spray large nonstick skillet with nonfat cooking spray. Pour vegetable broth into skillet and sprinkle with garlic powder and ginger. Cook over medium-high heat, stirring frequently, until it comes to a boil. Add peppers and onions; cook 6 to 8 minutes, stirring frequently, until vegetables are tender. Stir in hoisin sauce and mix well. Roll up in fat-free tortillas, if desired.

Serves: 4

VIGOROUS VEGETABLES

Nutrition per Serving		Exchanges
Calories	30	1 vegetable
Carbohydrate	7 grams	
Cholesterol	0 milligrams	
Dietary Fiber	1 gram	
Protein	1 gram	
Sodium	223 milligrams	

SHOPPING LIST:
2 oz. vegetable broth, ginger, garlic powder, 1 red bell pepper, 1 yellow bell pepper, 1 green bell pepper, 1 Vidalia onion, hoisin sauce

SWEET VEGETABLE TZIMMES

EASY - DO AHEAD

INGREDIENTS:
4 large sweet potatoes, peeled and sliced
6 large carrots, thinly sliced
¼ cup raisins
¼ cup golden raisins
¼ cup pitted prunes
¼ cup chopped dates
½ cup orange juice
¼ cup brown sugar
2 tbsp. honey

DIRECTIONS:
Preheat oven to 350 degrees. Lightly spray a 9x13-inch baking dish with nonfat cooking spray. Layer sweet potatoes, carrots, raisins, prunes, and dates in baking pan. Sprinkle orange juice, brown sugar, and honey over top and cover with foil or lid. Bake in preheated oven 1½ hours, until vegetables and fruits are tender.

Serves: 8

Nutrition per Serving		Exchanges
Calories	206	1 starch
Carbohydrate	51 grams	2⅓ fruit
Cholesterol	0 milligrams	
Dietary Fiber	5 grams	
Protein	3 grams	
Sodium	33 milligrams	

SHOPPING LIST:
4 large sweet potatoes, 6 large carrots, 2 oz. raisins, 2 oz. golden raisins, 2 oz. pitted prunes, 2 oz. chopped dates, 4 oz. orange juice, brown sugar, 1 oz. honey

VIGOROUS VEGETABLES

VEGGIE PATTIES

EASY - DO AHEAD

INGREDIENTS:
- ¾ cup shredded zucchini
- ¾ cup shredded carrots
- 1½ tsp. onion powder
- 2 tsp. minced garlic
- 15 oz. can fat-free black beans, mashed
- ½ cup fat-free cooked rice
- ¼ cup egg substitute
- 2 tbsp. fat-free bread crumbs
- 1 tsp. Italian seasoning

DIRECTIONS:
Preheat broiler on high heat. Line broiler pan with foil and lightly spray with nonfat cooking spray. In a large bowl, combine all ingredients and mix well. (If mixture is too moist to shape, refrigerate 1 hour.) Shape mixture into 8 patties and place on prepared pan. Broil 4 to 6 inches from heat for 5 to 6 minutes per side, until lightly browned. Great as a sandwich on fat-free roll with lettuce, tomato, and deli-style mustard or fat-free honey-mustard sauce.

Serves: 4

Nutrition per Serving		Exchanges
Calories	188	1 starch
Carbohydrate	34 grams	4 vegetable
Cholesterol	0 milligrams	
Dietary Fiber	6 grams	
Protein	12 grams	
Sodium	37 milligrams	

SHOPPING LIST:
1 zucchini, 1 to 2 carrots, onion powder, minced garlic, 15 oz. can fat-free black beans, fat-free rice, 2 oz. egg substitute, fat-free bread crumbs, Italian seasoning

PINEAPPLE BAKED BEANS

EASY - DO AHEAD

INGREDIENTS:

2 16-oz. cans fat-free baked beans
1 cup pineapple chunks in juice, drained
2 tbsp. molasses
2 tsp. mustard
¼ cup brown sugar
½ tsp. cinnamon

DIRECTIONS:

Preheat oven to 350 degrees. Lightly spray 1½-quart casserole with nonfat cooking spray. Combine baked beans, pineapple, molasses, and mustard in prepared casserole. In a small bowl, combine brown sugar and cinnamon and blend well. Sprinkle mixture over beans and mix well. Bake in preheated oven for 30 minutes, until bubbly and cooked through.

Serves: 8

Nutrition per Serving		Exchanges
Calories	155	2 starch
Carbohydrate	36 grams	⅓ fruit
Cholesterol	0 milligrams	
Dietary Fiber	9 grams	
Protein	6 grams	
Sodium	469 milligrams	

SHOPPING LIST:

2 16-oz. cans fat-free baked beans, 8 oz. pineapple chunks in juice, molasses, mustard, brown sugar, cinnamon

VIGOROUS VEGETABLES

RANCH-STYLE BEANS

AVERAGE - DO AHEAD

INGREDIENTS:
- 1 cup stewed tomatoes, with liquid
- 1 tbsp. onion powder
- ½ cup brown sugar
- 1 tbsp. mustard
- 1½ tsp. apple cider vinegar
- 3 cups fat-free baked beans
- ¾ cup fat-free canned red kidney beans

DIRECTIONS:
Preheat oven to 400 degrees. Lightly spray 1-quart casserole with nonfat cooking spray. Lightly spray large nonstick skillet with nonfat cooking spray. Pour tomatoes with liquid into skillet; sprinkle with onion powder and heat over medium-high heat, about 3 to 5 minutes. Stir in sugar, mustard, vinegar, baked beans, and kidney beans; cover and simmer over low heat for 10 minutes. Spoon beans into prepared casserole and bake in preheated oven 15 to 20 minutes, until bubbly.

Serves: 6

Nutrition per Serving

Calories	243
Carbohydrate	54 grams
Cholesterol	0 milligrams
Dietary Fiber	7 grams
Protein	9 grams
Sodium	669 milligrams

Exchanges
3⅓ starch

SHOPPING LIST:
8 oz. stewed tomatoes, onion powder, brown sugar, mustard, apple cider vinegar, 2 15-oz. cans fat-free baked beans, 15 oz. can fat-free red kidney beans

BUTTERMILK MASHED POTATOES

AVERAGE

INGREDIENTS:
> 3 lbs. baking potatoes, peeled and cubed
> 2 tbsp. Buttermilk Blend Mix
> ½ cup water
> ½ cup chopped green onion
> ½ tsp. pepper

DIRECTIONS:
> Place potatoes in a large saucepan or Dutch oven; add just
> enough water to cover potatoes. Cover and bring to a boil
> over high heat; reduce heat to low and simmer 25 to 30 min-
> utes, until potatoes are tender. Drain potatoes and mash
> well; sprinkle Buttermilk Blend into potatoes and add
> water. Mix potatoes with masher or blender until creamy
> and smooth. Add green onions and pepper and mix lightly.
> Serve immediately.

Serves: 6

Nutrition per Serving		Exchanges
Calories	201	2 starch
Carbohydrate	46 grams	1 fruit
Cholesterol	< 1 milligram	
Dietary Fiber	3 grams	
Protein	4 grams	
Sodium	25 milligrams	

VIGOROUS VEGETABLES

SHOPPING LIST:
> 3 lb. baking potatoes, Buttermilk Blend Mix, 1 to 2 green
> onions, pepper

CHEDDAR POTATO CRISPS

EASY - DO AHEAD

INGREDIENTS:

4 lbs. potatoes, peeled and sliced
1 tsp. onion powder
pepper to taste
¾ cup sliced mushrooms
1 cup fat-free Cheddar cheese, shredded

DIRECTIONS:

Preheat oven to 350 degrees. Lightly spray 9x13-inch baking dish with nonfat cooking spray. Arrange half the potatoes on the bottom of the dish; sprinkle with onion powder and pepper. Top with mushrooms, ½ cup cheese and remaining potatoes. Lightly spray potatoes with nonfat cooking spray. Bake 50 to 60 minutes in preheated oven, until potatoes are tender. Remove from oven and increase temperature to 400 degrees. Sprinkle remaining cheese over potatoes and bake until cheese is melted.

Serves: 10

Nutrition per Serving		Exchanges
Calories	177	2¼ starch
Carbohydrate	38 grams	
Cholesterol	0 milligrams	
Dietary Fiber	3 grams	
Protein	7 grams	
Sodium	120 milligrams	

VIGOROUS VEGETABLES

SHOPPING LIST:

4 lb. potatoes, onion powder, pepper, 3 to 4 mushrooms, 8 oz. fat-free shredded Cheddar cheese

CINNAMON-HONEY SWEET POTATOES

EASY - DO AHEAD

INGREDIENTS:

5 large sweet potatoes, peeled and sliced
1 tsp. cinnamon
½ tsp. ginger
1 tbsp. orange juice
¼ cup honey

DIRECTIONS:

Preheat oven to 350 degrees. Lightly spray a 9-inch baking dish with nonfat cooking spray. Arrange potato slices in bottom of dish. Sprinkle with cinnamon, ginger, orange juice, and honey. Bake, covered, in preheated oven for 50 to 60 minutes, until potatoes are soft and tender.

Serves: 8

Nutrition per Serving		Exchanges
Calories	122	⅓ starch
Carbohydrate	30 grams	1⅔ fruit
Cholesterol	0 milligrams	
Dietary Fiber	3 grams	
Protein	1 gram	
Sodium	9 milligrams	

SHOPPING LIST:

5 large sweet potatoes, cinnamon, ginger, orange juice, 2 oz. honey

CREAMY MASHED POTATOES

EASY - DO AHEAD

INGREDIENTS:
  8 medium baking potatoes
  1 cup fat-free cream cheese, softened
  ¼ cup fat-free sour cream
  salt and pepper, to taste
  ½ cup fat-free Parmesan cheese

DIRECTIONS:
  Preheat oven to 350 degrees. Lightly spray a 2-quart casserole with nonfat cooking spray. Wash potatoes and cut into quarters. Place in large saucepan and cover with water. Bring to a boil over high heat; reduce heat to medium and cook 20 to 25 minutes, until potatoes are tender. Drain and cool to room temperature. Peel potatoes and set aside. In a a large bowl, combine cream cheese and sour cream and mix until blended smooth. Add potatoes and mash or blend with electric mixer until all ingredients are blended. Season with salt and pepper to taste. Spoon potato mixture into prepared casserole; sprinkle top with Parmesan cheese and bake in preheated oven for 30 minutes. If recipe is prepared ahead of time, refrigerate until ready to bake; bake 10 to 15 minutes longer if refrigerated before cooking.

Serves: 8

VIGOROUS VEGETABLES

Nutrition per Serving

Calories	193
Carbohydrate	38 grams
Cholesterol	0 milligrams
Dietary Fiber	4 grams
Protein	10 grams
Sodium	254 milligrams

Exchanges
2½ starch

SHOPPING LIST:
  8 medium baking potatoes, 8 oz. fat-free cream cheese, 2 oz. fat-free sour cream, salt and pepper, 2 oz. fat-free Parmesan cheese

GINGER SWEET POTATOES

EASY - DO AHEAD

INGREDIENTS:
2 lbs. yams, thinly sliced
1¼ cups fat-free chicken broth
3 tsp. ginger, divided
1 tbsp. sugar
½ tsp. cinnamon

DIRECTIONS:
Preheat oven to 375 degrees. Lightly spray a 9-inch baking dish with nonfat cooking spray. Arrange potato slices in baking dish. Combine chicken broth and 1½ teaspoons ginger in a small bowl; pour over potatoes. Bake in preheated oven about 1 hour, until tender. In a small bowl, combine remaining ginger, sugar, and cinnamon; sprinkle over potatoes and bake 20 to 30 minutes, until lightly browned and glazed.

Serves: 4

Nutrition per Serving		Exchanges
Calories	282	2 vegetable
Carbohydrate	67 grams	4 fruit
Cholesterol	0 milligrams	
Dietary Fiber	10 grams	
Protein	4 grams	
Sodium	244 milligrams	

SHOPPING LIST:
2 lb. yams, 14½ oz. can fat-free chicken broth, ginger, sugar, cinnamon

VIGOROUS VEGETABLES

ITALIAN POTATO BOATS

EASY - DO AHEAD

INGREDIENTS:
2 medium baking potatoes
2 tbsp. fat-free pasta sauce
2 tbsp. fat-free Parmesan cheese
2 tbsp. fat-free shredded mozzarella cheese

DIRECTIONS:
Preheat oven to 400 degrees. Lightly spray baking sheet with nonfat cooking spray. Cut potatoes in half lengthwise. Dip each potato half into pasta sauce and sprinkle with Parmesan cheese. Place, cheese-side down, on baking sheet and bake 25 to 30 minutes, until potatoes are tender. Turn potatoes over; top with mozzarella cheese and bake 5 to 10 minutes, until cheese is melted.

Serves: 2

Nutrition per Serving		Exchanges
Calories	141	2 starch
Carbohydrate	30 grams	
Cholesterol	0 milligrams	
Dietary Fiber	3 grams	
Protein	6 grams	
Sodium	126 milligrams	

SHOPPING LIST:
2 medium baking potatoes, 1 oz. fat-free pasta sauce, ½ fat-free Parmesan cheese, ½ oz. fat-free shredded m zarella cheese

LEMON NEW POTATOES

AVERAGE

INGREDIENTS:

2 lbs. new potatoes
⅓ cup fat-free margarine, melted
1 tsp. grated lemon rind
1 tsp. lemon juice
2 tbsp. minced chives
½ tsp. salt
⅛ tsp. pepper
⅛ tsp. ground cardamom

DIRECTIONS:

Scrub potatoes well and pare a band around the middle of each potato. Place potatoes in large saucepan and cover with water. Bring to a boil over high heat; reduce heat to low; cover and simmer 20 minutes, until potatoes are tender. Drain potatoes and return to pan over medium heat and shake until potatoes are dry. In a small bowl, combine melted margarine with lemon rind and lemon juice. Pour mixture over potatoes; sprinkle with chives, salt, pepper, and cardamom. Toss gently and serve immediately.

Serves: 6

Nutrition per Serving		Exchanges
Calories	155	1 starch
Carbohydrate	35 grams	1⅓ fruit
Cholesterol	0 milligrams	
Dietary Fiber	3 grams	
Protein	3 grams	
Sodium	268 milligrams	

SHOPPING LIST:

2 lb. new potatoes, fat-free margarine, lemon rind, lemon juice, chives, salt, pepper, cardamom

PARMESAN POTATOES

EASY - DO AHEAD

INGREDIENTS:
3 lbs. red potatoes, quartered
1 cup chopped onion
¼ tsp. garlic powder
⅛ tsp. pepper
¼ cup fat-free margarine, melted
¾ cup fat-free Parmesan cheese

DIRECTIONS:
Preheat oven to 450 degrees. Lightly spray a 10x15-inch baking dish with nonfat cooking spray. Place potatoes and onions in prepared dish and mix lightly. Sprinkle potatoes and onions with garlic powder and pepper; drizzle with margarine. Top with Parmesan cheese. Bake in preheated oven for 25 to 30 minutes, until lightly browned.

Serves: 6

Nutrition per Serving		Exchanges
Calories	255	3⅓ starch
Carbohydrate	55 grams	
Cholesterol	0 milligrams	
Dietary Fiber	6 grams	
Protein	9 grams	
Sodium	162 milligrams	

SHOPPING LIST:
3 lb. red potatoes, 1 large onion, garlic powder, pepper, 2 oz. fat-free margarine, 3 oz. fat-free Parmesan cheese

VIGOROUS VEGETABLES

POTATO CASSEROLE

EASY - DO AHEAD

INGREDIENTS:

1 cup skim milk
3 cups shredded potatoes
2 tbsp. fat-free margarine
1 tbsp. onion flakes
¼ tsp. pepper
½ cup fat-free shredded Cheddar cheese

DIRECTIONS:

Preheat oven to 350 degrees. Lightly spray a 9x13-inch baking dish with nonfat cooking spray. Place skim milk in medium saucepan and heat over medium-high heat to a boil. Add potatoes and cook until milk is totally absorbed. Stir in margarine, onion flakes, and pepper; mix well. Pour into prepared pan and cover top with cheese. Bake in preheated oven 1 hour, until browned.

Serves: 12

Nutrition per Serving		Exchanges
Calories	56	⅔ starch
Carbohydrate	11 grams	
Cholesterol	< 1 milligram	
Dietary Fiber	< 1 gram	
Protein	3 grams	
Sodium	74 milligrams	

SHOPPING LIST:

8 oz. skim milk, 1 lb. potatoes, fat-free margarine, onion flakes, pepper, 2 oz. fat-free shredded Cheddar cheese

VIGOROUS VEGETABLES

POTATO SNACKS WITH ROASTED GARLIC DRESSING

EASY - DO AHEAD

INGREDIENTS:
1 lb. baking potatoes
¼ tsp. garlic powder
¼ tsp. onion powder
¼ tsp. dry mustard
½ tsp. paprika
¼ tsp. sugar
1 cup fat-free Roasted Garlic Dressing

DIRECTIONS:
Preheat oven to 450 degrees. Line baking sheet with foil and lightly spray with nonfat cooking spray. Slice potatoes lengthwise into 6 to 8 slices and place in a single layer on baking sheet. In a small bowl, combine garlic powder, onion powder, dry mustard, paprika, and sugar; mix until blended. Lightly spray potatoes with nonfat cooking spray and immediately sprinkle with mixed seasonings. Bake in preheated oven for 10 to 15 minutes, until browned; remove from oven. Flip potatoes with spatula; sprinkle with remaining seasoning mixture and bake an additional 15 minutes, until browned and crisp on both sides. Serve with Roasted Garlic Dressing.

Serves: 6

Nutrition per Serving		Exchanges
Calories	179	1½ starch
Carbohydrate	41 grams	1 fruit
Cholesterol	0 milligrams	
Dietary Fiber	4 grams	
Protein	3 grams	
Sodium	179 milligrams	

SHOPPING LIST:
1 lb. baking potatoes, garlic powder, onion powder, dry mustard, paprika, sugar, 8 oz. fat-free Roasted Garlic Dressing

SPINACH BAKED POTATOES

EASY - DO AHEAD

INGREDIENTS:

4 large baking potatoes
½ cup skim milk, warmed
1 cup fat-free cottage cheese
¼ tsp. garlic powder
2 cups chopped spinach, cooked and drained
¼ cup fat-free Parmesan cheese
½ cup fat-free shredded Cheddar cheese

DIRECTIONS:

Preheat oven to 400 degrees. Lightly spray baking sheet with nonfat cooking spray. Pierce potatoes several times with fork and bake in preheated oven for 1 hour (or microwave on high 20 to 25 minutes, until cooked through). Remove from oven and cool slightly. Cut potato in half and carefully scoop out pulp. In a medium bowl, combine potato pulp with warm milk and mix until smooth. Stir in cottage cheese, garlic powder, spinach, and 2 tablespoons Parmesan cheese; mix well. Spoon mixture into potato skins and sprinkle with remaining Parmesan and Cheddar cheese. Place on prepared baking sheet and bake in preheated oven for 15 to 20 minutes, until cheese is melted. This can be prepared ahead of time; cook 10 to 15 minutes longer if potatoes are cold.

Serves: 4

Nutrition per Serving		Exchanges
Calories	269	3 starch
Carbohydrate	53 grams	1 vegetable
Cholesterol	2 milligrams	½ meat
Dietary Fiber	7 grams	
Protein	16 grams	
Sodium	345 milligrams	

VIGOROUS VEGETABLES

SHOPPING LIST:

4 large baking potatoes, 4 oz. skim milk, 8 oz. fat-free cottage cheese, garlic powder, 2 10-oz. packages frozen chopped spinach, 1 oz. fat-free Parmesan cheese, 2 oz. fat-free shredded Cheddar cheese

YOGURT MASHED POTATOES

INGREDIENTS:

2 lbs. red potatoes, cleaned
½ cup fat-free plain yogurt
1 tsp. white horseradish
½ tsp. minced garlic
2 tsp. freeze-dried chives
salt and pepper to taste

DIRECTIONS:

Place potatoes in a large saucepan or Dutch oven and cover with water. Bring water to a boil over medium-high heat; reduce temperature to medium-low; cover and cook 10 to 15 minutes, until potatoes are soft and tender. Drain potatoes and place in a large bowl. Mash potatoes with fork or potato masher. In a small bowl, combine yogurt, horseradish, and garlic; mix until blended. Stir yogurt mixture and chives into mashed potatoes. Season with salt and pepper. Serve immediately.

Serves: 6

Nutrition per Serving		Exchanges
Calories	160	2 starch
Carbohydrate	36 grams	
Cholesterol	< 1 milligram	
Dietary Fiber	3 grams	
Protein	4 grams	
Sodium	25 milligrams	

VIGOROUS VEGETABLES

SHOPPING LIST:

2 lbs. red potatoes, 4 oz. fat-free yogurt, white horseradish, minced garlic, freeze-dried chives, salt, pepper

DELICIOUS DESSERTS

APPLE-CARROT CAKE

EASY - DO AHEAD - FREEZE

INGREDIENTS:

2 tbsp. apple butter
1 cup chunky-style apple-
  sauce
¾ cup egg substitute
½ cup sugar
½ cup brown sugar
1 tsp. vanilla

2 cups flour
1 tsp. baking soda
1 tsp. baking powder
2 tsp. cinnamon
3 cups grated carrots
powdered sugar (optional)

DIRECTIONS:

Preheat oven to 350 degrees. Lightly spray a 9x13-inch baking dish with nonfat cooking spray. In large bowl, combine
apple butter, applesauce, egg substitute, sugar, brown sugar,
and vanilla; blend until smooth. Gradually add flour, baking soda, baking powder, and cinnamon to apple mixture;
blend until all dry ingredients are moistened. Fold in carrots; mix lightly. Pour batter into prepared pan; bake in preheated oven 35 to 40 minutes, until knife inserted in center
comes out clean. Cool to room temperature; sprinkle with
powdered sugar, if desired.

Serves: 12

Nutrition per Serving		Exchanges
Calories	175	1⅓ starch
Carbohydrate	40 grams	1⅓ fruit
Cholesterol	0 milligrams	
Dietary Fiber	2 grams	
Protein	4 grams	
Sodium	129 milligrams	

SHOPPING LIST:

1 oz. unsweetened apple butter, 8 oz. chunky-style applesauce, 6 oz. egg substitute, ¼ lb. sugar, ¼ lb. brown sugar,
vanilla, ½ lb. flour, baking soda, baking powder, cinnamon,
1 package shredded carrots (or 4 to 5 carrots), powdered
sugar (optional)

BLACK FOREST CAKE

AVERAGE - DO AHEAD - FREEZE

INGREDIENTS:

½ cup egg substitute
1 cup Lighter Bake
¾ cup + 4 tsp. skim milk
½ cup sugar
1 cup brown sugar
1½ tbsp. vanilla
1 cup boiling water
2 tsp. baking soda

1¾ cups flour
1 cup unsweetened cocoa
  powder
1 tsp. baking powder
2 cups frozen pitted sweet
  cherries, thawed
1 cup powdered sugar

DIRECTIONS:

Preheat oven to 350 degrees. Lightly spray 16-cup bundt or tube pan with nonfat cooking spray. In large bowl, combine egg substitute, Lighter Bake, ¾ cup milk, sugar, brown sugar, and vanilla and mix until blended. Add boiling water and baking soda to egg mixture; blend well. In a medium bowl, combine flour, cocoa, and baking powder; mix well. Add flour mixture to liquid mixture; mix until all dry ingredients are moistened and batter is blended smooth. Pour ½ batter in prepared pan; top with 1 cup cherries and remaining batter. Bake in preheated oven for 45 to 50 minutes, until knife inserted in center comes out clean. Remove from pan; cool completely. In a medium bowl, combine powdered sugar with enough skim milk (about 4 teaspoons) to desired consistency. Drizzle glaze over cooled cake.

Serves: 16

Nutrition per Serving

Calories	219
Carbohydrate	53 grams
Cholesterol	< 1 milligram
Dietary Fiber	< 1 gram
Protein	4 grams
Sodium	153 milligrams

Exchanges

1⅓ starch
2 fruit

SHOPPING LIST:

4 oz. egg substitute, 8 oz. Lighter Bake, 7 oz. skim milk, ¼ lb. sugar, ½ lb. brown sugar, vanilla, baking soda, flour, 4 oz. unsweetened cocoa powder, baking powder, 16 oz. frozen pitted sweet cherries, ½ lb. powdered sugar

BUTTERSCOTCH CAKE

EASY - DO AHEAD

INGREDIENTS:
½ cup skim milk
¼ cup apple butter
1 cup flour
¾ cup sugar
2 tsp. baking powder
2 tsp. cinnamon, divided
1 cup brown sugar
½ cup fat-free Cool Whip (optional)

DIRECTIONS:
Preheat oven to 350 degrees. Lightly spray 8-inch square baking dish with nonfat cooking spray. In a large bowl, combine milk and apple butter; mix until smooth. Add flour, sugar, baking powder, and 1½ teaspoons cinnamon; mix until all ingredients are blended. In a small bowl, combine brown sugar and ½ teaspoon cinnamon. Spread batter into prepared pan; sprinkle brown sugar mixture over top and bake in preheated oven for 40 to 45 minutes, until cooked through. Cool 15 to 20 minutes before serving. Top with fat-free Cool Whip, if desired.

Serves: 12

Nutrition per Serving		Exchanges
Calories	172	⅓ starch
Carbohydrate	42 grams	2½ fruit
Cholesterol	< 1 milligram	
Dietary Fiber	< 1 gram	
Protein	1 gram	
Sodium	67 milligrams	

SHOPPING LIST:
4 oz. skim milk, 2 oz. apple butter, flour, sugar, baking powder, cinnamon, ½ lb. brown sugar, 4 oz. fat-free Cool Whip (optional)

CHOCOLATE CHERRY CAKE

EASY - DO AHEAD - FREEZE

INGREDIENTS:

¾ cup Lighter Bake
½ cup egg substitute
1 tsp. vanilla
1¼ cups water
1 cup brown sugar
⅔ cup sugar
2¼ cups flour

⅔ cup unsweetened cocoa
powder
1 tsp. baking soda
½ tsp. baking powder
20 oz. lite cherry pie filling
chocolate powdered sugar
(optional)

DIRECTIONS:

Preheat oven to 350 degrees. Lightly spray a 9x13-inch baking dish with nonfat cooking spray. In a large bowl, combine Lighter Bake, egg substitute, vanilla, water, brown sugar, and sugar; mix until blended and creamy. Add flour, ⅔ cup cocoa, baking soda, and baking powder to mixture and blend until dry ingredients are moistened and blended. Spread ½ batter into prepared pan. Top with cherry pie filling and spread remaining batter on top. Bake in preheated oven for 30 to 40 minutes, until knife inserted in center comes out clean. Cool to room temperature. Sprinkle with chocolate powdered sugar, if desired.

Serves: 16

Nutrition per Serving		Exchanges
Calories	271	1 starch
Carbohydrate	66 grams	3¼ fruit
Cholesterol	0 milligrams	
Dietary Fiber	1 gram	
Protein	3 grams	
Sodium	117 milligrams	

DELICIOUS DESSERTS

SHOPPING LIST:

6 oz. Lighter Bake, 4 oz. egg substitute, vanilla, ½ lb. brown sugar, sugar, flour, 8 oz. unsweetened cocoa powder, baking soda, baking powder, 20 oz. lite cherry pie filling, chocolate powdered sugar (optional)

DEVILS FOOD FUDGE CAKE

AVERAGE - DO AHEAD - FREEZE

INGREDIENTS:

¼ cup Lighter Bake
¼ cup apple butter
1 cup water
⅜ cup egg substitute
1½ tsp. vanilla
1⅛ cups flour
⅝ cup sugar
½ cup brown sugar

1 cup unsweetened cocoa powder, divided
1½ tsp. baking powder
¼ tsp. baking soda
2½ cups chocolate powdered sugar
¼ cup skim milk

DIRECTIONS:

Preheat oven to 350 degrees. Lightly spray a 10-inch baking dish with nonfat cooking spray. In a large bowl, combine Lighter Bake, apple butter, water, egg substitute, and vanilla and mix until blended smooth. Add flour, sugar, brown sugar, ¾ cup cocoa, baking powder, and baking soda; mix well. Spread batter into prepared pan and bake in preheated oven for 25 to 30 minutes, until knife inserted in center comes out clean. Cool completely.

In a medium bowl, combine chocolate powdered sugar, ¼ cup cocoa, and milk; mix until smooth. Spread over cooled cake.

Serves: 16

Nutrition per Serving		Exchanges
Calories	180	1 starch
Carbohydrate	46 grams	2 fruit
Cholesterol	0 milligrams	
Dietary Fiber	< 1 gram	
Protein	3 grams	
Sodium	63 milligrams	

SHOPPING LIST:

2 oz. Lighter Bake, 2 oz. apple butter, 3 oz. egg substitute, 1 egg, vanilla, ⅓ lb. flour, ¼ lb. sugar, ¼ lb. brown sugar, 4 oz. unsweetened cocoa powder, baking powder, baking soda, 1 lb. chocolate powdered sugar, 2 oz. skim milk

DELICIOUS DESSERTS

PEACH STREUSEL CAKE

EASY - DO AHEAD - FREEZE

INGREDIENTS:

3½ cups Pioneer Baking Mix, divided
½ cup sugar
¾ cup brown sugar, divided
⅓ cup nonfat dry milk powder
1 cup water
2 tsp. vanilla
½ cup egg substitute
21 oz. peach pie filling
¾ tsp. cinnamon
2 tbsp. reconstituted Butter Buds

DIRECTIONS:

Preheat oven to 375 degrees. Lightly spray a 9x13-inch baking dish with nonfat cooking spray. In a large bowl, combine 3 cups baking mix, sugar, ½ cup brown sugar, and milk powder; mix well. Gradually add water, vanilla, and egg substitute; mix until blended smooth. Spread half the batter into prepared dish; top with peach pie filling. Cover peaches with remaining batter. In a small bowl, combine ½ cup baking mix, ¼ cup brown sugar, and cinnamon; mix well. Stir in Butter Buds until mixture becomes crumbly. Sprinkle on top of cake and bake in preheated oven for 20 to 30 minutes, until knife inserted in center comes out clean. Apple or cherry pie filling can be substituted for peach.

Serves: 16

Nutrition per Serving	
Calories	300
Carbohydrate	78 grams
Cholesterol	< 1 milligram
Dietary Fiber	< 1 gram
Protein	4 grams
Sodium	509 milligrams

Exchanges
1⅓ starch
3⅔ fruit

SHOPPING LIST:

Pioneer Baking Mix, sugar, brown sugar, nonfat dry milk powder, vanilla, 4 oz. egg substitute, 21 oz. peach pie filling, cinnamon, Butter Buds Flavored Granules

PEPPERMINT CHEESECAKE

AVERAGE - DO AHEAD

INGREDIENTS:

1½ cups fat-free graham
   cracker crumbs
3 tbsp. reconstituted Butter
   Buds granules
3 cups fat-free cream cheese,
   softened
1 cup sugar

1 cup egg substitute
1½ cups fat-free sour cream
1 tsp. vanilla
½ tsp. peppermint extract
red food coloring (optional)
¼ cup hard peppermint
   candies, crushed

DIRECTIONS:

Preheat oven to 350 degrees. Lightly spray 10-inch spring-form pan with nonfat cooking spray. In a medium bowl, combine graham cracker crumbs with liquid Butter Buds; mix until blended. Press mixture onto bottom of springform pan.

In large bowl, combine cream cheese and sugar; mix until blended and fluffy. Add egg substitute, ¼ cup at a time, mixing well after each addition. Add sour cream and vanilla and mix until blended. Remove 1 cup mixture and place in small bowl. Stir in peppermint extract and food coloring, if desired. Pour plain cheese mixture over crust; drop peppermint batter by tablespoons onto cheese mixture, Using knife, swirl batters together. Bake in preheated oven 55 to 60 minutes, until knife inserted in center comes out clean. Cool pie to room temperature and refrigerate overnight before serving. Sprinkle crushed peppermint candies on top just before serving.

Serves: 12

Nutrition per Serving		Exchanges
Calories	162	1 milk
Carbohydrate	27 grams	1 fruit
Cholesterol	0 milligrams	½ meat
Dietary Fiber	1 gram	
Protein	12 grams	
Sodium	408 milligrams	

SHOPPING LIST:

fat-free graham crackers (18 squares), Butter Buds Flavored Granules, 24 oz. fat-free cream cheese, ½ lb. sugar, 8 oz. egg substitute, 12 oz. fat-free sour cream, vanilla, peppermint extract, red food coloring (optional), hard peppermint candies

DELICIOUS
DESSERTS

BANANA PUDDING PIE

AVERAGE - DO AHEAD

INGREDIENTS:
2 cups fat-free crushed granola
½ tsp. cinnamon
1 tbsp. Lighter Bake
2 medium bananas, sliced
¾ cup skim milk
1 cup fat-free banana yogurt
3⅜ oz. instant fat-free vanilla pudding mix

DIRECTIONS:
Lightly spray 9-inch pie pan with nonfat cooking spray. In a medium bowl, combine granola and cinnamon; stir in Lighter Bake until mixture is blended. Press granola mixture into bottom of pie pan. Arrange banana slices on top of crust. In a medium bowl, combine milk, yogurt, and pudding mix; beat until mixture is thick and creamy. Spoon over bananas and smooth evenly. Refrigerate several hours before serving.

Serves: 8

Nutrition per Serving		Exchanges
Calories	167	½ milk
Carbohydrate	40 grams	2 fruit
Cholesterol	1 milligram	
Dietary Fiber	< 1 gram	
Protein	3 grams	
Sodium	206 milligrams	

DELICIOUS DESSERTS

SHOPPING LIST:
Health Valley fat-free granola, cinnamon, Lighter Bake, 2 medium bananas, 6 oz. skim milk, 8 oz. fat-free banana yogurt, 3⅜ oz. fat-free instant vanilla pudding mix

CHOCOLATE MARSHMALLOW COOKIE PIE

EASY - DO AHEAD

INGREDIENTS:

1½ cups crushed SnackWell's fat-free cinnamon graham cookies
2 cups miniature marshmallows
2 cups + 2 tbsp. skim milk
2½ cups fat-free Cool Whip
8 oz. package instant fat-free chocolate pudding mix
15 whole fat-free chocolate wafer cookies

DIRECTIONS:

Lightly spray a 9-inch pie plate with nonfat cooking spray. Sprinkle crushed cinnamon graham cookies in bottom of pan and press down firmly. In a medium microwave-safe bowl, combine marshmallows and 2 tablespoons milk. Microwave on high 45 seconds. Stir mixture until marshmallows are slightly melted. Refrigerate marshmallows 15 to 20 minutes; stir in 1 cup Cool Whip and mix well. In a large bowl, combine pudding with 2 cups milk and whisk until blended. Let pudding stand 1 minute until thickened. Stir in remaining Cool Whip and blend well. Spread pudding mixture over graham crumbs. Arrange cookies on top of pudding; top with marshmallow mixture. Refrigerate pie until set, about 4 to 6 hours.

Serves: 8

Nutrition per Serving		Exchanges
Calories	234	1⅓ starch
Carbohydrate	50 grams	2 fruit
Cholesterol	1 milligram	
Dietary Fiber	1 gram	
Protein	4 grams	
Sodium	93 milligrams	

SHOPPING LIST:

1 box SnackWell's fat-free cinnamon graham cookies, 16 oz. miniature marshmallows, 17 oz. skim milk, 20 to 24 oz. fat-free Cool Whip, 8 oz. fat-free chocolate instant pudding mix, 1 box fat-free chocolate wafer cookies

LEMON-ORANGE PIE

EASY - DO AHEAD

INGREDIENTS:
1 fat-free graham cracker crust (page 340)
⅜ cup sugar
2 tbsp. cornstarch
1½ cups orange juice
1½ tbsp. lemon juice
powdered sugar

DIRECTIONS:
Prepare pie crust according to directions (see Graham Cracker Crust page 340). In a medium saucepan over medium-low heat, combine sugar and cornstarch. Gradually add orange juice and cook, stirring constantly, until mixture thickens. Add lemon juice and mix well; remove from heat and cool to room temperature. Pour into prepared pie crust and refrigerate several hours before serving. Sprinkle top with powdered sugar just before serving.

Serves: 8

Nutrition per Serving		Exchanges
Calories	129	⅔ starch
Carbohydrate	30 grams	1⅓ fruit
Cholesterol	0 milligrams	
Dietary Fiber	2 grams	
Protein	2 grams	
Sodium	36 milligrams	

DELICIOUS DESSERTS

SHOPPING LIST:
fat-free graham cracker crust (or ingredients for homemade graham cracker crust with orange marmalade, page 340), sugar, cornstarch, 12 oz. orange juice, ¾ oz. lemon juice, powdered sugar

SAUCY APPLE PIE TART

EASY - DO AHEAD

INGREDIENTS:
⅓ cup sugar
⅔ cup brown sugar, divided
¾ tsp. cinnamon
¼ tsp. nutmeg
1 cup lite applesauce
20 oz. canned apple slices
1 whole fat-free pie crust
¾ cup flour
3 tbsp. apple butter

DIRECTIONS:
Preheat oven to 400 degrees. In a medium bowl, combine sugar, ⅓ cup brown sugar, cinnamon, nutmeg, and applesauce; mix well. Stir in apple slices. Pour mixture into pie shell. In a small bowl, combine flour and ⅓ cup brown sugar; cut in apple butter until mixture becomes crumbly. Sprinkle topping over top of pie and bake in preheated oven 40 minutes, until golden brown.

Serves: 8

Nutrition per Serving		Exchanges
Calories	226	1 starch
Carbohydrate	55 grams	2½ fruit
Cholesterol	0 milligrams	
Dietary Fiber	3 grams	
Protein	3 grams	
Sodium	35 milligrams	

SHOPPING LIST:
sugar, brown sugar, cinnamon, nutmeg, 8 oz. lite applesauce, 20 oz. canned apple slices, 1 fat-free pie crust, flour, 1½ oz. apple butter

CHOCOLATE CRUST

EASY - DO AHEAD - FREEZE

INGREDIENTS:
- ¼ cup corn syrup
- 3 tbsp. sugar
- 2 tbsp. brown sugar
- ¼ cup egg substitute
- 1 cup flour
- 2 tbsp. unsweetened cocoa powder

DIRECTIONS:

Preheat oven to 350 degrees. Lightly spray a 9-inch spring-form pan or pie plate with nonfat cooking spray. In a large bowl, combine corn syrup, sugar, brown sugar, and egg substitute until blended. Add flour and cocoa to sugar mixture; stir until well mixed. Spread batter into bottom of prepared pan and bake in preheated oven for 5 to 8 minutes. Fill pie shell with favorite filling and bake accordingly. If using pudding or other chilled filling, bake crust 15 to 20 minutes at 350 degrees.

Serves: 12

Nutrition per Serving		Exchanges
Calories	81	⅔ starch
Carbohydrate	19 grams	½ fruit
Cholesterol	0 milligrams	
Dietary Fiber	< 1 gram	
Protein	2 grams	
Sodium	13 milligrams	

SHOPPING LIST:

2 oz. corn syrup, sugar, brown sugar, 2 oz. egg substitute, flour, unsweetened cocoa powder

GRAHAM CRACKER CRUST

EASY - DO AHEAD

INGREDIENTS:
1 cup fat-free graham cracker crumbs
3 tbsp. orange marmalade, melted*
¼ tsp. cinnamon
1 tbsp. sugar

DIRECTIONS:
Preheat oven to 350 degrees. Lightly spray a 9-inch pie plate with nonfat cooking spray. Combine crumbs, melted orange marmalade, cinnamon, and sugar in medium bowl; mix until blended. Press crumb mixture into prepared pan and bake in preheated oven for 8 to 10 minutes.
*Apple butter or apricot preserves can be substituted for orange marmalade.

Serves: 8

Nutrition per Serving		Exchanges
Calories	45	⅓ starch
Carbohydrate	11 grams	⅓ fruit
Cholesterol	0 milligrams	
Dietary Fiber	1 gram	
Protein	1 gram	
Sodium	6 milligrams	

SHOPPING LIST:
fat-free graham crackers (12 squares), 1½ oz. orange marmalade, cinnamon, sugar

DELICIOUS DESSERTS

CHOCOLATE BERRY SHORTCAKES

AVERAGE - DO AHEAD

INGREDIENTS:
    4 cups frozen berry mix, sliced
    ½ cup sugar, divided
    2 tbsp. orange juice
    2¼ cups Pioneer Baking Mix
    ½ cup unsweetened cocoa powder
    1 cup skim milk
    1 tsp. vanilla
    2½ cups fat-free strawberry frozen yogurt

DIRECTIONS:
    Preheat oven to 400 degrees. Lightly spray baking sheet with nonfat cooking spray. In a medium bowl, combine mixed berries with ¼ cup sugar, and orange juice. In a large bowl, combine baking mix, cocoa, milk, ¼ cup sugar, and vanilla; blend until smooth. Roll dough into ball; dust with additional baking mix if dough is too sticky. Sprinkle counter or surface with baking mix; roll or pat dough into ½-inch-thick rectangle. Cut into rounds with cookie cutter or glass and place on prepared baking sheet. Bake in preheated oven for 10 to 12 minutes, until lightly browned. Cool cakes to room temperature. To serve, cut shortcakes in half; top with mixed berries and frozen yogurt. Top with remaining shortcakes and serve.

Serves: 10

Nutrition per Serving		Exchanges
Calories	334	2 starch
Carbohydrate	83 grams	¾ fruit
Cholesterol	< 1 milligram	
Dietary Fiber	1 gram	
Protein	8 grams	
Sodium	507 milligrams	

SHOPPING LIST:
    20 oz. frozen berry mix, sugar, 1 oz. orange juice, Pioneer Baking Mix, unsweetened cocoa powder, 8 oz. skim milk, vanilla, 20 oz. favorite flavor frozen yogurt

DELICIOUS DESSERTS

CHOCOLATE CARROT BROWNIES

EASY - DO AHEAD - FREEZE

INGREDIENTS:

1 tbsp. Lighter Bake
¼ cup sugar
¼ cup brown sugar
¼ cup skim milk
½ cup egg substitute
1½ tsp. vanilla
1 cup flour
¼ cup unsweetened cocoa powder
1½ tsp. baking powder
1 cup shredded carrots

DIRECTIONS:

Preheat oven to 350 degrees. Lightly spray a 9-inch baking dish with nonfat cooking spray. In a large bowl, combine Lighter Bake, sugar, brown sugar, milk, egg substitute, and vanilla; blend until smooth. In a medium bowl, combine flour, cocoa, and baking powder; mix until blended. Add flour mixture to large bowl and mix until dry ingredients are moistened. Fold in carrots and mix lightly. Pour batter into prepared pan and bake in preheated oven 20 to 25 minutes, until knife inserted in center comes out clean.

Serves: 16

Nutrition per Serving		Exchanges
Calories	66	¾ starch
Carbohydrate	15 grams	
Cholesterol	0 milligrams	
Dietary Fiber	< 1 gram	
Protein	2 grams	
Sodium	48 milligrams	

SHOPPING LIST:

Lighter Bake, sugar, brown sugar, 2 oz. skim milk, 4 oz. egg substitute, vanilla, flour, unsweetened cocoa powder, baking powder, prepackaged shredded carrots (or ½ lb. carrots)

CHOCOLATE FUDGE BROWNIES

EASY - DO AHEAD - FREEZE

INGREDIENTS:
¾ cup unsweetened apple butter
1 cup sugar
1 cup brown sugar
2 tsp. vanilla
1 cup egg substitute
¾ cup unsweetened cocoa powder
1 cup flour
½ tsp. baking powder

DIRECTIONS:
Preheat oven to 350 degrees. Lightly spray a 9x13-inch baking dish with nonfat cooking spray. In a large bowl, combine apple butter, sugar, brown sugar, vanilla, and egg substitute and mix until blended smooth. Stir in cocoa, flour, and baking powder; mix until all ingredients are blended. Spoon batter into prepared dish and bake 30 to 35 minutes. Cool to room temperature; sprinkle with powdered sugar, if desired.

Serves: 24

Nutrition per Serving		Exchanges
Calories	112	⅔ starch
Carbohydrate	27 grams	1 fruit
Cholesterol	0 milligrams	
Dietary Fiber	< 1 gram	
Protein	2 grams	
Sodium	24 grams	

SHOPPING LIST:
6 oz. unsweetened apple butter, ½ lb. sugar, ½ lb. brown sugar, vanilla, 8 oz. egg substitute, 8 oz. unsweetened cocoa powder, flour, baking powder

DELICIOUS DESSERTS

CINNAMON COOKIE SNACKS

EASY - DO AHEAD - FREEZE

INGREDIENTS:

¼ cup Lighter Bake
¼ cup apple butter
1 cup sugar, divided
¼ cup brown sugar
3 tbsp. Buttermilk Blend
  Mix
¾ cup water

1 tsp. vanilla
2 cups flour
1 tsp. cinnamon, divided
¼ tsp. nutmeg
¼ tsp. baking powder
¼ tsp. baking soda

DIRECTIONS:

Combine Lighter Bake, apple butter, ¾ cup sugar, brown sugar, Buttermilk Blend, water, and vanilla in a large bowl; mix until blended smooth. Add flour, ½ teaspoon cinnamon, nutmeg, baking powder, and baking soda; mix until all ingredients are blended. Cover and refrigerate 2 to 4 hours. Preheat oven to 375 degrees. Lightly spray baking sheets with nonfat cooking spray. In a small bowl, combine ¼ cup sugar with ½ teaspoon cinnamon; mix well. Roll dough into balls and press flat onto baking sheet. Sprinkle cookies with cinnamon-sugar mixture and bake in preheated oven 8 to 10 minutes, until lightly browned.

Serves: 36

Nutrition per Serving		Exchanges
Calories	61	¼ starch
Carbohydrate	14 grams	1 fruit
Cholesterol	0 milligrams	
Dietary Fiber	< 1 gram	
Protein	1 gram	
Sodium	13 milligrams	

SHOPPING LIST:

2 oz. Lighter Bake, 2 oz. apple butter, ½ lb. sugar, brown sugar, Buttermilk Blend Mix, vanilla, ½ lb. flour, cinnamon, nutmeg, baking powder, baking soda

GINGERSNAPS

INGREDIENTS:
1 cup apple butter
¾ cup egg substitute
1 cup brown sugar
3¼ cups flour
½ tsp. baking soda
½ tsp. baking powder
1½ tsp. ginger
1½ tsp. cinnamon
½ tsp. allspice

DIRECTIONS:
In a large bowl, combine apple butter, egg substitute, and brown sugar; mix until blended smooth. Add flour, baking soda, baking powder, ginger, cinnamon, and allspice to butter mixture and mix until dry ingredients are moistened and blended. Wrap dough in plastic wrap and refrigerate at least 3 hours or overnight.

Preheat oven to 350 degrees. Lightly spray baking sheets with nonfat cooking spray. Roll dough into balls and flatten with sugar-dipped glass or roll out on floured surface and cut with cookie cutters. Place on prepared baking sheets and bake in preheated oven 10 to 12 minutes, until lightly browned.

Serves: 36

DELICIOUS DESSERTS

Nutrition per Serving		Exchanges
Calories	83	⅔ starch
Carbohydrate	19 grams	⅔ fruit
Cholesterol	0 milligrams	
Dietary Fiber	< 1 gram	
Protein	2 grams	
Sodium	25 milligrams	

SHOPPING LIST:
8 oz. apple butter, 6 oz. egg substitute, ½ lb. brown sugar, flour, baking soda, baking powder, ginger, cinnamon, allspice

GINGERBREAD

AVERAGE - DO AHEAD - FREEZE

INGREDIENTS:

⅓ cup Lighter Bake
2 tbsp. apple butter
1½ cups brown sugar
½ cup molasses
¼ cup egg substitute
2 tsp. vanilla
2⅓ cups flour

1½ tsp. baking soda
½ tsp. baking powder
1½ tsp. ginger
1 tsp. cinnamon
½ tsp. allspice
¾ cup boiling water

DIRECTIONS:

Preheat oven to 375 degrees. Lightly spray 9-inch square pan with nonfat cooking spray. In a large bowl, combine Lighter Bake, apple butter, brown sugar, molasses, egg substitute, and vanilla; blend until smooth. In a separate medium bowl, combine flour, baking soda, baking powder, ginger, cinnamon, and allspice; mix well. Alternately add flour mixture and boiling water to sugar mixture; mix well. Pour batter into prepared pan and bake in preheated oven 35 to 40 minutes, until knife inserted in center comes out clean.

Serves: 16

Nutrition per Serving		Exchanges
Calories	189	⅔ starch
Carbohydrate	45 grams	2⅓ fruit
Cholesterol	0 milligrams	
Dietary Fiber	< 1 gram	
Protein	2 grams	
Sodium	102 milligrams	

DELICIOUS DESSERTS

SHOPPING LIST:

3 oz. Lighter Bake, 1 oz. apple butter, ¾ lb. brown sugar, 4 oz. molasses, 2 oz. egg substitute, vanilla, flour, baking soda, baking powder, ginger, cinnamon, allspice

GLAZED SPICE COOKIES

EASY - DO AHEAD - FREEZE

INGREDIENTS:

¾ cup apple butter
½ cup corn syrup
½ cup sugar
1 cup brown sugar
½ cup egg substitute
¾ cup skim milk, divided
2 tsp. vanilla, divided

4½ cups flour
1 tsp. baking powder
1 tsp. baking soda
1½ tsp. cinnamon
1 tsp. ground ginger
¼ tsp. nutmeg
3 cups powdered sugar

DIRECTIONS:

In a large bowl, combine apple butter, corn syrup, sugar, brown sugar, egg substitute, ½ cup milk, and 1 teaspoon vanilla; blend until smooth. Add flour, baking powder, baking soda, cinnamon, ginger, and nutmeg; mix until all ingredients are blended. Wrap dough in plastic wrap and refrigerate 2 hours or overnight. Preheat oven to 350 degrees. Lightly spray baking sheets with nonfat cooking spray. Roll dough into 2-inch balls; place on cookie sheet and flatten. Bake in preheated oven for 6 to 8 minutes, until cookies are lightly browned. Cool on wire rack before icing. In a medium bowl, combine powdered sugar, ¼ cup milk and 1 teaspoon vanilla; mix until smooth. Spread icing on top of cooled cookies and store in airtight container.

Serves: 48

Nutrition per Serving		Exchanges
Calories	117	⅔ starch
Carbohydrate	27 grams	1 fruit
Cholesterol	0 milligrams	
Dietary Fiber	< 1 gram	
Protein	2 grams	
Sodium	35 milligrams	

SHOPPING LIST:

6 oz. apple butter, 4 oz. corn syrup, sugar, brown sugar, 4 oz. egg substitute, 6 oz. skim milk, vanilla, 1 lb. flour, baking powder, baking soda, cinnamon, ginger, nutmeg, 1½ lbs. powdered sugar

HONEY CAKE COOKIES

AVERAGE - DO AHEAD - FREEZE

INGREDIENTS:

½ cup apple butter
¼ cup Lighter Bake
½ cup sugar, divided
2 tbsp. brown sugar
¼ cup orange juice

2 cups flour
1½ tsp. baking powder
¾ tsp. cinnamon
¾ cup honey
¼ cup water

DIRECTIONS:

In a large bowl, combine apple butter, Lighter Bake, ¼ cup sugar, brown sugar, and orange juice; mix until blended smooth. Add flour, baking powder, and cinnamon; mix well. Cover dough with plastic wrap and refrigerate 1 hour.

Preheat oven to 375 degrees. Lightly spray baking sheets with nonfat cooking spray. Roll dough into 2-inch balls and place on prepared sheets. Bake in preheated oven for 10 to 15 minutes, until lightly browned. Cool completely.

In a small saucepan, combine ¼ cup sugar, honey, and water; bring to a boil over high heat, stirring constantly; cook until sugar is dissolved. Dip cooled cookies in honey mixture and place on wire racks until dry. Store in airtight container.

Serves: 24

Nutrition per Serving		Exchanges
Calories	109	1⅔ fruit
Carbohydrate	26 grams	
Cholesterol	0 milligrams	
Dietary Fiber	< 1 gram	
Protein	1 gram	
Sodium	22 milligrams	

SHOPPING LIST:

4 oz. apple butter, 2 oz. Lighter Bake, ¼ lb. sugar, brown sugar, 2 oz. orange juice, ½ lb. flour, baking powder, cinnamon, 6 oz. honey

MARBLE PUMPKIN SQUARES

AVERAGE - DO AHEAD

INGREDIENTS:

⅜ cup fat-free cream cheese
3 tbsp. sugar
¼ cup egg substitute
½ cup apple butter
1 cup brown sugar
2 large egg whites

1½ tsp. vanilla
1 cup flour
1 tsp. cinnamon
¼ tsp. pumpkin pie spice
¾ cup canned pumpkin

DIRECTIONS:

Preheat oven to 350 degrees. Lightly spray an 8-inch square baking dish with nonfat cooking spray. In a small bowl, combine cream cheese, sugar, and egg substitute; mix until blended smooth. In a large bowl, combine apple butter, brown sugar, egg whites, and vanilla; mix until blended. Add flour, cinnamon, and pumpkin pie spice; mix until blended. Stir in pumpkin and mix until blended. Spread batter into prepared baking dish; top with cream cheese mixture and swirl into batter. Bake in preheated oven for 25 to 30 minutes, until toothpick inserted in center comes out clean. Cool 15 to 20 minutes before cutting.

Serves: 8

Nutrition per Serving		Exchanges
Calories	241	⅔ meat
Carbohydrate	55 grams	3⅔ fruit
Cholesterol	0 milligrams	
Dietary Fiber	1 gram	
Protein	5 grams	
Sodium	108 milligrams	

SHOPPING LIST:

3 oz. fat-free cream cheese, sugar, 2 oz. egg substitute, 4 oz. apple butter, ½ lb. brown sugar, 2 eggs, vanilla, ¼ lb. flour, cinnamon, pumpkin pie spice, 14 oz. canned pumpkin

MOLASSES COOKIES

EASY - DO AHEAD - FREEZE

INGREDIENTS:
¼ cup apple butter
¼ cup Lighter Bake
¼ cup sugar
½ cup brown sugar
¼ cup molasses
¼ cup egg substitute
2 cups flour
2 tsp. cinnamon
1 tsp. ginger
½ tsp. baking soda

DIRECTIONS:
Preheat oven to 350 degrees. Lightly spray cookie sheet with nonfat cooking spray. In a large bowl, combine apple butter, Lighter Bake, sugar, brown sugar, molasses, and egg substitute; mix until blended. Add flour, cinnamon, ginger, and baking soda; mix until dry ingredients are blended. Form dough into 1-inch balls and dip in sugar; place on cookie sheets and flatten with fork dipped in sugar. Bake in preheated oven for 10 to 15 minutes, until lightly browned.

Serves: 24

Nutrition per Serving		Exchanges
Calories	85	⅓ starch
Carbohydrate	20 grams	1 fruit
Cholesterol	0 milligrams	
Dietary Fiber	< 1 gram	
Protein	1 gram	
Sodium	23 milligrams	

SHOPPING LIST:
2 oz. apple butter, 2 oz. Lighter Bake, sugar, brown sugar, 2 oz. molasses, 2 oz. egg substitute, ½ lb. flour, cinnamon, ginger, baking soda

DELICIOUS DESSERTS

STRAWBERRY-OATMEAL BARS

EASY - DO AHEAD

INGREDIENTS:
1½ cups multi-grain oatmeal
1 cup brown sugar
1½ cups flour
¼ tsp. baking soda
½ cup Lighter Bake
3 cups strawberries, chopped
1½ cups sugar
2 tbsp. cornstarch
¼ cup water
1 tsp. vanilla

DIRECTIONS:
Preheat oven to 350 degrees. Lightly spray a 9x13-inch baking dish with nonfat cooking spray. In a medium bowl, combine oatmeal, brown sugar, flour, and baking soda. Using 2 knives or a pastry blender, cut in Lighter Bake until mixture is crumbly. Press half the mixture into prepared pan. In a medium saucepan, combine strawberries, sugar, cornstarch, and water. Cook until thickened and blended. Stir in vanilla. Pour into crust; sprinkle with remaining crumb mixture. Bake 20 to 30 minutes, until lightly browned and crisp.

Serves: 16

Nutrition per Serving		Exchanges
Calories	251	⅔ starch
Carbohydrate	62 grams	3⅓ fruit
Cholesterol	0 milligrams	
Dietary Fiber	2 grams	
Protein	2 grams	
Sodium	27 milligrams	

SHOPPING LIST:
multi-grain oatmeal (Quaker), ½ lb. brown sugar, flour, baking soda, 4 oz. Lighter Bake, 1½ pints strawberries, sugar, cornstarch, vanilla

DELICIOUS DESSERTS

....

APPLE-BERRY CRISP

EASY - DO AHEAD

INGREDIENTS:

⅓ cup sugar
3 tbsp. cornstarch
2½ tsp. cinnamon, divided
½ tsp. nutmeg
2 16-oz. cans apple slices
1 cup blueberries (fresh or
frozen)

½ cup corn syrup
½ cup multi-grain oatmeal
⅓ cup brown sugar
1¼ cups flour
3 tbsp. apple butter

DIRECTIONS:

Preheat oven to 350 degrees. Lightly spray an 8-inch baking
dish with nonfat cooking spray. In a large bowl, combine
sugar, cornstarch, 1½ teaspoons cinnamon, and nutmeg.
Add apples, blueberries, and corn syrup; toss ingredients to
mix well. Spoon mixture into prepared baking dish. In a
small bowl, combine oatmeal, brown sugar, flour, and 1 teaspoon cinnamon; mix well. Using 2 knives or pastry
blender, cut in apple butter until mixture is crumbly. Sprinkle over apple-blueberry mixture. Bake in preheated oven
for 45 to 50 minutes, until apples are tender and top is
lightly browned. Best served warm.

Serves: 8

Nutrition per Serving		Exchanges
Calories	313	1 starch
Carbohydrate	76 grams	4 fruit
Cholesterol	0 milligrams	
Dietary Fiber	4 grams	
Protein	3 grams	
Sodium	20 milligrams	

SHOPPING LIST:

sugar, cornstarch, cinnamon, nutmeg, 2 16-oz. cans apple
slices, ½ pint fresh or 8 oz. frozen blueberries, 4 oz. corn
syrup, multi-grain oatmeal (Quaker), brown sugar, flour,
1½ oz. apple butter

DELICIOUS DESSERTS

BLUEBERRY-PEACH CRISP

EASY - DO AHEAD

INGREDIENTS:
½ cup Grape-Nuts cereal
½ cup multi-grain oatmeal
⅓ cup brown sugar
¼ cup + 1 tbsp. flour
1½ tsp. cinnamon
3 tbsp. Lighter Bake
32 oz. frozen peach slices, thawed and drained
8 oz. frozen blueberries, unthawed
8 oz. frozen strawberries, sliced, unthawed

DIRECTIONS:
Preheat oven to 375 degrees. Lightly spray 8-inch baking dish with nonfat cooking spray. In a large bowl, combine Grape-Nuts, oatmeal, sugar, ¼ cup flour, and cinnamon; mix well. Stir in Lighter Bake and mix until dry ingredients are moistened and mixture is crumbly. In a separate bowl, combine peaches, blueberries, and strawberries; toss with 1 tablespoon flour. Spoon mixture into prepared pan and top with crumb topping. Bake in preheated oven for 30 to 35 minutes; serve warm or at room temperature, with fat-free Cool Whip or frozen yogurt, if desired.

Serves: 8

Nutrition per Serving		Exchanges
Calories	198	1 starch
Carbohydrate	49 grams	2⅓ fruit
Cholesterol	0 milligrams	
Dietary Fiber	6 grams	
Protein	3 grams	
Sodium	57 milligrams	

DELICIOUS DESSERTS

SHOPPING LIST:
Grape-Nuts cereal, Quaker multi-grain oatmeal, brown sugar, flour, cinnamon, 1½ oz. Lighter Bake, 2 16-oz. packages frozen peach slices, 8 oz. frozen blueberries, 8 oz. frozen strawberries

CRANBERRY-APPLE CRISP

EASY - DO AHEAD

INGREDIENTS:
3 cups canned apple slices
3 cups cranberries
¾ cup sugar
2 tsp. cinnamon, divided
¼ cup flour, divided
2 tbsp. brown sugar
¾ cup Grape-Nuts
1½ tbsp. Lighter Bake

DIRECTIONS:
Preheat oven to 375 degrees. Lightly spray a 9x13-inch baking dish with nonfat cooking spray. In a large bowl, combine apples, cranberries, sugar, 1½ teaspoons cinnamon, and 1 tablespoon flour; mix well. Pour mixture into prepared dish. In the same bowl, combine remaining flour, brown sugar, and Grape-Nuts; mix well. Stir in Lighter Bake and mix until crumbly. Sprinkle over apple mixture and bake in preheated oven 40 minutes, until lightly browned. Let stand at room temperature 5 to 10 minutes before serving.

Serves: 8

Nutrition per Serving		Exchanges
Calories	212	⅔ starch
Carbohydrate	53 grams	2⅔ fruit
Cholesterol	0 milligrams	
Dietary Fiber	3 gram	
Protein	2 grams	
Sodium	79 milligrams	

DELICIOUS DESSERTS

SHOPPING LIST:
2 20-oz. cans apple slices, 1½ pint cranberries (or 3 10-oz. pkgs. frozen cranberries), sugar, cinnamon, flour, brown sugar, Grape-Nuts cereal, ¾ oz. Lighter Bake

CHOCOLATE FLAN

AVERAGE - DO AHEAD

INGREDIENTS:

1 cup + 1 tbsp. sugar
1 ¾ cups water, divided
2 tbsp. unsweetened cocoa
  powder
28 oz. fat-free sweetened
  condensed milk

1 cup egg substitute
¾ tsp. vanilla
¼ tsp. almond extract

DIRECTIONS:

Preheat oven to 350 degrees. Lightly spray an 8-inch cake pan with nonfat cooking spray. Combine 1 cup sugar and ¼ cup water in a medium saucepan and cook over medium heat, stirring constantly, about 15 minutes. Pour sugar mixture into prepared pan and cool completely. In a small saucepan, combine 1½ cups water, 1 tablespoon sugar, and cocoa; bring to a boil over medium-high heat, stirring frequently, and cook until sugar and cocoa are dissolved and blended. Remove from heat and cool completely.

In an electric blender or food processor, combine milk, egg substitute, vanilla, and almond extract; process until blended. Add cocoa mixture and process until blended smooth. Pour cocoa mixture over sugar in cake pan; place cake pan in a shallow baking dish and fill with 1-inch of water. Cover with foil and bake in preheated oven for 1½ hours, until knife inserted in center comes out clean. Remove pan from water and cool to room temperature; cover and refrigerate at least 8 hours before serving. Loosen Flan with spatula and invert onto serving plate.

Serves: 8

Nutrition per Serving

Calories	392
Carbohydrate	88 grams
Cholesterol	0 milligrams
Dietary Fiber	0 grams
Protein	10 grams
Sodium	143 milligrams

Exchanges

1¼ milk
4⅔ fruit

SHOPPING LIST:

½ lb. sugar, unsweetened cocoa powder, 2 14-oz. cans fat-free sweetened condensed milk, 8 oz. egg substitute, vanilla, almond extract

DECADENT ALMOND-CHOCOLATE MOUSSE

AVERAGE - DO AHEAD

INGREDIENTS:

2 tsp. unflavored gelatin
⅓ cup sugar
¼ cup unsweetened cocoa powder
½ cup water
½ cup evaporated skim milk
1½ tsp. vanilla
1½ tsp. almond extract
½ cup fat-free Cool Whip

DIRECTIONS:

Combine gelatin, sugar, cocoa, and ½ cup water in a medium saucepan; cook over high heat until mixture comes to a boil. Pour chocolate mixture into 2-quart bowl; gradually add milk and mix until blended. Cover bowl and freeze about 1 hour. Using an electric mixer, whip chocolate mixture until fluffy; stir in vanilla and almond extract. Top mousse with 2 tablespoons fat-free Cool Whip.

Serves: 4

Nutrition per Serving		Exchanges
Calories	121	1⅔ starch
Carbohydrates	25 grams	
Cholesterol	1 milligram	
Dietary Fiber	0 grams	
Protein	5 grams	
Sodium	45 milligrams	

SHOPPING LIST:

1 package unflavored gelatin, sugar, 1 oz. unsweetened cocoa powder, 4 oz. evaporated skim milk, vanilla, almond extract, 4 oz. fat-free Cool Whip

DELICIOUS DESSERTS

MEXICAN FLAN

AVERAGE - DO AHEAD

INGREDIENTS:
 ½ cup egg substitute
 2 large egg whites
 1½ cups skim milk
 1½ tsp. vanilla
 ½ cup honey, divided
 ½ tsp. cinnamon

DIRECTIONS:
 Preheat oven to 325 degrees. Lightly spray four 6-ounce custard cups with nonfat cooking spray. Place custard cups in 8-inch square baking dish. In a medium bowl, combine egg substitute, egg whites, milk, vanilla, and ¼ cup honey; mix until blended. In a small bowl, combine ¼ cup honey with cinnamon; mix well. Spoon 1 tablespoon honey-cinnamon mixture into bottom of each custard cup; divide egg mixture evenly among custard cups. Pour boiling water into baking dish (1-inch-deep) and bake in preheated oven for 40 to 45 minutes, until knife inserted in center comes out clean. Refrigerate if not serving immediately.

Serves: 4

Nutrition per Serving		Exchanges
Calories	189	½ milk
Carbohydrate	40 grams	½ meat
Cholesterol	2 milligrams	2¼ fruit
Dietary Fiber	0 grams	
Protein	7 grams	
Sodium	117 milligrams	

DELICIOUS DESSERTS

SHOPPING LIST:
 4 oz. egg substitute, 2 eggs, 12 oz. skim milk, vanilla, 4 oz. honey, cinnamon

PEACHY GINGERBREAD PUDDING

AVERAGE - DO AHEAD

INGREDIENTS:
¼ cup apple butter
1¾ cups skim milk
⅓ cup brown sugar
½ cup egg substitute
1½ tsp. ginger
½ tsp. cinnamon
1 tsp. vanilla
4 cups fat-free French bread, cubed
16 oz. peach slices in juice, drained
1½ tbsp. sugar

DIRECTIONS:
Preheat oven to 350 degrees. Lightly spray an 8-inch baking dish with nonfat cooking spray. In a large bowl, combine apple butter, milk, brown sugar, egg substitute, ginger, cinnamon, and vanilla; mix until blended. Add bread cubes; mix until well coated. Let stand 15 to 20 minutes. Fold peaches into bread mixture. Pour mixture into prepared pan; sprinkle with sugar. Bake in preheated oven 30 minutes, until top is browned and knife inserted in center comes out clean. Serve with fat-free Cool Whip or fat-free frozen yogurt.

Serves: 8

Nutrition per Serving		Exchanges
Calories	188	2 starch
Carbohydrate	39 grams	⅔ fruit
Cholesterol	< 1 milligram	
Dietary Fiber	2 grams	
Protein	6 grams	
Sodium	205 milligrams	

SHOPPING LIST:
2 oz. apple butter, 14 oz. skim milk, brown sugar, 4 oz. egg substitute, ginger, cinnamon, vanilla, 1 lb. fat-free French bread, 16 oz. peach slices in juice, sugar

DELICIOUS DESSERTS

SWEET POTATO PUDDING

EASY - DO AHEAD

INGREDIENTS:
¾ cup mashed sweet potatoes
1 cup mashed bananas
1 cup evaporated skim milk
3 tbsp. brown sugar
⅓ cup egg substitute
1 tbsp. sugar
1 tsp. cinnamon
¼ cup Craisins

DIRECTIONS:
Preheat oven to 300 degrees. Lightly spray a 1-quart casserole with nonfat cooking spray. In a medium bowl, combine potatoes, bananas, milk, brown sugar, and egg substitute; beat until blended smooth. Pour mixture into prepared casserole. In a small bowl, combine sugar, cinnamon, and Craisins; toss until coated. Sprinkle over potato mixture and bake in preheated oven 45 minutes, until knife inserted in center comes out clean.

Serves: 6

Nutrition per Serving		Exchanges
Calories	166	1⅔ starch
Carbohydrate	37 grams	½ fruit
Cholesterol	2 milligrams	
Dietary Fiber	2 grams	
Protein	5 grams	
Sodium	70 milligrams	

DELICIOUS DESSERTS

SHOPPING LIST:
6 oz. canned sweet potatoes, 1 to 2 bananas, 8 oz. evaporated skim milk, brown sugar, 3 oz. egg substitute, sugar, cinnamon, Craisins

BERRY-BERRY ICE

AVERAGE - DO AHEAD - FREEZE

INGREDIENTS:
2 cups water
1 cup sugar
1 cup frozen blueberries
1 cup frozen raspberries
1 cup frozen strawberries
1 cup frozen blackberries
1½ tbsp. lemon juice

DIRECTIONS:
Combine water and sugar in medium saucepan and bring to a boil over high heat; reduce heat to low and simmer, uncovered, 8 to 10 minutes. Remove from heat and cool to room temperature. Combine berries and lemon juice in a food processor or blender and process until blended. Add sugar-water to berries and process until smooth. Pour mixture into large bowl; cover and freeze 2 to 3 hours. Place frozen mixture in food processor or blender and process until smooth and creamy. Freeze mixture overnight; slightly soften in refrigerator or at room temperature before serving. This can be made with any combination of frozen berries to equal 4 cups.

Serves: 8

Nutrition per Serving		Exchanges
Calories	127	2⅓ fruit
Carbohydrate	33 grams	
Cholesterol	0 milligrams	
Dietary Fiber	3 grams	
Protein	1 gram	
Sodium	1 milligram	

SHOPPING LIST:
½ lb. sugar, 10 oz. frozen blueberries, 10 oz. frozen raspberries, 10 oz. frozen strawberries, 10 oz. frozen blackberries, ¾ oz. lemon juice

DELICIOUS DESSERTS

DESSERT PEARS

EASY - DO AHEAD

INGREDIENTS:
3 medium pears, peeled, cored and cut in half
½ cup raisins
½ cup orange juice
¼ cup honey
2 tsp. reconstituted butter-flavored granules
⅛ tsp. cinnamon
⅛ tsp. nutmeg

DIRECTIONS:
Preheat oven to 350 degrees. Lightly spray 9x13-inch baking dish with nonfat cooking spray. Place pears, cut-side up, in dish. Spoon 1 tablespoon raisins in center of each pear. In a small bowl, combine orange juice, honey, and liquid butter; mix until blended. Pour mixture over pears; sprinkle with cinnamon and nutmeg. Cover with foil and bake in preheated oven for 25 to 30 minutes. Serve warm.

Serves: 6

Nutrition per Serving		Exchanges
Calories	139	2⅓ fruit
Carbohydrate	36 grams	
Cholesterol	0 milligrams	
Dietary Fiber	3 grams	
Protein	1 gram	
Sodium	2 milligrams	

DELICIOUS DESSERTS

SHOPPING LIST:
3 medium pears, 2 oz. raisins, 4 oz. orange juice, 2 oz. honey, butter-flavored granules, cinnamon, nutmeg

FRUIT FLAUTAS

AVERAGE - DO AHEAD

INGREDIENTS:

8 oz. pineapple tidbits in juice
½ cup sliced strawberries
½ medium papaya, peeled and cut in 1-inch pieces
1 medium banana, peeled and cubed
1 kiwi fruit, peeled and cubed

2 tbsp. lemon juice
1¼ tbsp. cornstarch
1 tbsp. brown sugar
¾ tsp. cinnamon
6 fat-free flour tortillas
powdered sugar

DIRECTIONS:

Preheat oven to 400 degrees. Line baking sheet with foil and lightly spray with nonfat cooking spray. Drain pineapple, reserving liquid. In a large bowl, combine pineapple, strawberries, papaya, banana, and kiwi; mix lightly. In a small saucepan, combine reserved pineapple juice, lemon juice, and cornstarch, stirring until blended. Heat over medium heat until mixture thickens; stir in brown sugar and cinnamon; mix until sugar is dissolved and blended smooth. Fold in fruit. Wrap tortillas in foil and heat in oven 3 to 5 minutes, just until warmed through. Place fruit mixture down the center of each tortilla and roll up tightly. Place, seam-side down, on baking sheet and bake in preheated oven for 8 to 10 minutes, until lightly browned. Sprinkle with powdered sugar and serve immediately.

Serves: 6

Nutrition per Serving		Exchanges
Calories	183	1⅔ starch
Carbohydrate	43 grams	1 fruit
Cholesterol	0 milligrams	
Dietary Fiber	3 grams	
Protein	5 grams	
Sodium	343 milligrams	

SHOPPING LIST:

8 oz. pineapple tidbits in juice, ¼ pint strawberries, papaya, 1 banana, 1 kiwi, 1 oz. lemon juice, cornstarch, brown sugar, cinnamon, 6 fat-free flour tortillas, powdered sugar

PINEAPPLE-BERRY COMPOTE

EASY - DO AHEAD

INGREDIENTS:
½ cup sugar
⅔ cup water
¼ cup pineapple juice
1 cup blueberries
1 cup sliced strawberries
2 cups pineapple tidbits in juice, drained
powdered sugar (optional)

DIRECTIONS:
In a small saucepan, combine sugar and water and pineapple juice; heat over medium-high heat and bring mixture to a boil. Reduce heat to low; cover and simmer 5 minutes. Cover and refrigerate 1 hour. In a medium bowl, combine blueberries, strawberries, and pineapple; pour sauce over fruit just before serving. Sprinkle lightly with powdered sugar, if desired.

Serves: 4

Nutrition per Serving		Exchanges
Calories	205	3⅔ fruit
Carbohydrate	54 grams	
Cholesterol	0 milligrams	
Dietary Fiber	3 grams	
Protein	1 gram	
Sodium	5 milligrams	

DELICIOUS DESSERTS

SHOPPING LIST:
¼ lb. sugar, 2 oz. pineapple juice, ½ pint blueberries, ½ pint strawberries, 20 oz. pineapple tidbits in juice, powdered sugar (optional)

VANILLA STRAWBERRIES

EASY - DO AHEAD

INGREDIENTS:

4 cups sliced strawberries
⅓ cup sugar
⅓ cup fat-free vanilla yogurt
⅓ cup fat-free strawberry yogurt
2 tbsp. balsamic vinegar

DIRECTIONS:

Combine all ingredients in a large bowl; mix well. Refrigerate until ready to serve.

Serves: 8

Nutrition per Serving		Exchanges
Calories	63	1 fruit
Carbohydrate	15 grams	
Cholesterol	< 1 milligram	
Dietary Fiber	2 grams	
Protein	1 gram	
Sodium	13 milligrams	

SHOPPING LIST:

2 pints strawberries, sugar, 3 oz. fat-free vanilla yogurt, 3 oz. fat-free strawberry yogurt, 1 oz. balsamic vinegar

DELICIOUS DESSERTS

DELIGHTFUL DRINKS

ALMOND PEACH SMOOTHIE

EASY

INGREDIENTS:
1 cup skim milk
1 cup sliced peaches
½ tsp. almond extract
1 cup fat-free frozen vanilla yogurt

DIRECTIONS:
Combine all ingredients in blender and process until smooth and creamy.

Serves: 2

Nutrition per Serving		Exchanges
Calories	173	1 milk
Carbohydrate	34 grams	1½ fruit
Cholesterol	2 milligrams	
Dietary Fiber	1 gram	
Protein	9 grams	
Sodium	123 milligrams	

SHOPPING LIST:
8 oz. skim milk, 2 fresh peaches, almond extract, 8 oz. fat-free frozen vanilla yogurt

PINEAPPLE-BLUEBERRY SMOOTHIE

EASY

INGREDIENTS:
1 cup fat-free blueberry yogurt
⅓ cup pineapple juice
¾ cup blueberries
1 tsp. sugar

DIRECTIONS:
Combine all ingredients in blender and process until smooth.

Serves: 2

Nutrition per Serving		Exchanges
Calories	106	½ milk
Carbohydrate	22 grams	1 fruit
Cholesterol	3 milligrams	
Dietary Fiber	1 gram	
Protein	4 grams	
Sodium	74 milligrams	

SHOPPING LIST:
8 oz. fat-free blueberry yogurt, 3 oz. pineapple juice, ⅓ pint blueberries, sugar

DELIGHTFUL DRINKS

PAPAYA-PEACH SMOOTHIE

EASY

INGREDIENTS:
½ whole papaya, peeled, seeded, and chopped
1 peach, pitted, peeled, and chopped
2 tbsp. Cultured Buttermilk Mix
½ cup water
2 tbsp. lime juice
2½ tbsp. sugar
5 ice cubes

DIRECTIONS:
Combine all ingredients in a blender and process until smooth and creamy. Serve immediately.

Serves: 2

Nutrition per Serving		Exchanges
Calories	99	1⅔ fruit
Carbohydrate	25 grams	
Cholesterol	1 milligram	
Dietary Fiber	1 gram	
Protein	1 gram	
Sodium	17 milligrams	

SHOPPING LIST:
1 small papaya, 1 peach, Cultured Buttermilk Mix, 1 oz. lime juice, sugar

PURPLE PLUM SMOOTHIE

EASY - DO AHEAD

INGREDIENTS:
6 medium pitted plums
1 cup fat-free vanilla yogurt
2 tbsp. honey
1 tbsp. wheat germ
6 ice cubes

DIRECTIONS:
Combine all ingredients in a blender and process until smooth.

Serves: 4

Nutrition per Serving		Exchanges
Calories	116	½ milk
Carbohydrate	26 grams	1⅓ fruit
Cholesterol	1 milligram	
Dietary Fiber	2 grams	
Protein	3 grams	
Sodium	36 milligrams	

SHOPPING LIST:
6 medium plums, 8 oz. fat-free vanilla yogurt, 1 oz. honey, wheat germ

SWEET AND SPICY
BANANA SMOOTHIE

EASY

INGREDIENTS:
  ¾ cup skim milk
  ½ cup fat-free banana yogurt
  1 medium banana
  ½ tsp. cinnamon
  ⅛ tsp. nutmeg
  6 ice cubes

DIRECTIONS:
  Combine all ingredients in a blender and process until smooth. Great breakfast drink!

  Serves: 2

Nutrition per Serving		Exchanges
Calories	110	¾ fruit
Carbohydrate	22 grams	¾ milk
Cholesterol	3 milligrams	
Dietary Fiber	1 gram	
Protein	6 grams	
Sodium	83 milligrams	

SHOPPING LIST:
  6 oz. skim milk, 4 oz. fat-free banana yogurt, 1 banana, cinnamon, nutmeg

BLUEBERRY SHAKE

EASY

INGREDIENTS:
2 cups skim milk
1¼ cups blueberries
¾ tsp. sugar

DIRECTIONS:
Combine all ingredients in a blender and process until smooth and creamy.

Serves: 2

Nutrition per Serving		Exchanges
Calories	142	1 milk
Carbohydrate	26 grams	1 fruit
Cholesterol	4 milligrams	
Dietary Fiber	2 grams	
Protein	9 grams	
Sodium	131 milligrams	

SHOPPING LIST:
1 pint skim milk, ½ to ¾ pint blueberries, sugar

BLUEBERRY-BANANA SHAKE

EASY

INGREDIENTS:

1 cup fat-free banana-flavored yogurt
1 large banana, cut into chunks
½ cup frozen blueberries
¼ cup orange juice

DIRECTIONS:

Combine all ingredients in a blender and process until smooth. Serve immediately.

Serves: 2

Nutrition per Serving		Exchanges
Calories	157	½ milk
Carbohydrate	35 grams	2 fruit
Cholesterol	3 milligrams	
Dietary Fiber	3 grams	
Protein	5 grams	
Sodium	72 milligrams	

SHOPPING LIST:

8 oz. fat-free banana yogurt, 1 large banana, 4 oz. frozen blueberries, 2 oz. orange juice

DELIGHTFUL DRINKS

CHOCOLATE-BANANA SHAKE

EASY

INGREDIENTS:
1 large banana
1 cup skim milk
1 tbsp. sugar
2½ tsp. unsweetened cocoa powder
¾ tsp. vanilla
4 ice cubes

DIRECTIONS:
Combine all ingredients in a blender and process until smooth. Serve immediately.

Serves: 2

Nutrition per Serving		Exchanges
Calories	154	½ milk
Carbohydrate	34 grams	2 fruit
Cholesterol	2 milligrams	
Dietary Fiber	1 gram	
Protein	5 grams	
Sodium	65 milligrams	

SHOPPING LIST:
1 large banana, 8 oz. skim milk, sugar, unsweetened cocoa powder, vanilla

FRUIT FROSTY

EASY - DO AHEAD

INGREDIENTS:
- ¼ cup skim milk
- ¼ cup water
- 2 oz. frozen fruit juice concentrate (any flavor)
- 2 ice cubes
- 1¼ tbsp. sugar
- ¼ tsp. vanilla

DIRECTIONS:

Combine all ingredients in a blender and process until smooth. Serve immediately or refrigerate and reblend before serving.

Serves: 2

Nutrition per Serving		Exchanges
Calories	86	¼ milk
Carbohydrate	20 grams	1 fruit
Cholesterol	< 1 milligram	
Dietary Fiber	< 1 gram	
Protein	2 grams	
Sodium	17 milligrams	

SHOPPING LIST:

2 oz. skim milk, 2 oz. frozen fruit concentrate (any flavor), sugar, vanilla

FRUITY BREAKFAST SHAKE

EASY

INGREDIENTS:
1½ cups fat-free yogurt
½ cup skim milk
1 medium banana, cut into chunks
½ cup sliced strawberries
½ cup pineapple chunks in juice
2 tsp. sugar
1 tsp. vanilla
⅔ cup crushed ice (or 5 to 6 ice cubes)

DIRECTIONS:
Place all ingredients in a blender and process until mixture is blended smooth.

Serves: 2

Nutrition per Serving		Exchanges
Calories	222	1½ milk
Carbohydrate	42 grams	1½ fruit
Cholesterol	4 milligrams	
Dietary Fiber	2 grams	
Protein	13 grams	
Sodium	164 milligrams	

SHOPPING LIST:
12 oz. fat-free yogurt, 4 oz. skim milk, 1 banana, ¼ pint strawberries, 4 oz. pineapple chunks in juice, sugar, vanilla

DELIGHTFUL DRINKS

LEMONADE SLUSHIES

EASY

INGREDIENTS:
 6 oz. frozen pink lemonade concentrate, thawed
 1 cup cranberry juice cocktail
 6 ice cubes

DIRECTIONS:
 Combine all ingredients in a blender and process until mixture is blended.

Serves: 2

Nutrition per Serving		Exchanges
Calories	237	4 fruit
Carbohydrate	62 grams	
Cholesterol	0 milligrams	
Dietary Fiber	2 grams	
Protein	0 grams	
Sodium	6 milligrams	

SHOPPING LIST:
 6 oz. frozen pink lemonade concentrate, 8 oz. cranberry juice cocktail

DELIGHTFUL DRINKS

ORANGE BANANA-BERRY SHAKE

EASY

INGREDIENTS:
⅓ cup fat-free strawberry-banana yogurt
1 cup sliced bananas
⅓ cup orange juice
1¾ tbsp. honey
¾ cup frozen strawberries, thawed and drained
2¾ cups ice cubes

DIRECTIONS:
Combine yogurt, bananas, orange juice, honey, strawberries and 1¼ cups ice cubes in a blender; process until smooth. Add remaining ice cubes and blend until thick and creamy.

Serves: 2

Nutrition per Serving		Exchanges
Calories	162	¼ milk
Carbohydrate	40 grams	2⅓ fruit
Cholesterol	1 milligram	
Dietary Fiber	3 grams	
Protein	2 grams	
Sodium	26 milligrams	

SHOPPING LIST:
4 oz. fat-free strawberry-banana yogurt, 2 small bananas, 3 oz. orange juice, honey, 6 oz. frozen strawberries

DELIGHTFUL DRINKS

ORANGE FREEZE

EASY

INGREDIENTS:
1 cup fat-free orange yogurt
1 cup orange juice
¾ tsp. vanilla
1 cup crushed ice

DIRECTIONS:
Combine all ingredients in a blender and process until smooth.

Serves: 2

Nutrition per Serving		Exchanges
Calories	106	½ milk
Carbohydrate	20 grams	1 fruit
Cholesterol	3 milligrams	
Dietary Fiber	1 gram	
Protein	5 grams	
Sodium	71 milligrams	

SHOPPING LIST:
8 oz. fat-free orange yogurt, 8 oz. orange juice, vanilla

DELIGHTFUL DRINKS

PEACHY GOOD SHAKE

EASY

INGREDIENTS:
    1¾ cups frozen unsweetened peach slices
    ⅓ cup frozen unsweetened raspberries
    ¾ cup skim milk
    ½ cup peach yogurt
    1½ tsp. honey
    ¾ tsp. vanilla
    ⅛ tsp. cinnamon

DIRECTIONS:
    Combine all ingredients in a blender and process until smooth and thick. Serve immediately.

Serves: 2

Nutrition per Serving		Exchanges
Calories	151	¾ milk
Carbohydrate	32 grams	1½ fruit
Cholesterol	3 milligrams	
Dietary Fiber	3 grams	
Protein	6 grams	
Sodium	83 milligrams	

SHOPPING LIST:
    12 oz. frozen unsweetened peach slices, 8 oz. frozen unsweetened raspberries, 6 oz. skim milk, 4 oz. fat-free peach yogurt, honey, vanilla, cinnamon

PINEAPPLE-BANANA SHAKE

EASY

INGREDIENTS:
1 cup pineapple chunks in juice, drained
1 small banana, cut into chunks
½ cup skim milk
½ cup egg substitute

DIRECTIONS:
Combine all ingredients in a blender and process until creamy.

Serves: 2

Nutrition per Serving		Exchanges
Calories	125	1 milk
Carbohydrate	24 grams	¾ fruit
Cholesterol	1 milligram	
Dietary Fiber	2 grams	
Protein	8 grams	
Sodium	113 milligrams	

SHOPPING LIST:
8 oz. pineapple chunks in juice, 1 small banana, 4 oz. skim milk, 4 oz. egg substitute

DELIGHTFUL DRINKS

CRANBERRY-ORANGE COCKTAIL

EASY

INGREDIENTS:

½ cup cranberry juice, chilled
½ cup orange juice, chilled
2 orange slices
1 tbsp. maraschino cherries

DIRECTIONS:

In a pitcher or blender, combine cranberry and orange juice until blended. Pour into two 6-ounce glasses; garnish with orange slices and cherries.

Serves: 2

Nutrition per Serving		Exchanges
Calories	79	1⅓ fruit
Carbohydrate	19 grams	
Cholesterol	0 milligrams	
Dietary Fiber	1 gram	
Protein	1 gram	
Sodium	3 milligrams	

SHOPPING LIST:

4 oz. cranberry juice, 4 oz. orange juice, 1 small orange, maraschino cherries

DELIGHTFUL DRINKS

REFRESHINGLY BERRY ICED TEA

EASY - DO AHEAD

INGREDIENTS:
1 cup raspberries
2 cups iced tea
1½ cups cranberry juice

DIRECTIONS:
Place ½ cup raspberries into blender and purée until smooth. Pour in iced tea and cranberry juice; process until mixed. Pour into pitcher and chill 1 to 2 hours. When ready to serve, place several raspberries into each glass; fill with berry tea.

Serves: 4

Nutrition per Serving		Exchanges
Calories	70	1¼ fruit
Carbohydrate	18 grams	
Cholesterol	0 milligrams	
Dietary Fiber	1 gram	
Protein	< 1 gram	
Sodium	7 milligrams	

SHOPPING LIST:
½ pint raspberries, 1 pint unsweetened iced tea, 12 oz. cranberry juice

SPARKLING CRANBERRY LEMONADE

EASY - DO AHEAD

INGREDIENTS:
8 to 10 ice cubes
1 cup cranberry juice
1 cup sugar-free lemonade
1 cup sodium-free club soda

DIRECTIONS:
Divide ice cubes among three 12-ounce glasses. In a pitcher or blender, combine cranberry juice, lemonade, and club soda; mix until blended. Pour over ice and serve. Garnish with a fresh lemon slice, if desired.

Serves: 3

Nutrition per Serving		Exchanges
Calories	48	¾ fruit
Carbohydrate	12 grams	
Cholesterol	0 milligrams	
Dietary Fiber	0 grams	
Protein	0 grams	
Sodium	20 milligrams	

SHOPPING LIST:
8 oz. cranberry juice, 8 oz. sugar-free lemonade, 8 oz. sodium-free club soda

DELIGHTFUL DRINKS

SPARKLING ORANGE TEA

EASY - DO AHEAD

INGREDIENTS:
4 tsp. instant tea powder
1 cup orange juice
12 oz. club soda
4 to 6 ice cubes
orange slices (optional)

DIRECTIONS:
Combine tea powder and orange juice in pitcher or blender. Stir in club soda. Place 2 to 3 ice cubes in two 12-ounce glasses; pour in drink and serve. Garnish with orange slices, if desired.

Serves: 2

Nutrition per Serving		Exchanges
Calories	60	1 fruit
Carbohydrate	14 grams	
Cholesterol	0 milligrams	
Dietary Fiber	1 gram	
Protein	1 gram	
Sodium	53 milligrams	

SHOPPING LIST:
instant tea powder, 8 oz. orange juice, 12 oz. club soda, 1 small orange (optional)

DELIGHTFUL DRINKS

HOLIDAY NOG

EASY - DO AHEAD

INGREDIENTS:
3 cups skim milk, divided
¼ cup egg substitute
2 egg whites
¼ cup sugar
¾ tsp. vanilla
½ tsp. rum extract
1 tsp. cinnamon
½ tsp. nutmeg

DIRECTIONS:
In a large saucepan over medium heat, combine 2½ cups skim milk, egg substitute, egg whites, and sugar; cook until mixture becomes thick. Remove from heat and stir in vanilla and rum extract. Cover mixture and refrigerate several hours or overnight. If mixture becomes too thick, add remaining milk and mix well. Divide among glasses and sprinkle with cinnamon and nutmeg.

Serves: 4

Nutrition per Serving		Exchanges
Calories	129	1 milk
Carbohydrate	22 grams	¾ fruit
Cholesterol	3 milligrams	
Dietary Fiber	0 grams	
Protein	9 grams	
Sodium	135 milligrams	

SHOPPING LIST:
24 oz. skim milk, 2 oz. egg substitute, 2 eggs, sugar, vanilla, rum extract, cinnamon, nutmeg

DELIGHTFUL DRINKS

HOT AND SPICY CRANBERRY CIDER

EASY - DO AHEAD

INGREDIENTS:

2 cups apple cider
¾ cup cranberry juice cocktail
1 tbsp. brown sugar
1 whole cinnamon stick
¼ tsp. whole cloves
4 lemon slices

DIRECTIONS:

Combine all ingredients in a large saucepan and heat to boiling over high heat. Reduce heat to low and simmer 15 to 20 minutes. Remove cinnamon sticks and cloves from cider. Serve ½ cup per person and top with lemon slice.

Serves: 2

Nutrition per Serving		Exchanges
Calories	98	1⅔ fruit
Carbohydrate	25 grams	
Cholesterol	0 milligrams	
Dietary Fiber	0 grams	
Protein	0 grams	
Sodium	6 milligrams	

SHOPPING LIST:

1 pint apple cider, 6 oz. cranberry juice cocktail, brown sugar, cinnamon stick, whole cloves, 1 lemon

HOT COCOA

EASY - DO AHEAD

INGREDIENTS:
  2 tbsp. unsweetened cocoa powder
  2 tbsp. sugar
  ⅔ cup water
  1⅓ cups skim milk
  cinnamon, nutmeg, miniatute marshmallows (optional)

DIRECTIONS:
  Combine cocoa and sugar in a small saucepan and stir to mix. Gradually pour water into cocoa mixture and heat over medium-low heat until mixture begins to boil. Cook, stirring constantly, 2 minutes. Add milk; increase heat to high and cook until blended (do not boil). Sprinkle cinnamon, nutmeg, or miniature marshmallows on top, and serve.

Serves: 2

Nutrition per Serving		Exchanges
Calories	113	¾ milk
Carbohydrate	23 grams	1 fruit
Cholesterol	3 milligrams	
Dietary Fiber	0 grams	
Protein	7 grams	
Sodium	87 milligrams	

SHOPPING LIST:
  unsweetened cocoa powder, sugar, 11 to 12 oz. skim milk, cinnamon (optional), nutmeg (optional), miniature marshmallows (optional)

DELIGHTFUL DRINKS

"KOOKING"
FOR
KIDS

✦ ✦ ✦

KIDS "KOOKING"
MADE FUN AND SAFE

- Always have an adult helper when cooking.

- Read through the entire recipe before you begin cooking, and ask your adult helper about any instructions you do not understand.

- Whenever a recipe calls for the use of any electric appliances, knives, or stove-top cooking, you must have adult assistance and supervision.

- Wash your hands in warm soapy water, rinse, and dry well.

- Gather all the ingredients and equipment you will need to prepare the recipe before you get started.

- Measure all your ingredients and line them up on the counter if possible. This will help to eliminate the possibility that you will leave anything out!

- NEVER pick up a knife by the blade, and make sure the sharp edge is facing down when you cut.

- Use a cutting board when slicing or chopping any ingredients.

- Wash all utensils thoroughly after cutting poultry, fish, or meat.

- Wash sharp knives separately from other utensils or ask your adult helper to assist you.

- When you are cooking on top of the stove, turn the pot handle toward the center of the stove, making sure the handle is not over another burner.

- Put large pans on large burners and small pans on small burners.

- Always use thick, dry pot holders when handling hot pans.

- If oven racks need to be adjusted, move them before you turn the oven on.

- It is best to have your adult helper put dishes in and out of the oven.

- Remove casseroles or baking dishes from oven with thick oven mitts. Pull the rack out slightly—don't reach into a hot oven or place a hot pan on the countertop. Have racks or trivets handy for hot dishes.

- Always remove casserole or pot lids away from you, to let the steam out. Keep your face away from the steam.

- Always ask your adult helper with help draining foods cooked in hot water. These pots tend to be very heavy and difficult to handle, so make sure you have assistance.

- Always turn off the stove or oven as soon as you are finished cooking.

- Before using or plugging in any electrical appliance, make sure your hands are clean and dry. Unplug immediately after use, with clean and dry hands.

- Do not put your hands in the bowl when using an electric mixer. Turn off the mixer and make sure it is unplugged whenever you are putting them in or taking them out.

- When using a blender, make sure the top is securely in place before turning the machine on. Turn the blender off and wait for the blades to stop moving before scraping down the sides.

- Clean up as you go for quicker clean-up.

- Wash and dry all the utensils you use and put them in their proper place. Wash the counters and leave a sparkling, clean kitchen.

- Enjoy your cooking experience and wonderful creations!

••••••••••••••••••••

APPLE FRENCH TOAST

AVERAGE - DO AHEAD

INGREDIENTS:
2 cups apple slices
⅓ cup sugar
¾ tsp. cinnamon
6 slices fat-free bread
1 cup egg substitute
1½ cups skim milk
1 tbsp. vanilla

DIRECTIONS:
1. Preheat oven to 350 degrees.
2. Place apple slices in a medium bowl.
3. In a small bowl, combine sugar and cinnamon; mix well.
4. Sprinkle 2 tablespoons cinnamon-sugar mixture over apples and toss until well coated.
5. Lightly spray 9-inch baking dish with nonfat cooking spray.
6. Place apple slices on bottom of dish.
7. Layer bread over apple slices to cover whole dish.
8. In a medium bowl, combine egg substitute, milk, and vanilla; mix until blended.
9. Pour mixture over bread slices, covering all pieces of bread.
10. Sprinkle with remaining cinnamon-sugar mixture.
11. Bake in preheated oven for 40 to 45 minutes, until golden brown.

Serves: 6

Nutrition per Serving		Exchanges
Calories	195	2 starch
Carbohydrate	41 grams	⅔ fruit
Cholesterol	0 milligrams	
Dietary Fiber	3 grams	
Protein	6 grams	
Sodium	208 milligrams	

"KOOKING" FOR KIDS

SHOPPING LIST:
20 oz. can apple slices, sugar, cinnamon, ½ lb. fat-free bread, 8 oz. egg substitute, 12 oz. skim milk, vanilla

PIG AND EGGS IN A BLANKET

EASY

INGREDIENTS:
  8 large egg whites
  2 tbsp. skim milk
  4 fat-free hot dogs
  4 fat-free flour tortillas
  1 cup fat-free shredded Cheddar cheese
  1 cup chopped tomatoes

DIRECTIONS:
  1. In a large microwave-safe bowl, combine egg whites and skim milk; beat until blended. Cover with plastic wrap; poke several holes through top.
  2. Microwave on high 6 to 8 minutes, turning halfway through cooking. Eggs should be set in omelet form; if you prefer scrambled, stir and crumble eggs halfway through cooking.
  3. Microwave hot dogs according to package directions (about 45 seconds to 1 minute per hot dog); cool slightly and cut into bite-sized pieces.
  4. Place tortilla on microwave-safe dish; top with ¼ cooked eggs, ¼ hot dog bites and ¼ cup shredded cheese. Microwave on high 30 to 45 seconds, until cheese is melted. Top with ¼ cup chopped tomatoes and serve.

Serves: 4

Nutrition per Serving		Exchanges
Calories	248	1⅔ starch
Carbohydrate	34 grams	1 vegetable
Cholesterol	15 milligrams	2½ meat
Dietary Fiber	2 grams	
Protein	26 grams	
Sodium	1,311 milligrams	

SHOPPING LIST:
  8 eggs, 1 oz. skim milk, 1 package fat-free hot dogs, 4 10" flour tortillas, 4 oz. fat-free shredded Cheddar cheese, 1 large tomato

APPLE-CHEESE SANDWICHES

EASY

INGREDIENTS:
1 cup fat-free shredded Cheddar cheese
1 cup chopped apple
¼ cup fat-free mayonnaise
8 slices fat-free bread
¼ cup reconstituted butter-flavored granules

DIRECTIONS:
1. Lightly spray large nonstick skillet with nonfat cooking spray.
2. In a medium bowl, combine cheese, apple, and mayonnaise; mix until blended.
3. Spread cheese mixture on 4 bread slices and top with remaining bread.
4. Brush top of each sandwich with 1 teaspoon liquid butter.
5. Coat skillet with 1 tablespoon liquid butter and heat over medium-high heat.
6. Place sandwiches in skillet, butter-side down, and cook until bottom is lightly browned.
7. Brush top piece of bread with liquid butter; carefully flip sandwiches over; Cook until lightly browned on both sides and cheese is melted.

Serves: 4

Nutrition per Serving		Exchanges
Calories	247	1 meat
Carbohydrate	43 grams	2 starch
Cholesterol	0 milligrams	1 fruit
Dietary Fiber	2 grams	
Protein	14 grams	
Sodium	689 milligrams	

SHOPPING LIST:
4 oz. fat-free shredded Cheddar cheese, 1 medium apple, 2 oz. fat-free mayonnaise, ½ lb. fat-free bread, butter-flavored granules

BARBECUED BEEF TORTILLA WRAPS

AVERAGE

INGREDIENTS:
6 fat-free flour tortillas
¾ cup barbecue sauce
1 lb. fat-free roast beef, thinly sliced
1½ cups fat-free shredded Cheddar cheese

DIRECTIONS:
1. Preheat oven to 350 degrees.
2. Wrap tortillas in foil; seal tightly.
3. Heat tortillas in oven for 3 to 5 minutes, until soft and heated.
4. Remove tortillas from oven.
5. Combine barbecue sauce and roast beef in microwave-safe dish and heat on high 2 to 3 minutes, until heated through. (If you do not have a microwave, combine sauce and beef in small saucepan and heat over medium heat, about 5 to 6 minutes.)
6. Divide roast beef with sauce among tortillas and top each with ½ cup cheese.
7. Roll tortilla up, burrito-style, and serve.

Serves: 6

Nutrition per Serving		Exchanges
Calories	267	1 fruit
Carbohydrate	40 grams	1⅔ starch
Cholesterol	27 milligrams	2⅓ meat
Dietary Fiber	2 grams	
Protein	23 grams	
Sodium	1,955 milligrams	

SHOPPING LIST:
fat-free flour tortillas, 6 oz. barbecue sauce, 1 lb. fat-free deli roast beef (thinly sliced), 6 oz. fat-free shredded Cheddar cheese

CHEESE SQUARES

EASY - DO AHEAD

INGREDIENTS:
16 slices fat-free bread
2 whole egg whites
2 cups fat-free shredded Cheddar cheese
1 tbsp. fat-free margarine, melted

DIRECTIONS:
1. Preheat oven to 400 degrees.
2. Lightly spray baking sheet with nonfat cooking spray.
3. Remove crust from bread and cut into squares.
4. Place bread slices on baking sheet.
5. In a small bowl, combine egg whites, cheese, and margarine; blend until smooth.
6. Spread mixture on bread slices.
7. Bake in preheated oven 8 to 10 minutes, until cheese is bubbly and lightly browned.

Serves: 8

Nutrition per Serving		Exchanges
Calories	127	1½ starch
Carbohydrate	20 grams	1 meat
Cholesterol	0 milligrams	
Dietary Fiber	0 grams	
Protein	4 grams	
Sodium	490 milligrams	

SHOPPING LIST:
1 lb. fat-free bread, 2 eggs, 8 oz. fat-free shredded Cheddar cheese, fat-free margarine

"KOOKING" FOR KIDS

CHEESE-WRAPPED HOT DOG

EASY - DO AHEAD - FREEZE

INGREDIENTS:
4 fat-free frozen bread rolls, thawed
4 fat-free hot dogs
4 oz. fat-free American cheese slices
2 tsp. mustard

DIRECTIONS:
1. Preheat oven to 400 degrees.
2. Line baking sheet with foil and lightly spray with non-fat cooking spray.
3. Lightly sprinkle counter with flour; sprinkle rolling pin with flour.
4. Roll out each bread roll to flat rectangle, spread ½ tsp. mustard on each bread roll.
5. Place 1 slice cheese and 1 hot dog onto each bread square.
6. Wrap bread dough around hot dog and seal tightly.
7. Place, seam-side down, on baking sheet and bake in pre-heated oven 15 to 20 minutes; turn hot dogs after 10 minutes and cook until lightly browned on all sides.

Serves: 4

Nutrition per Serving		Exchanges
Calories	173	1⅓ starch
Carbohydrate	21 grams	2 meat
Cholesterol	15 milligrams	
Dietary Fiber	1 gram	
Protein	17 grams	
Sodium	871 milligrams	

SHOPPING LIST:
fat-free frozen bread rolls, fat-free hot dogs, 4 oz. fat-free American cheese slices, mustard

FOOTLONG SUBMARINE

EASY - DO AHEAD

INGREDIENTS:
1 lb. fat-free French bread
1 tbsp. deli-style mustard
4 oz. fat-free sliced Swiss cheese
¾ lb. fat-free deli turkey, thinly sliced
¾ lb. fat-free deli roast beef, thinly sliced
1 large tomato, thinly sliced
¼ cup low-sodium dill pickles, sliced
1 cup shredded lettuce

DIRECTIONS:
1. Cut bread in half horizontally.
2. Spread 2 teaspoons mustard on each half of bread.
3. Spread cheese slices on bottom half of bread.
4. Layer turkey, roast beef, tomato, and pickles on top of cheese.
5. Sprinkle shredded lettuce over meat and vegetables.
6. Place remaining half of bread on top.
7. Place 8 toothpicks in equal intervals on sandwich loaf to secure.
8. Cut into 8 sandwich slices and serve.
Great with homemade potato chips!

Serves: 8

Nutrition per Serving		Exchanges
Calories	267	2 starch
Carbohydrate	38 grams	2 vegetable
Cholesterol	30 milligrams	1½ meat
Dietary Fiber	2 grams	
Protein	20 grams	
Sodium	1,371 milligrams	

SHOPPING LIST:
1 lb. fat-free French bread loaf, deli-style mustard, 4 oz. fat-free Swiss cheese slices, ¾ lb. fat-free deli turkey, ¾ lb. fat-free deli roast beef, 1 large tomato, sandwich sliced low-sodium dill pickles, packaged preshredded lettuce

ITALIAN PIZZA DOGS

EASY

INGREDIENTS:

1½ cups Boboli pizza sauce
6 fat-free hot dogs
2 tbsp. reconstituted butter-flavored granules
½ tsp. garlic powder

6 fat-free buns (or 12 slices fat-free bread)
1½ cups fat-free shredded pizza cheese

DIRECTIONS:

1. Place pizza sauce in small saucepan or microwave-safe dish and cook until heated through (about 1 minute in microwave on high, or 5 to 6 minutes in saucepan over medium-high heat).
2. Line baking sheet with foil and lightly spray with non-fat cooking spray.
3. Place hot dogs on baking sheet.
4. Brush hot dogs with pizza sauce and broil 10 to 15 minutes, until browned on all sides (turn hot dogs halfway through cooking time).
5. In small bowl, combine liquid butter with garlic powder.
6. Brush both sides of bread or buns with butter-garlic mixture and toast lightly.
7. Brush bottom half of bun with pizza sauce; place hot dog on top; brush with sauce and top with cheese.
8. Place under broiler for 1 to 2 minutes, until cheese is melted.

Serves: 6

Nutrition per Serving		Exchanges
Calories	283	3 starch
Carbohydrate	45 grams	1¾ meat
Cholesterol	15 milligrams	
Dietary Fiber	2 grams	
Protein	22 grams	
Sodium	1,189 milligrams	

SHOPPING LIST:

12 oz. Boboli pizza sauce, Best Foods fat-free hot dogs, butter-flavored granules, garlic powder, 6 fat-free buns or 12 slices fat-free bread, 6 oz. fat-free shredded pizza cheese

"KOOKING" FOR KIDS

•••••••••••••••••••••
399

OVEN-GRILLED
TURKEY-CHEESE SANDWICHES

EASY - DO AHEAD

INGREDIENTS:

8 slices fat-free bread
2 tbsp. deli-style mustard
4 oz. fat-free sliced Swiss cheese

½ lb. fat-free deli turkey, thinly sliced
2 tbsp. reconstituted Butter Buds

DIRECTIONS:

1. Preheat oven to 450 degrees.
2. Line baking sheet with foil and lightly spray with non-fat cooking spray.
3. Place bread slices on sheet and spread with mustard.
4. Top ½ of the bread slices with 1 slice cheese and turkey slices; place remaining bread slices on top.
5. Brush top of bread with liquid Butter Buds.
6. Place in preheated oven and bake 5 minutes, until lightly browned.
7. Remove from oven and flip sandwiches over with spatula.
8. Brush top with remaining Butter Buds and bake 3 to 5 minutes, until cheese is melted and bread is lightly browned.
9. Sandwiches can be prepared ahead, covered with plastic wrap, and refrigerated; brush with Butter Buds when ready to bake and serve.

Serves: 4

Nutrition per Serving		Exchanges
Calories	271	2½ starch
Carbohydrate	38 grams	1⅔ meat
Cholesterol	20 milligrams	
Dietary Fiber	2 grams	
Protein	19 grams	
Sodium	1,257 milligrams	

SHOPPING LIST:

½ lb. fat-free bread, 1 oz. deli-style mustard, 4 oz. fat-free sliced Swiss cheese, ½ lb. fat-free deli turkey (thinly sliced), Butter Buds

SMILING CRAB SANDWICHES

EASY - DO AHEAD

INGREDIENTS:
1 cup fat-free cream cheese, softened
1 tbsp. chili sauce
1 tsp. horseradish
6½ oz. can fat-free crabmeat
3 fat-free bagels
½ cup sliced carrots
¼ cup sliced water chestnuts
¼ cup chopped celery

DIRECTIONS:
1. In a small bowl, combine cream cheese, chili sauce, and horseradish; mix until blended.
2. Stir in crabmeat; mix well.
3. Toast bagel halves in oven or toaster.
4. Spread crabmeat mixture onto each bagel half.
5. Place 2 carrot slices on for "eyes," 1 round water chestnut slice for "nose," and several pieces of chopped celery to form a "mouth."

Serves: 6

Nutrition per Serving		Exchanges
Calories	156	1⅔ starch
Carbohydrate	25 grams	1 meat
Cholesterol	3 milligrams	
Dietary Fiber	1 gram	
Protein	12 grams	
Sodium	593 milligrams	

SHOPPING LIST:
8 oz. fat-free cream cheese, chile sauce, horseradish, 6½ oz. fat-free crabmeat, 3 fat-free bagels, 1 to 2 carrots, canned sliced water chestnuts, 1 stalk celery

SPICY CHICKEN FINGERS

EASY - DO AHEAD - FREEZE

INGREDIENTS:
½ cup egg substitute
1½ cups crumbled Kellogs Cornflakes
1½ tsp. Cajun seasoning
1½ lb. fat-free chicken tenders

DIRECTIONS:
1. Preheat oven to 425 degrees.
2. Line baking sheet with foil and lightly spray with non-fat cooking spray.
3. Pour egg substitute into small bowl.
4. Combine Cornflake crumbs and Cajun seasoning on large paper plate.
5. Dip chicken tenders in egg substitute and then roll in crumb mixture until coated on all sides; place on prepared baking sheet.
6. Bake in preheated oven 15 minutes, until crisp and cooked through. Great served with ketchup, barbecue sauce, or honey-mustard sauce!

Serves: 4

Nutrition per Serving		Exchanges
Calories	284	1⅔ starch
Carbohydrate	25 grams	5 meat
Cholesterol	106 milligrams	
Dietary Fiber	< 1 gram	
Protein	40 grams	
Sodium	810 milligrams	

"KOOKING" FOR KIDS

SHOPPING LIST:
4 oz. egg substitute, crumbled Kellogs Cornflakes, Cajun seasoning, 1½ lb. fat-free chicken tenders

TORTILLA PIZZA

EASY - DO AHEAD

INGREDIENTS:
4 fat-free flour tortillas
15 oz. can fat-free refried beans, any flavor
2 cups fat-free shredded pizza cheese
1 cup cherry tomatoes
1 tbsp. black olives
¼ cup chopped green chilies

DIRECTIONS:
1. Preheat oven to 450 degrees.
2. Line baking sheet(s) with foil and lightly spray with nonfat cooking spray.
3. Place tortillas on baking sheet(s).
4. Spread ½ cup beans on each tortilla.
5. Sprinkle each tortilla with ½ cup cheese.
6. Place 2 cherry tomatoes for "eyes," 1 black olive in center for "nose," and 1 tablespoon green chilies in the form of a "smile."
7. Bake in preheated oven for 5 to 7 minutes, until cheese is melted and tortillas are crisp.

Serves: 4

Nutrition per Serving		Exchanges
Calories	299	2 starch
Carbohydrate	43 grams	2 meat
Cholesterol	0 milligrams	3 vegetable
Dietary Fiber	5 grams	
Protein	28 grams	
Sodium	1,287 milligrams	

SHOPPING LIST:
fat-free flour tortillas, 15 oz. can fat-free refried beans (any flavor), 8 oz. fat-free shredded pizza cheese, ½ pint cherry tomatoes, black olives, 2 oz. chopped green chilies

"KOOKING" FOR KIDS

VEGGIE-MACARONI BAKE

EASY - DO AHEAD - FREEZE

INGREDIENTS:
5 cups cooked macaroni
16 oz. frozen mixed vegetables, thawed and drained
28 oz. fat-free pasta sauce
½ cup fat-free Parmesan cheese
2 cups fat-free shredded mozzarella cheese

DIRECTIONS:
1. Preheat oven to 375 degrees.
2. Lightly spray 9x13-inch baking dish with nonfat cooking spray.
3. Cook macaroni according to package directions; pour into colander and drain well.
4. In a large bowl, combine macaroni, vegetables, and pasta sauce; sprinkle with Parmesan cheese and toss until well mixed.
5. Spoon macaroni mixture into prepared dish; sprinkle with mozzarella cheese.
6. Bake in preheated oven 20 to 25 minutes, until cheese is melted.
7. Carefully remove from oven and let stand 5 minutes before serving.

Serves: 6

Nutrition per Serving		Exchanges
Calories	325	2 starch
Carbohydrate	53 grams	1 meat
Cholesterol	0 milligrams	
Dietary Fiber	5 grams	
Protein	23 grams	
Sodium	769 milligrams	

SHOPPING LIST:
8 oz. macaroni, 16 oz. frozen mixed vegetables, 28 oz. fat-free pasta sauce, 2 oz. fat-free Parmesan cheese, 8 oz. fat-free shredded mozzarella cheese

FRESH CINNAMON APPLESAUCE

AVERAGE - DO AHEAD

INGREDIENTS:
¼ cup apple juice
4 cups sliced apples
¼ cup sugar
1 tsp. cinnamon

DIRECTIONS:
1. Pour apple juice into blender.
2. Add 1 cup apple slices to blender and process until smooth.
3. Gradually add remaining apple slices to blender and process until mixture is smooth.
4. Add sugar and cinnamon to apple mixture; process until blended.

Serves: 8

Nutrition per Serving		Exchanges
Calories	59	1 fruit
Carbohydrate	16 grams	
Cholesterol	0 milligrams	
Dietary Fiber	1 gram	
Protein	< 1 gram	
Sodium	< 1 milligram	

SHOPPING LIST:
2 oz. apple juice, 4 medium apples, sugar, cinnamon

FROZEN FRUIT SALAD

EASY - DO AHEAD - FREEZE

INGREDIENTS:
1 cup fat-free sour cream
⅜ cup sugar
1 tbsp. lemon juice
1 medium banana, mashed
½ cup crushed pineapple in juice, drained
2 maraschino cherries, chopped

DIRECTIONS:
1. Combine sour cream, sugar, and lemon juice in a large bowl; mix well.
2. Fold in banana, pineapple, and chopped cherries; mix until ingredients are blended.
3. Line muffin cups with paper liners.
4. Fill muffin cups with fruit mixture.
5. Freeze fruit cups at least 3 hours, until firm.
6. Remove from cups just before serving.

Serves: 8

Nutrition per Serving		Exchanges
Calories	78	¼ milk
Carbohydrate	15 grams	¾ fruit
Cholesterol	0 milligrams	
Dietary Fiber	< 1 gram	
Protein	2 grams	
Sodium	21 milligrams	

SHOPPING LIST:
8 oz. sour cream, sugar, lemon juice, 1 banana, 4 oz. crushed pineapple in juice, maraschino cherries

HAWAIIAN COLESLAW

EASY - DO AHEAD

INGREDIENTS:
¼ cup fat-free mayonnaise
½ cup fat-free sour cream
1 tsp. sugar
½ tsp. dry mustard
⅛ tsp. pepper
2 cups shredded cabbage
2 cups broccoli slaw
½ cup shredded carrots
8 oz. pineapple tidbits in juice, drained
1 cup miniature marshmallows

DIRECTIONS:
1. In a large bowl, combine mayonnaise, sour cream, sugar, mustard, and pepper; mix until blended smooth.
2. Add cabbage, broccoli slaw, and carrots to bowl; toss until well mixed.
3. Stir in pineapple and marshmallows.
4. Cover and refrigerate several hours before serving.

Serves: 6

Nutrition per Serving		Exchanges
Calories	84	2 vegetable
Carbohydrate	17 grams	½ fruit
Cholesterol	0 milligrams	
Dietary Fiber	2 grams	
Protein	3 grams	
Sodium	112 milligrams	

SHOPPING LIST:
2 oz. fat-free mayonnaise, 4 oz. fat-free sour cream, sugar, dry mustard, pepper, packaged preshredded cabbage, packaged preshredded broccoli slaw, packaged preshredded carrots, 8 oz. pineapple tidbits in juice, miniature marshmallows

PINEAPPLE TUNA SALAD

EASY - DO AHEAD

INGREDIENTS:
12 oz. fat-free tuna
⅔ cup diced celery
2½ oz. crushed pineapple in juice
2 tbsp. fat-free mayonnaise
2 tbsp. fat-free sour cream
1 tsp. onion powder
1 tsp. dried parsley

DIRECTIONS:
1. Place tuna in medium bowl and mash with fork.
2. Add diced celery, pineapple with juice, mayonnaise, sour cream, onion powder, and parsley; mix well.
3. Chill several hours before serving. Serve on fat-free bread slices, crackers, bagels, or pita pockets.

Serves: 4

Nutrition per Serving		Exchanges
Calories	135	⅓ fruit
Carbohydrate	4 grams	3½ meat
Cholesterol	15 milligrams	
Dietary Fiber	1 gram	
Protein	26 grams	
Sodium	379 milligrams	

SHOPPING LIST:
2 6-oz. cans fat-free tuna, 2 stalks celery, 2½ oz. crushed pineapple in juice, 1 oz. fat-free mayonnaise, 1 oz. fat-free sour cream, onion powder, dried parsley

"KOOKING" FOR KIDS

COLD TUNA SHELLS

AVERAGE - DO AHEAD

INGREDIENTS:

8 oz. jumbo pasta shells
¼ cup fat-free sour cream
¼ cup fat-free mayonnaise
2 6½-oz. cans fat-free tuna, drained
2 tsp. onion powder
1 tsp. lemon juice
⅛ tsp. pepper
1 cup frozen peas, thawed and drained

DIRECTIONS:

1. Cook pasta shells according to package directions; drain well in colander and dry carefully with paper towels.
2. In a medium bowl, combine sour cream, mayonnaise, tuna, onion powder, lemon juice, and pepper; mix until blended.
3. Carefully fold in peas; mix lightly.
4. Spoon 1 tablespoon mixture into each pasta shell and place on serving platter.
5. Cover filled shells with plastic wrap and refrigerate 2 to 3 hours before serving.

Serves: 8

Nutrition per Serving

Calories	190
Carbohydrate	26 grams
Cholesterol	8 milligrams
Dietary Fiber	1 gram
Protein	18 grams
Sodium	235 milligrams

Exchanges

1⅔ starch
2 meat

SHOPPING LIST:

8 oz. jumbo pasta shells, 2 oz. fat-free sour cream, 2 oz. fat-free mayonnaise, 2 6½-oz. cans fat-free tuna, onion powder, lemon juice, pepper, 10 oz. frozen peas

CINNAMON APPLE CRACKER SNACKS

EASY - DO AHEAD

INGREDIENTS:
24 fat-free crackers
¼ cup sugar
½ tsp. cinnamon
⅛ tsp. nutmeg
2 small red apples, thinly sliced
1½ oz. fat-free shredded Cheddar cheese

DIRECTIONS:
1. Preheat oven to 350 degrees.
2. Line a baking sheet with foil.
3. Place crackers on baking sheet in a single layer.
4. In a medium bowl, combine sugar, cinnamon, and nutmeg; stir until well mixed.
5. Toss apples with cinnamon-sugar mixture.
6. Top each cracker with 2 apple slices and sprinkle with cheese.
7. Bake in preheated oven 5 minutes, until cheese is melted.

Serves: 12

Nutrition per Serving		Exchanges
Calories	70	½ starch
Carbohydrate	13 grams	½ meat
Cholesterol	0 milligrams	⅓ fruit
Dietary Fiber	1 gram	
Protein	4 grams	
Sodium	167 milligrams	

SHOPPING LIST:
fat-free crackers, sugar, cinnamon, nutmeg, 2 small red apples, 6 oz. fat-free shredded Cheddar cheese

"KOOKING" FOR KIDS

GARLIC-CHEESE POTATO CHIPS

EASY - DO AHEAD

INGREDIENTS:
20 oz. Simply Potatoes—sliced home fries
2 tsp. garlic powder
¼ cup fat-free Parmesan cheese

DIRECTIONS:
1. Preheat oven to 425 degrees.
2. Line baking sheet with foil and lightly spray with non-fat cooking spray.
3. Spread potato slices in single layer on baking sheet (if necessary, use 2 baking sheets).
4. Lightly spray potato slices with nonfat cooking spray; immediately sprinkle with garlic powder and Parmesan cheese.
5. Bake in preheated oven for 10 to 15 minutes.
6. Remove from oven and carefully flip potato slices over.
7. Return to oven and bake until lightly browned, about 15 minutes.
8. Turn oven off and let potatoes stand in hot oven until crisp.

Serves: 6

Nutrition per Serving		Exchanges
Calories	116	1½ starch
Carbohydrate	26 grams	
Cholesterol	0 milligrams	
Dietary Fiber	2 grams	
Protein	4 grams	
Sodium	38 milligrams	

SHOPPING LIST:
20 oz. Simply Potatoes (sliced home fries), garlic powder, 1 oz. fat-free Parmesan cheese

"KOOKING" FOR KIDS

MINI PIZZA SNACKS

EASY - DO AHEAD

INGREDIENTS:
24 fat-free crackers
½ cup Boboli pizza sauce
½ cup fat-free shredded pizza cheese

DIRECTIONS:
1. Preheat oven to 400 degrees.
2. Line baking sheet with foil and spray lightly with non-fat cooking spray.
3. Arrange crackers in a single layer on baking sheet.
4. Squirt pizza sauce onto crackers and spread smooth with the back of a spoon.
5. Sprinkle cheese on top.
6. Bake in preheated oven 3 to 5 minutes, until cheese is melted.

Serves: 6

Nutrition per Serving		Exchanges
Calories	61	⅔ starch
Carbohydrate	10 grams	
Cholesterol	0 milligrams	
Dietary Fiber	< 1 gram	
Protein	3 grams	
Sodium	203 milligrams	

SHOPPING LIST:
fat-free cracker rounds, 4 oz. Boboli pizza sauce (small packets), 2 oz. fat-free shredded pizza cheese

MUNCHIE MIX

EASY - DO AHEAD

INGREDIENTS:

¾ cup Corn Chex
1½ cups fat-free goldfish
  pretzel mix
¾ cup Cheerios
½ cup Golden Grahams
¾ fat-free pretzel nuggets

1½ tbsp. low-sodium soy
  sauce
2 tsp. Dijon mustard
1 tsp. garlic powder
1 tsp. onion powder

DIRECTIONS:

1. Preheat oven to 350 degrees.
2. Lightly spray a 10x15x1-inch baking sheet with nonfat cooking spray.
3. In a large bowl, combine Corn Chex, goldfish pretzel mix, Cheerios, Golden Grahams, and pretzel nuggets; toss until mixed.
4. In a small bowl, combine soy sauce, mustard, garlic powder, and onion powder; mix until blended.
5. Pour sauce over cereal mixture; spread into prepared pan.
6. Bake in preheated oven 5 minutes.
7. Remove mixture from oven and mix lightly.
8. Return to oven and bake an additional 5 minutes.
9. Cool completely and store in airtight container.

Serves: 6

Nutrition per Serving		Exchanges
Calories	120	1½ starch
Carbohydrate	25 grams	
Cholesterol	0 milligrams	
Dietary Fiber	1 gram	
Protein	3 grams	
Sodium	589 milligrams	

SHOPPING LIST:

Corn Chex cereal, fat-free goldfish pretzel mix, Cheerios, Golden Grahams, fat-free pretzel nuggets, low-sodium soy sauce, Dijon mustard, garlic powder, onion powder

HONEY-CRUNCH DIP

EASY - DO AHEAD

INGREDIENTS:
1 cup fat-free vanilla yogurt
2¾ tbsp. honey
½ tsp. almond extract
1½ tbsp. fat-free almond-flavored granola
crushed assorted fruit

DIRECTIONS:
1. Combine all ingredients in a medium bowl and mix until blended smooth.
2. Refrigerate several hours before serving.
3. Serve with sliced cantaloupe, honeydew melon, strawberries, and sliced peaches.

Serves: 6

Nutrition per Serving		Exchanges
Calories	50	⅔ starch
Carbohydrate	11 grams	
Cholesterol	1 milligram	
Dietary Fiber	0 grams	
Protein	1 gram	
Sodium	24 milligrams	

SHOPPING LIST:
8 oz. fat-free vanilla yogurt, honey, almond extract, fat-free almond-flavored granola, assorted fruit

SWEET AND SPICY PUMPKIN DIP

EASY - DO AHEAD

INGREDIENTS:
1 cup fat-free cream cheese, softened
1 cup powdered sugar
1 cup canned pumpkin
1¼ tsp. cinnamon
¼ tsp. nutmeg

DIRECTIONS:
1. Beat cream cheese with electric mixer or spoon until very smooth and creamy.
2. Gradually add sugar, beating well after each addition.
3. Stir in pumpkin, cinnamon, and nutmeg.
4. Refrigerate 1 to 2 hours before serving.
Great dip with fat-free snickerdoodles, gingersnaps, or cinnamon-raisin bagel chips.

Serves: 8

Nutrition per Serving		Exchanges
Calories	84	1 starch
Carbohydrate	17 grams	
Cholesterol	0 milligrams	
Dietary Fiber	1 gram	
Protein	4 grams	
Sodium	202 milligrams	

SHOPPING LIST:
8 oz. fat-free cream cheese, ½ lb. powdered sugar, 8 oz. canned pumpkin, cinnamon, nutmeg

"KOOKING" FOR KIDS

BANANA-BERRY YOGURT POPS

EASY - DO AHEAD - FREEZE

INGREDIENTS:
1 cup fat-free vanilla yogurt
2 small bananas, cut into 1-inch pieces
3 oz. strawberry-banana frozen juice concentrate
paper cups
popsicle sticks

DIRECTIONS:
1. Place bananas and frozen juice concentrate in blender or food processor and process until smooth.
2. Add yogurt to blender and process until smooth and creamy.
3. Pour mixture into ice cube tray or paper cups (about ¾-full) and freeze about 1 hour, until slightly frozen.
4. Insert popsicle stick in center and freeze 6 to 8 hours, until firm.

You can substitute any flavor frozen juice concentrate and experiment with different flavored yogurt.

Serves: 4

Nutrition per Serving		Exchanges
Calories	110	⅓ milk
Carbohydrate	25 grams	1⅓ fruit
Cholesterol	1 milligram	
Dietary Fiber	1 gram	
Protein	3 grams	
Sodium	36 milligrams	

SHOPPING LIST:
2 small bananas, 3 oz. strawberry-banana (or any flavor) frozen juice concentrate, 8 oz. fat-free vanilla (or favorite flavor) yogurt, paper cups, popsicle sticks

CRUNCHY BANANA POPS

EASY - DO AHEAD - FREEZE

INGREDIENTS:
1 cup fat-free banana yogurt
1½ cups fat-free granola
¾ tsp. cinnamon
3 large bananas, cut in half

DIRECTIONS:
1. Place yogurt in small dish.
2. Place granola in small dish; sprinkle with cinnamon and mix.
3. Line a baking sheet with plastic wrap or waxed paper.
4. Roll each banana half in yogurt.
5. Roll banana in granola mixture and place on prepared sheet.
6. Place baking sheet in freezer; freeze until firm.
7. Wrap each banana pop in plastic wrap and store in freezer.

Serves: 6

Nutrition per Serving		Exchanges
Calories	165	1 starch
Carbohydrate	40 grams	1⅔ fruit
Cholesterol	< 1 milligram	
Dietary Fiber	1 gram	
Protein	3 grams	
Sodium	27 milligrams	

SHOPPING LIST:
8 oz. fat-free banana yogurt, fat-free granola, cinnamon, 3 large bananas

FROZEN BERRY YOGURT POPS

EASY - DO AHEAD - FREEZE

INGREDIENTS:
   2 cups fat-free yogurt
   4 cups fresh strawberries, blueberries,
      raspberries, or combination of any berries

DIRECTIONS:
   1. Combine yogurt and berries in food processor or blender.
   2. Process or blend until smooth.
   3. Fill ice tray or paper cups with yogurt mixture.
   4. Insert popsicle sticks in center, if desired, and freeze several hours, until firm.

Serves: 8

Nutrition per Serving

Calories	54	
Carbohydrate	10 grams	
Cholesterol	1 milligram	
Dietary Fiber	2 grams	
Protein	4 grams	
Sodium	44 milligrams	

Exchanges
½ milk
⅓ fruit

SHOPPING LIST:
   16 oz. fat-free yogurt, 2 pints berries

"KOOKING" FOR KIDS

FROZEN ORANGEADE PIE

EASY - DO AHEAD - FREEZE

INGREDIENTS:
8 oz. fat-free Cool Whip Lite
16 oz. frozen orange juice concentrate, thawed
14 oz. fat-free sweetened condensed milk
2 fat-free graham cracker pie crusts
1 medium orange, sliced thin

DIRECTIONS:
1. Place Cool Whip into large bowl.
2. Add orange juice and milk to Cool Whip and blend until smooth.
3. Spread mixture into pie crusts; cover and freeze overnight.
4. Let pie stand at room temperature 10 minutes; garnish with orange slices and serve.

Serves: 16

Nutrition per Serving		Exchanges
Calories	202	2⅓ starch
Carbohydrate	43 grams	½ fruit
Cholesterol	0 milligrams	
Dietary Fiber	2 grams	
Protein	7 grams	
Sodium	65 milligrams	

SHOPPING LIST:
8 oz. fat-free Cool Whip Lite, 16 oz. frozen orange juice concentrate, 14 oz. fat-free sweetened condensed milk, 2 fat-free graham cracker pie crusts, 1 orange

FRUIT 'N YOGURT PARFAIT

EASY - DO AHEAD

INGREDIENTS:

1½ cups fat-free strawberry-banana yogurt
8 oz. crushed pineapple in juice, drained
1 medium banana
¼ cup fat-free granola
11 oz. mandarin oranges in juice, drained
¼ cup sliced strawberries

DIRECTIONS:

1. Combine yogurt and pineapple in a small bowl and mix until blended.
2. Spoon 2 tablespoons yogurt mixture into each of 4 parfait glasses.
3. Place banana slices on top of yogurt.
4. Sprinkle 1 tablespoon granola over banana in each cup.
5. Spoon another 2 tablespoons yogurt over granola.
6. Top with oranges.
7. Spoon remaining yogurt mixture over oranges.
8. Top with strawberry slices.

Serves: 4

Nutrition per Serving		Exchanges
Calories	157	½ milk
Carbohydrate	36 grams	2 fruit
Cholesterol	2 milligrams	
Dietary Fiber	3 grams	
Protein	5 grams	
Sodium	54 milligrams	

"KOOKING" FOR KIDS

SHOPPING LIST:

12 oz. fat-free strawberry-banana yogurt, 8 oz. crushed pineapple in juice, 1 banana, fat-free granola, 11 oz. mandarin oranges in juice, strawberries

KOOL-AID POPSICLES

EASY - DO AHEAD - FREEZE

INGREDIENTS:
- 3 oz. Jell-O gelatin, any flavor
- 1 cup boiling water
- 1 package Kool-Aid, same flavor as Jell-O
- 1 cup sugar

DIRECTIONS:
1. Place Jell-O in boiling water and mix until Jell-O is dissolved.
2. Combine Jell-O, Kool-Aid, and sugar in a large glass or plastic measuring bowl with spout.
3. Add enough water to equal 2 quarts.
4. Pour into paper cups, ice tray, or popsicle holders; freeze until hard.

Serves: 6

Nutrition per Serving		Exchanges
Calories	167	3 fruit
Carbohydrate	43 grams	
Cholesterol	0 milligrams	
Dietary Fiber	0 grams	
Protein	1 gram	
Sodium	< 1 milligram	

SHOPPING LIST:
3 oz. any flavor Jello-O, 1 package any flavor Kool-Aid, sugar

"KOOKING" FOR KIDS

. . . .

421

CHERRY COBBLER

EASY - DO AHEAD

INGREDIENTS:
21 oz. lite cherry pie filling
1¼ cups Pioneer baking mix
1½ tbsp. sugar
¼ cup skim milk
¼ fat-free cherry yogurt

DIRECTIONS:
1. Lightly spray 2-quart glass casserole with nonfat cooking spray.
2. Preheat oven to 425 degrees.
3. Place cherry pie filling in casserole; heat in microwave on high 2 to 3 minutes, until heated through.
4. In a medium bowl, combine baking mix, sugar, milk, and yogurt until blended.
5. Drop dough by tablespoons onto cherry pie filling.
6. Bake in preheated oven 15 to 20 minutes, until biscuits are lightly browned.
7. Serve with fat-free Cool Whip or fat-free frozen yogurt, if desired.

Serves: 6

Nutrition per Serving		Exchanges
Calories	244	3 fruit
Carbohydrate	63 grams	1 starch
Cholesterol	< 1 milligram	
Dietary Fiber	< 1 gram	
Protein	3 grams	
Sodium	514 milligrams	

SHOPPING LIST:
21 oz. lite cherry pie filling, Pioneer baking mix, sugar, 2 oz. skim milk, 2 oz. fat-free cherry yogurt

CHOCOLATE CHERRY SURPRISE CUPCAKES

EASY - DO AHEAD - FREEZE

INGREDIENTS:

2 cups Pioneer baking mix
½ cup sugar
¼ cup brown sugar
1 cup unsweetened cocoa powder
1 cup skim milk
2 tsp. vanilla
½ cup egg substitute
21 oz. lite cherry pie filling

DIRECTIONS:

1. Preheat oven to 375 degrees.
2. Lightly spray muffin cups with nonfat cooking spray.
3. In a large bowl, combine baking mix, sugar, brown sugar, cocoa, milk, vanilla, and egg substitute; mix until ingredients are blended smooth.
4. Place ⅓ cup batter into each muffin cup; top with 1 tablespoon pie filling and 2 tablespoons batter.
5. Bake in preheated oven 15 to 20 minutes, until toothpick inserted in center comes out clean.
6. Cool to room temperature and sprinkle with powdered sugar, if desired.

Serves: 18

Nutrition per Serving		Exchanges
Calories	119	1 starch
Carbohydrate	30 grams	¾ fruit
Cholesterol	< 1 milligram	
Dietary Fiber	< 1 gram	
Protein	3 grams	
Sodium	272 milligrams	

SHOPPING LIST:

Pioneer baking mix, sugar, brown sugar, 4 oz. unsweetened cocoa powder, 8 oz. skim milk, vanilla, 4 oz. egg substitute, 21 oz. lite cherry pie filling

CHOCOLATE KRISP SQUARES

EASY - DO AHEAD

INGREDIENTS:
1 tbsp. reconstituted butter-flavored granules
3 tbsp. Lighter Bake
10 oz. marshmallows
6 cups Cocoa Krispies

DIRECTIONS:
1. Lightly spray 9x13-inch baking dish with nonfat cooking spray.
2. Lightly spray large saucepan or Dutch oven with nonfat cooking spray.
3. Combine liquid butter and Lighter Bake in pan; heat over low heat until blended.
4. Add marshmallows and stir until marshmallows are completely melted.
5. Remove from heat.
6. Stir in cereal until mixed well.
7. Pat mixture into baking dish and let stand at room temperature until completely cooled and set.

Serves: 24

Nutrition per Serving		Exchanges
Calories	76	⅓ starch
Carbohydrate	19 grams	1 fruit
Cholesterol	0 milligrams	
Dietary Fiber	0 grams	
Protein	1 gram	
Sodium	74 milligrams	

SHOPPING LIST:
butter-flavored granules, 1½ oz. Lighter Bake, 10 oz. marshmallows, Cocoa Krispies cereal

CHOCOLATE STRAWBERRIES

EASY - DO AHEAD

INGREDIENTS:
1½ pints strawberries
¼ cup fat-free sour cream
¼ cup fat-free chocolate fudge sauce
1 tsp. frozen strawberry juice concentrate, thawed

DIRECTIONS:
1. Rinse strawberries and dry well. Remove stems, if desired.
2. In a small bowl, combine sour cream, chocolate fudge, and strawberry juice; blend until smooth.
3. Place dip in center of platter and surround with strawberries.

Serves 4

Nutrition per Serving		Exchanges
Calories	101	⅔ fruit
Carbohydrate	20 grams	⅔ starch
Cholesterol	0 milligrams	
Dietary Fiber	3 grams	
Protein	2 grams	
Sodium	41 milligrams	

SHOPPING LIST:
1½ pints strawberries, 4 oz. fat-free sour cream, 4 oz. fat-free chocolate fudge sauce, frozen strawberry juice concentrate

CINNAMON PEACH CRISP

EASY - DO AHEAD

INGREDIENTS:
16 oz. canned peach slices in juice, drained
1 cup fat-free granola
½ cup raisins
1 tsp. cinnamon
fat-free Cool Whip (optional)

DIRECTIONS:
1. Preheat oven to 350 degrees.
2. Lightly spray 9-inch baking dish with nonfat cooking spray.
3. Combine all ingredients in baking dish and mix lightly; cover with foil and bake 20 minutes.
4. Remove foil and bake 10 to 15 minutes, until lightly browned.
5. Serve hot or cold; top with fat-free Cool Whip, if desired.

Serves: 6

Nutrition per Serving		Exchanges
Calories	103	⅓ starch
Carbohydrate	26 grams	1⅓ fruit
Cholesterol	0 milligrams	
Dietary Fiber	2 grams	
Protein	1 gram	
Sodium	7 milligrams	

SHOPPING LIST:
16 oz. peach slices in juice, fat-free granola, raisins, cinnamon, fat-free Cool Whip (optional)

OATMEAL RAISIN BARS

AVERAGE - DO AHEAD - FREEZE

INGREDIENTS:

½ cup apple butter
¼ cup corn syrup
¼ cup egg substitute
½ cup brown sugar
1½ cup Pioneer baking mix

1 tsp. cinnamon
1 cup multi-grain oatmeal
½ cup Grape-Nuts
¾ cup raisins

DIRECTIONS:

1. Preheat oven to 300 degrees.
2. Lightly spray a 9x13-inch baking dish with nonfat cooking spray.
3. In a large bowl, combine apple butter, corn syrup, egg substitute, and brown sugar; mix until all ingredients are blended smooth.
4. Stir in baking mix, cinnamon, oatmeal, and Grape-Nuts; mix well.
5. Fold in raisins.
6. Spread batter into prepared pan.
7. Bake in preheated oven for 35 to 40 minutes.
8. Cool oatmeal bars at room temperature for 15 to 20 minutes before cutting.

Serves: 16

Nutrition per Serving		Exchanges
Calories	167	1 starch
Carbohydrate	42 grams	1⅔ fruit
Cholesterol	0 milligrams	
Dietary Fiber	1 gram	
Protein	3 grams	
Sodium	229 milligrams	

SHOPPING LIST:

4 oz. apple butter, 2 oz. corn syrup, 2 oz. egg substitute, ¼ lb. brown sugar, Pioneer baking mix, cinnamon, Quaker multi-grain oatmeal, Grape-Nuts, raisins

PINEAPPLE-STRAWBERRY PIE

AVERAGE - DO AHEAD

INGREDIENTS:

4 oz. strawberry gelatin
⅔ cup boiling water
½ cup cold water
ice cubes
8 oz. fat-free Cool Whip

¾ cup sliced strawberries
¼ cup pineapple tidbits in
juice, drained and dried
1 fat-free graham cracker
pie crust

DIRECTIONS:

1. Pour gelatin into large bowl.
2. Pour boiling water over gelatin and stir constantly until dissolved.
3. Pour ½ cup cold water into large 4-cup measuring cup; fill with ice cubes to make 1¼ cups.
4. Pour gelatin into cold water and mix until it becomes thick.
5. Stir 3½ cups Cool Whip into gelatin and mix until smooth.
6. Fold in fruit and mix lightly.
7. Refrigerate 3 to 4 hours, until mixture is thick.
8. Spoon mixture into crust and top with additional Cool Whip, if desired.

Serves: 8

Nutrition per Serving		Exchanges
Calories	150	2 fruit
Carbohydrate	30 grams	1 meat
Cholesterol	0 milligrams	
Dietary Fiber	2 grams	
Protein	9 grams	
Sodium	41 milligrams	

SHOPPING LIST:

4 oz. strawberry gelatin, 8 oz. fat-free Cool Whip, ½ pint strawberries, 8 oz. pineapple tidbits in juice, fat-free graham cracker pie crust

RAISIN-MARSHMALLOW TREATS

EASY - DO AHEAD

INGREDIENTS:
⅓ cup reconstituted butter-flavored granules
4 cups miniature marshmallows
¾ tsp. vanilla
6 cups Rice Krispies cereal

DIRECTIONS:
1. Lightly spray 10-inch baking dish with nonfat cooking spray.
2. Combine liquid butter and marshmallows in a medium saucepan and cook over low heat, stirring constantly, until marshmallows are melted and mixture is blended.
3. Remove from heat and stir in vanilla.
4. Gradually add cereal to marshmallow mixture and mix until evenly coated.
5. Press mixture into prepared pan; cool completely before cutting.

Serves: 24

Nutrition per Serving	
Calories	63
Carbohydrate	14 grams
Cholesterol	0 milligrams
Dietary Fiber	0 grams
Protein	1 gram
Sodium	88 milligrams

Exchanges
⅓ starch
⅔ fruit

SHOPPING LIST:
butter-flavored granules, 20 oz. miniature marshmallows, vanilla, Rice Krispies cereal

RASPBERRY OAT BARS

EASY - DO AHEAD

INGREDIENTS:
1 cup brown sugar
¾ cup apple butter
1½ cups multi-grain oatmeal
1¾ cups flour
½ tsp. baking soda
10 oz. low-sugar raspberry jam

DIRECTIONS:
1. Preheat oven to 400 degrees.
2. Lightly spray 9x13-inch baking dish with nonfat cooking spray.
3. In a large bowl, combine brown sugar and apple butter; mix until smooth.
4. Add oatmeal, flour, and baking soda to sugar mixture and mix until crumbly.
5. Press half of the crumb mixture into prepared pan.
6. Spread raspberry jam (or any flavor) and sprinkle with remaining crumb mixture.
7. Bake in preheated oven for 20 to 25 minutes, until lightly browned and cooked through.
8. Cool to room temperature; cut into bars.

Serves: 24

Nutrition per Serving		Exchanges
Calories	135	⅔ starch
Carbohydrate	32 grams	1⅓ fruit
Cholesterol	0 milligrams	
Dietary Fiber	1 gram	
Protein	2 grams	
Sodium	22 milligrams	

SHOPPING LIST:
½ lb. brown sugar, 6 oz. apple butter, Quaker multi-grain oatmeal, flour, baking soda, 10 oz. low-sugar raspberry jam

MOUTHWATERING
MENUS

2-WEEK MENU PLAN

BREAKFAST - DAY 1

½ cup Mini Shredded Wheat
½ cup skim milk
1 slice fat-free toast with 1 tsp. fat-free margarine
½ cup Cranberry-Orange Cocktail—page 381

LUNCH

Turkey Pita Pizza—page 289
½ cup cubed cantaloupe
carrots and celery with Dijon Ranch dressing - page 143

DINNER

Parmesan Fish Fillets—page 166
Herbed Rice—page 239
fat-free bread or roll

BREAKFAST - DAY 2

Fruity Breakfast Shake—page 375
½ fat-free bagel with 2 tsp. low-calorie preserves

LUNCH

Tomato Basil Roast Beef Sandwich—page 121
1 cup salad with 1-2 tbsp. fat-free salad dressing
1 apple

DINNER

Spaghetti with Peppers and Mushrooms—page 268
romaine lettuce with Italian and Cheese Croutons—page 124
1-2 tbsp. fat-free Creamy Caesar Salad Dressing—page 140
1 slice Italian bread

BREAKFAST - DAY 3

Spice Apple Pancakes with
Apple Raisin Pancake Sauce—page 40 and page 126
1 cup skim milk

LUNCH

Pasta Salad Bowl—page 87
1 slice Italian bread with 1 tsp. fat-free margarine
½ cup pineapple tidbits in juice, drained

DINNER

Breaded Baked Flounder—page 161
Spinach Baked Potato—page 324
1 cup salad with 1-2 tbsp. fat-free salad dressing

BREAKFAST - DAY 4

Warm Apple Granola Cereal—page 42
1 cup skim milk

LUNCH

1 cup Chicken Vegetable Noodle Soup—page 100
½ bagel with lettuce, tomato, cucumber, and mustard

DINNER

Mozzarella Sticks—page 24
Seafood Pineapple Pizza—page 283
1 cup salad with 1-2 tbsp. fat-free salad dressing

BREAKFAST - DAY 5

Veggie Egg White Omelet—page 49
½ cup steamed broccoli (cooked into omelet)
1 medium peach
skim milk

MOUTHWATERING
MENUS

LUNCH

Spinach Crab Frittata—page 46
1 slice Italian Bread or Sourdough
½ cantaloupe

DINNER

Creamy Garlic Chicken Breasts—page 196
Pasta Risotto—page 262
1 slice fat-free garlic bread

BREAKFAST - DAY 6

Date Bran Muffin—page 55
1 cup fat-free cottage cheese
½ cup pineapple chunks in juice

LUNCH

Mushroom-Couscous—page 86
1 slice fat-free bread
1 medium apple

DINNER

Turkey Chili—page 111
fat-free flour tortilla
sliced tomato and cucumbers

BREAKFAST - DAY 7

French Toast Sticks—page 38
powdered sugar or low-calorie syrup, optional
½ cup strawberries
6 oz. fat-free vanilla yogurt

LUNCH

Lobster Salad Sandwich—page 118
steamed asparagus
1 orange

MOUTHWATERING MENUS

DINNER

Oriental Chicken Tenders—page 181
½ cup fat-free rice
1 cup frozen broccoli, cauliflower, and water chestnuts

BREAKFAST - DAY 8

1 cup cooked Cream of Wheat
1 cup skim milk
¾ cup blueberries

LUNCH

Caesar Salad Sandwich—page 114
½ cup Chilled Melon Soup—page 101

DINNER

Chicken Fajitas with tortillas—page 172
½ cup gazpacho soup

BREAKFAST - DAY 9

Purple Plum Smoothie—page 369
½ bagel with 1 tsp. fat-free cream cheese

LUNCH

Cajun Chicken Salad Sandwich—115
1 cup bell pepper strips
12 large cherries

DINNER

Barbecue Stir-Fry—218
½ cup wild rice
fat-free roll or bread

BREAKFAST - DAY 10

Brown Sugar Cinnamon Pancakes—page 36
¾ cup raspberries and blueberries

MOUTHWATERING MENUS

LUNCH

Shrimp Spinach Salad with
  Hot Orange Dressing—page 91 and page 147
1 slice Italian bread

DINNER

Sloppy Joes—page 184
Sweet and Spicy Corn—page 300
1 fat-free pita pocket

BREAKFAST - DAY 11

1 cup fat-free yogurt with 2 tbsp. fat-free granola
2 tbsp. raisins
½ slice Italian bread or sourdough with 1 tsp. fat-free margarine

LUNCH

Chicken Vegetable Quesadilla—page 20
1 cup salad with 2 tbsp. Red Pepper Vinaigrette dressing—
  page 152

DINNER

Cheese-wrapped Hot Dogs—page 397
Pineapple Baked Beans—page 312
Coleslaw—page 81

BREAKFAST - DAY 12

3 scrambled egg whites with
¼ cup shredded fat-free cheddar cheese
1 slice fat-free whole wheat toast with fat-free margarine
1 cup orange juice

LUNCH

Curry Chicken Salad—page 84
fat-free garlic bagel chips
½ cup Tart 'n Tangy Carrot Salad—93

DINNER

Turkey Cheeseburgers—page 212
Cajun Fries—page 221
Colorful Coleslaw—page 82

BREAKFAST - DAY 13

½ cup Quaker Multi-grain Oatmeal
   with 1 tbsp. brown sugar, 2 tbsp. Craisins,
¼ cup skim milk
½ cantaloupe

LUNCH

1 cup Seafood Chowder—page 109
fat-free crackers with 2 oz. fat-free cheese

DINNER

Simple Italian Chicken—page 205
Italian Potato Boats—page 319
fat-free Caesar salad

BREAKFAST - DAY 14

1 slice Carrot-Zucchini Fruit Bread—page 65
6 oz. fat-free yogurt
½ cup strawberries

LUNCH

fat-free roast beef Sandwich on whole wheat bread
1 tbsp. fat-free Dijon mustard
Potato Snacks with Roasted Garlic Dressing—page 323

DINNER

Turkey Meat Loaf—page 187
Creamy Mashed Potatoes—page 317
steamed broccoli

MOUTHWATERING
MENUS

FAT-FREE SNACKING
(CHOOSE 2 EACH DAY)

Peachy Good Shake—page 379
Papaya Peach Smoothie—page 368
Munchie Mix—page 413
1 cup skim milk with 2 tsp. fat-free strawberry syrup
¾ oz. fat-free pretzels
1 soft pretzel with mustard and 1 oz. fat-free cheese
24 grapes (may be frozen)
fat-free crackers with ¾ oz. fat-free cheese
1 cup cranberry juice with seltzer water
chili popcorn (fat-free popcorn sprinkled with chili powder)
8 oz. fat-free flavored yogurt
1 Honey-Cake Cookie—page 348
1 Gingersnap—page 345
Vanilla Strawberries—page 364
pita chips with Roasted Red Pepper Spread—page 12
1 cup orange sections
1 slice Italian bread brushed with 1 tbsp. fat-free pasta sauce and
    ½ oz. fat-free mozzarella cheese
Pineapple-Cheese Bagel Snacks—page 30
pineapple-melon kabobs
1 cup fat-free broth
Frozen Berry Yogurt Pop—page 418
Crunchy Banana Pop—page 417
1 Raisin-Marshmallow Treat—page 429
1 Oatmeal Raisin Bar—page 427
1 Chocolate Krisp Square—page 424
1 frozen banana
2 Cinnamon Apple Cracker Snacks—page 410
1 Oatmeal Raisin Muffin—page 61
1 Cinnamon Berry Muffin—page 52
fresh veggies with fat-free dip

ADDITIONAL FAT-FREE DESSERTS

Here is a selection of simple fat-free desserts—others may be chosen from the dessert section.

- Banana split—4 oz. fat-free frozen yogurt, ½ banana, 2 teaspoons fat-free chocolate syrup
- Fat-free pudding
- Angel food cake with fresh fruit
- Baked banana—peel banana and slice in half. Place on foil. Mix 1 teaspoon fat-free margarine, ½ teaspoon lemon juice, and ⅛ teaspoon cinnamon; brush over banana and sprinkle with 1 tablespoon brown sugar
- Baked apple
- 6 oz. fat-free yogurt sprinkled with 2 tablespoons fat-free granola
- Fat-free frozen fruit pops
- Fat-free sorbet
- Fat-free brownie with ½ cup fat-free frozen yogurt
- Sliced canned apples sprinkled with cinnamon and sugar

INDEX

INDEX